D1609528

THE PUBLISHER GRATEFULLY ACKNOWLEDGES THE GENEROUS

CONTRIBUTION TOWARD THE PUBLICATION OF THIS BOOK

PROVIDED BY THE DIRECTOR'S CIRCLE OF THE UNIVERSITY

OF CALIFORNIA PRESS ASSOCIATES, WHOSE MEMBERS ARE

Elaine Mitchell Attias

Robert and Alice Bridges Foundation

June and Earl Cheit

Margit and Lloyd Cotsen

August Frugé

Thomas C. Given

Ann and Bill Harmsen

Charlene Harvey

Florence and Leo Helzel

Mrs. Charles Henri Hine

Marsha Rosenbaum and John Irwin

Suzanne Badenhoop and Guy Lampard

Nancy Livingston and Fred Levin,
  The Shenson Foundation

Sheila and David Littlejohn

Sally and Peter McAndrew

Jacqueline and Jack Miles

Thormund Miller

Nancy and Timothy Muller

Mauree Jane and Mark Perry

Frances and Loren Rothschild

Shirley and Ralph Shapiro

THE WINEMAKER'S DANCE

THE
WINEMAKER'S DANCE

EXPLORING TERROIR IN THE NAPA VALLEY

JONATHAN SWINCHATT AND DAVID G. HOWELL

Graphics by

JOSÉ F. VIGIL   KATE BARTON   TIMOTHY LESLE

University of California Press   Berkeley   Los Angeles   London

University of California Press
Berkeley and Los Angeles, California

University of California Press, Ltd.
London, England

Library of Congress Cataloging-in-Publication Data

Swinchatt, Jonathan P.
    The winemaker's dance : exploring terroir in the Napa Valley /
Jonathan Swinchatt and David G. Howell.
        p.   cm.
    Includes bibliographical references and index.
    ISBN 0-520-23513-4 (cloth: alk. paper)
    1. Wine and wine making—California—Napa Valley.
2. Viticulture—California—Napa Valley.   3. Geology—
California—Napa Valley.   4. Napa Valley (Calif.)   I. Howell,
D. G.   II. Title.
TP557 .S83   2004
641.2'2'79419—dc22   2003025283

Manufactured in Canada
13   12   11   10   09   08   07   06
10   9   8   7   6   5   4   3   2

A satellite image of the San Francisco Bay Area. Napa County is outlined in yellow.

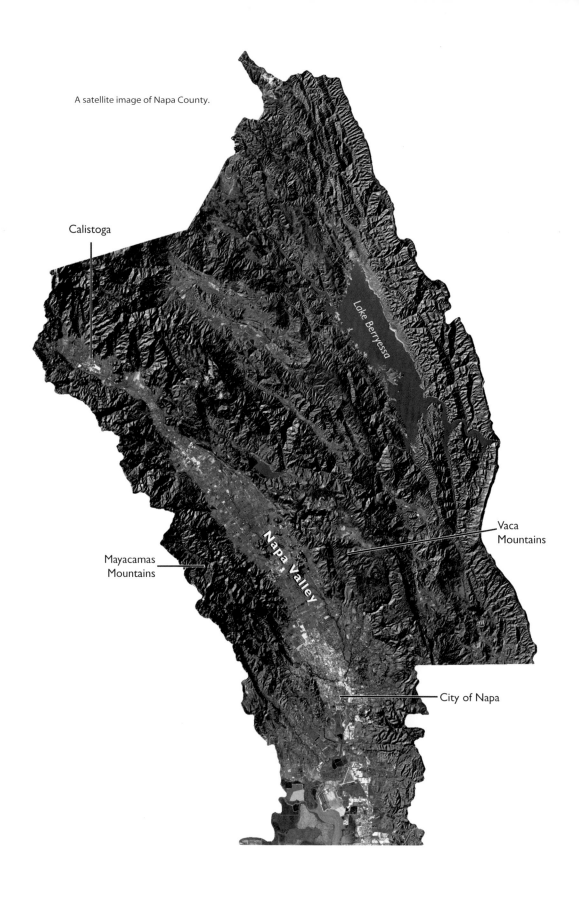

A satellite image of Napa County.

Calistoga

Lake Berryessa

Vaca
Mountains

Mayacamas
Mountains

Napa Valley

City of Napa

FOR NANCY, WHO SURELY KNOWS WHY,

AND SUSAN, FOR ALL THE RIGHT REASONS

AND IN MEMORY OF OUR FRIEND AND

COLLEAGUE JOSÉ F. VIGIL, WHOSE CREATIVE

GRAPHIC GENIUS INSPIRED OUR WORK

FOR THE PAST FIFTEEN YEARS.

CONTENTS

— ✦ —

ACKNOWLEDGMENTS

In preparing this book, we spoke with some eighty or ninety grape growers and winemakers, all of whom were immensely generous with their time and insight. Their input has been fundamental to the success of the project. While we hesitate to single out individuals, we must acknowledge some who truly went out of their way to provide us with information and additional connections.

Warren Winiarski, whom we first met while making the video *EarthNectar* in 1990, inspired our notion of the "winemaker's dance." Warren moves through his various roles in life so seamlessly that little appears to separate occupations as disparate as working in the vineyard and teaching Shakespeare in the summer for his alma mater, St. John's College.

Early on, Eric Sims of Robert Mondavi Winery, during a serendipitous meeting on a plane, offered us important contacts and direction. In particular, he pointed us toward consultant and winemaker David de Sante, who spent a whirlwind day filling us in on the history of Napa winemaking and bringing us quickly up to speed on new developments. Of the many people de Sante suggested we contact, none were more generous than Tony and Joanne Truchard, who have proven so well that you can indeed grow fine Cabernet in Carneros.

Ed Weber, agriculture specialist with the California State Extension Service in Napa, supplied insight into the fundamentals of modern winegrowing and proposed avenues of investigation that might otherwise have eluded us. Ed also connected us with, among others, Jan Krupp of Stagecoach Vineyards, a place that turned out to be particularly important in establishing the origin of certain unusual geologic features. After one of several tours of Stagecoach, we ended up in Krupp's dining room with some twenty-five barrel samples of wines made from Stagecoach grapes by a variety of winemakers, a truly eye-opening experience.

Philippe Melka, geologist turned winemaker, spoke with us many times of geology and vineyards, most memorably over a tasting of wines generously gathered from six of the properties where he has made wine. John Caldwell was there as well—he became our primary authority on rootstocks and clones as well as the source of many a shared laugh.

Chris Howell wrote such a thoughtful and challenging review of our original book proposal that we were prompted to seek him out for further information, which he provided unstintingly, both about his work at Cain Vineyards and about more general aspects of grape growing and winemaking. Chris and Napa Valley's resident geologist/winemaker John Livingston invited us to accompany them on a "Terroir Tour" of Napa, a package they offered at the 2001 Napa Valley Wine Auction. The buyers, Chuck McMinn of Vineyard 29 and his Silicon Valley colleague Chuck Haas, were most thoughtful in allowing us to tag along. Livingston, who has also written about Napa geology, has shared his insights openly with us since we first met him more than a decade ago.

Tony Soter highlighted examples of the diversity of Napa terroir and food on an expedition that ranged from Carneros to Calistoga and from Tra Vigne to Don Giovanni. It was a memorable day, one of several meetings with the person some see as Napa's resident philosopher.

Michael Silacci, director of winemaking at Opus One, spoke with us about many aspects of grape growing and winemaking, most specifically in relation to his current work and his previous position as winemaker at Stag's Leap Wine Cellars. Michael is one of several Napa winemakers, including Chris Howell and Philippe Melka, who began their careers in France and who bring a bit of European perspective to winemaking in Napa.

Our friend and colleague David Jones, geologist and proprietor of Lava Cap Winery in the foothills of the Sierra, got us started on this work by suggesting that we make a movie about geology and wine in California. The result was *EarthNectar,* with Davey conducting many of the interviews. Terry Wright, geologist and professor, has also generously shared his insights into Earth and terroir whenever we have had the pleasure of his company.

This list would not be complete without mention of three Napa stalwarts who were part of the *EarthNectar* story and who have been our friends ever since. Tom Burgess, Al Brounstein, and Craig Williams (Joseph Phelps Vineyards) have been supportive of our work in Napa from the beginning; our conversations and connections with them over the years have been integral to our growing understanding of Napa terroir.

In addition, the following people responded to our requests for time and information unhesitatingly, with both warmth and generosity: David Abreu, Joel Akin, Frank Altamura, Bart and Daphne Araujo, Daniel Baron, Bo Barrett, Heidi Peterson Barrett, Andy Beckstoffer, Ken Bernards, Daniel Bosch, Robert Brittan, Rosemary Cakebread, Cathy Corison, Karen Culler, Volker Eisele, Doug Fletcher, Bob Foley, Ric Forman, Paul and Suzie Frank, Bob Gallagher, Sara Gott, Dick Grace, Kirk Grace, Bill Harlan, Lee Hudson, Larry Hyde, Mia Klein, John Kongsgaard, Ann Kraemer, Steve Lagier, Paul Lukacs, Terry Mathison, Leo McLoskey, Colin McPhail, Carole Meredith, Dave Miner, Tim Mondavi, Bulmaro Montes, Manuel Montes, Christian Moueix, Mark Neal, Mary Novak, Jason Pahlmeyer, Philippe Pessereau, Glen Ragsdale, Steve Rogstad, Leslie Rudd, Ed Sbragia, Danny Schuster, John Shafer, Jeffrey Shifflett, Shari and Garren Staglin, Bob Steinhauer, Charles Thomas, Jeff Virnig, and John Williams.

During our many excursions into Napa, we would have been lost without the aid of Gabriele Ondine, who helped us with a variety of logistics. Jeff Adams of the Napa Valley Vintners Association kindly admitted us to a series of seminars offered to candidates for the Master of Wine degree. It was at one of these that we met wine writer Gerald Asher, whose insights into modern influences on the style and character of wine and the responsibility of the individual wine enthusiast are fundamental to the future of Napa, and perhaps world, winemaking.

The geologic foundations of this work reflect the extraordinary ability and dedication of the scientists of the U.S. Geological Survey and other professional geologists from the San Francisco Bay Area. We would particularly like to thank the following individuals for sharing with us their knowledge, insights, and interest in the rocks and what they tell: Richard Blakely, Earl Brabb, William Cotton, Russell Graymer, Wes Hildreth, Jack Hillhouse, Thomas Holzer, Robert Jachens, Chris Jones, Kenneth Lajoie, Vicky Langenheim, Robert McLaughlin, Patrick Muffler, Bonnie Murchey, Tom Noce, Richard Pike, James Rytuba, Andrei Sarna-Wojcicki, David Schwartz, David Wagner, Ray Wells, Carl Wentworth, and John Williams.

All quotations, unless otherwise designated, have been reconstructed from notes taken during interviews with the individuals listed here. Quotations have been edited slightly for clarity.

This book covers quite a broad scope, conceptually and graphically; the aid of our editors at the University of California Press has been central to its success. Blake Edgar quietly and carefully led us through the many steps of putting together a book that became significantly more complex than the original proposal indicated; Rose Vekony guided us, and the book, through the lengthy process of production with patience and grace; and Mary Renaud helped us present a variety of complicated notions more clearly while she tightened the text and smoothed our prose. Our deepest thanks to you and all your colleagues.

Lastly, a disclaimer: We have put plenty of opinions in this book—it might well turn out to be a bit controversial. The opinions are ours, and are not to be associated with any of the individuals who have aided us along the way. They provided insight; how we understood and shaped it is our doing alone.

INTRODUCTION

The Place and the Notion

The Napa Valley is perhaps as well known for its glamour, its lifestyle, and its chic and successful attitude as for its wine. The notion of the "wine country life" has made Napa the second largest tourist attraction in California, surpassed only by Disneyland. On almost any weekend, its highways are lined with cars and limousines. Its restaurants are as famous as any in New York or San Francisco; one, the French Laundry, is considered by some to be the finest dining establishment in the country. The Napa Valley Wine Auction attracts some of the highest rollers in the land and commands prices that run up to five hundred thousand dollars for a single bottle. The gossip and stories that arise from such a milieu are often amusing, sometimes scandalous, and always entertaining. It's easy to think of Napa as the site of one huge open party, welcoming all to jump in.

So easy, in fact, that one can forget that this small valley—all of about three miles wide and thirty miles long—is one of the great places on Earth for producing wine.

This has been so since George Yount planted the first vineyard in Napa some 150 years ago, near the town that took his name. By the end of the nineteenth century, winegrowers had planted vines in every part of the region—in the valley, along its edges, and scattered throughout the surrounding hills. Using *Vitis vinifera* vines brought from Europe, Napa rapidly made a name for itself on the world wine scene.

In the early years of the twentieth century, however, the ambition of this early generation of winemakers was first dampened by the temperance movement and then crushed by Prohibition. By the end of that era, in 1933, derelict wineries and abandoned equipment were witness to a devastated industry. But, together with the survivors—places such as the towering Greystone Cellars and the chateau of Inglenook—even the ruins suggested that winemaking was already a central part of the valley's history and fine wine its true vocation. And the intense energy of those early winemakers would carry down through the years, past the barriers of Prohibition and a variety of economic setbacks, to inspire the likes of Lee Stewart, Warren Winiarski, Robert Mondavi, Al Brounstein, Mike Grgich, Joe Heitz, and others who rejuvenated the valley in the 1950s and 1960s.

Why this happened in this particular small valley is a question not often asked and one that, to our knowledge, has never been answered. Nothing in the history of Napa suggests any singular event, any momentous recognition, that prompted the pioneer winemakers to gamble their money and prestige on an unknown place and assume that it would produce wine that would impress the world.

From our perspective, grounded in the landscape, the answer lies not in history but in the physical presence of the place. You need only contemplate the panorama from the top of Oakville Grade to sense the intrinsically attractive power of Napa. As Paul Lukacs observed to us, "You could stand where Gustave Niebaum stood and see both sides of the valley and much of its length" laid out before you. The Napa Valley is a self-contained piece of land that seems to gather together and embrace all that exists within its boundaries. Napa today, with block after block of neatly arranged vines spreading up and down the valley, dotted with wineries and small villages, stitched together by the two threads of the Silverado Trail and Highway 29, seems a natural place to develop a community of such shared and intense focus.

But it takes much more than energy and inspiration to make great wine. It also takes the right mix of elements that come together to form the near-mystical whole alluded to in that untranslatable French word *terroir*. Great wine can't be made just anywhere—the best winegrowing regions boast a certain balance of warm days and cool nights, sufficient rainfall at the appropriate times, well-drained sediments and soils, and levels of solar energy that can ripen grapes without pushing them into sugar overdose or shriveling them into raisins. And if a region is to be truly great, perhaps it also needs enough diversity of topography and substrate, enough variation of sun exposure and slope, to create microenvironments that, if carefully tended, can produce the nuances that make one fine wine different from its neighbor.

The Napa Valley is indeed graced by these attributes. Its rainfall is concentrated in the winter, when it can replenish groundwater and reservoirs without damaging grapes. Napa has a broad diversity of bedrock, and geologic processes have arranged the sediments and soils derived from it to provide the well-drained substrate that vines adore. And its complex topography reflects the land's geologic origins and creates microenvironments galore. Napa's climate is also generally benevolent (though some might argue that it borders on being too hot).

The "winemaker's dance" is the name we have given to the way winegrowers and winemakers interact with the physical elements of terroir—the flowing movement of vision and action that begins with winter pruning and moves through the growing season, into the harvest, and through the winery into barrel and bottle. The involvement is intense, fueled by information, passion, and the ability to integrate diverse modes of knowing. Imagine for a moment the array of information that flows through every winemaker's life—analytical reports, technical data, conversations with vineyard managers and winemaking assistants, sensory input from vineyard and winery, intuitive insights, opinions in the media. It's a world in which the feel of a leaf is balanced against the volume of drip irrigation, in which the taste and sensation of grape pulp and skin are put up against degrees Brix (a measure of sugar content) in which the words of a wine critic are read in relation to the winemaker's vision. The movement of breeze on the skin, the crunch of soil beneath the boot, the touch of a vine tendril, a glimpse of the grapes—all are as important as the spreadsheet that reports tonnage, the analyses of acid and pH, and the sophisticated new technologies now being introduced.

The winemaker's dance is an engagement with land, vine, and human understanding that is fundamental to unraveling the relationship of terroir and wine. The dance touches all aspects of the winegrowing and winemaking process, freely blending observation, information, and intuition. The resulting mix leads to a wine that does, indeed, reflect everything that has gone into its birth. The better the dancer— that is, the more fully in contact the winegrower or winemaker is with the land and all it represents—the truer the wine will be to the place from which it comes. In this view, the human element of terroir is the link that connects Earth, climate, vine, and winery, the connective tissue that binds them all to form the system we identify as terroir.

At its core, the notion of terroir refers to all the qualities that characterize place: topography, bedrock, sediments and soils, temperature, and rainfall. Some wine writers and professionals include viticultural practices, and others recognize the impact of both winegrower and winemaker. The broadest definitions incorporate aspects of culture, attitude, and spirit. James E. Wilson confronts this maze of misunderstanding in *Terroir: The Role of Geology, Climate, and Culture in the Making of French Wines* (Berkeley: University of California Press, 1999), his exhaustive study of the interplay of geology and wine in France. While Wilson provides the finest review of the geology of French wine available, he unfortunately further muddies the already turbulent waters of terroir by offering a range of vague and confusing definitions and further yet by using the term inconsistently (by his own admission) throughout the book. Wilson also implies that certain soils are the source of specific wine characteristics, although he never demonstrates any substantive connection between the two. This is not surprising—establishing the links between terroir and wine character is an elusive and difficult task—but the lack of substantive correlation in Wilson's book becomes apparent only on close reading. One can easily come away with the impression that the correlation of wine character with soil type is well documented.

In our view, while the connection of terroir and wine character is quite real, the specific nature of that connection—which elements of terroir produce specific characteristics in a wine—has yet to be determined. In the chapters that follow, we hope to shine light on this intriguing and murky realm of terroir and wine from a variety of perspectives. We examine how terroir and wine are connected, what we know and what we surmise, what we need to know, and what may forever lie beyond our ken. Make no mistake, however—this is not a guidebook, though perhaps it will offer enough guidance for ambitious readers to undertake a personal exploration of Napa terroir, both on the ground and from the bottle.

Our take on terroir has evolved since we first encountered the term in the late 1980s while working on a video project involving Earth and wine in the Napa Valley. In those days, many winegrowers and winemakers suspected that soil must somehow influence the character of wine, but its importance was not broadly recognized in California or the rest of the country. Most saw the role of soil as supporting the vine, storing water, and providing a few nutrients—end of story. Yet it was obviously not quite that simple.

A few winegrowers by then had decided that certain vineyards imparted such a distinct character that their wines deserved special recognition. Heitz's Martha's Vineyard and Bella Oaks Cabernets, Al Brounstein's three (sometimes four) Diamond Creek Cabernets, Phelps Eisele and Backus, Dunn Howell Mountain, and Stag's Leap Wine Cellars SLV all drew attention to the notion that substrate and place might provide more than simple sustenance. Outside Napa, Paul Draper at Ridge Vineyards and Steve Kistler in Sonoma were exploring this notion with particular vigor. Bill Bonetti, winemaker at Sonoma Cutrer, in 1989 quoted to us the French saying that "the Chardonnay grape is mainly a tool for extracting flavor from the soil." There was a feeling in the air that soil does influence wine character, but no one knew where to go with the idea.

Our perspective was jarred early one morning as we stood high on a ridge on the east side of the Napa Valley, the fog hanging thick and brilliantly white below us, the ridge exposed to the bright and hard winter sun. In answer to some lost interview question, our friend and colleague David Jones, owner of Lava Cap Winery and then professor of geology at the University of California at Berkeley, blurted out, "What you're tasting in a bottle of wine is a hundred million years of geologic history." *Vinull!*

We laughed immediately at such an absurd notion, but as Jones slowly repeated his statement, the reality beneath drew our attention. For all the complexity of the notion of terroir, this observation sliced through physical and historical boundaries that have held our thinking to narrower limits. Jones was suggesting that the character of a wine made from a single, identifiable patch of ground, with concern for quality, reflects not only what we can see and feel today—soil, sun, temperature, and rainfall, for example—but also all the "deep history" of the wine's birthplace, the dynamic mix of forces and events that forms its geologic and geographic heritage. To the three of us that morning, who had spent much of our lives studying Earth, this notion seemed so obvious that we wondered why no one had put it quite that way before.

If indeed we consider grapes as "a tool for extracting flavor from the soil," the notion that in wine we are actually getting a taste of Earth history begins to enter the realm of the thinkable. Soils—often taking tens or hundreds of thousands of years to develop fully—are complex mixtures of minerals, plants, and microorganisms in a dynamic state. The mineral components of soils are derived from the breakdown of rocks, which, in turn, are the product of a long and complicated evolutionary history. Assuming for the moment that the quality and character of grapes do reflect the place where they grow, then the wine made from them also will reflect that place. Thus the bottle of wine that we might be drinking tonight can, with a little effort on our part, reconnect us with both its roots and our own, for we both, ultimately, come from Earth. *Atonement w/ Dionysus*

Although many of us are cut off from nature by fast-paced urban lives, we all nonetheless depend on the land. We are supported and nourished by Earth, not in any mystical sense, but in the most pragmatic way. Everything that provides us with physical nourishment comes in some way from the land. The cells of our bodies are renewed every seven years, built from the food we eat. The air we breathe is intrinsic to that renewal, with the oxygen in the atmosphere in part a by-product of plant photosynthesis and thus also a product of the land. We may no longer be connected to place—the region where we live—by what we eat; our food, once local and seasonal, is now global and year-round. But wherever we live, however surrounded we are by the built environment, however disconnected from Earth we might feel, our bodies are still of the Earth. We are more directly connected with the notion and reality of terroir than we might think.

The land and its history, however, are only part of terroir. The notion also embraces other physical characteristics of place, such as rainfall, temperature, sun exposure, and slope. Additionally, we include the vine itself and the way it is cultivated as well as the history and culture of place. The grape grower and winemaker are also intrinsic parts of terroir, because their vision and actions influence the degree to which place is expressed in the grapes and the wine.

The concept of terroir does not specify how these elements are linked or precisely how they affect the character of the wine—they simply are part of the system, the context in which the wine is made and which, to varying degrees, the wine embodies. Terroir is a concept similar to the notion of "ecosystem," which is shorthand for all the aspects of a place that influence the growth and development of the plants and animals within its boundaries—including, of course, those plants and animals. Humans within the ecosystem boundaries, and all their actions, are an intrinsic part of the ecosystem—and so with terroir. As Warren Winiarski, owner of Stag's Leap Wine Cellars and one of the valley's most thoughtful winemakers, so directly states, "Without people, there is no terroir. It all rests on the '3 Gs'—ground, grapes, and guys," the necessary elements for the expression of the land in a bottle of wine. (We quickly note that, in Winiarski's lexicon, "guys" encompasses both genders.) For many, terroir also has a spiritual character, an aspect that can only be sensed rather than understood analytically.

The physical side of all this—the elements of land and climate, for example—is the easy part; we can describe physical things fairly objectively. Some features of grape growing and winemaking also have a clear and objective nature. The type of rootstock and clone used in a particular vineyard can be identified and described; but the reason they were chosen and the way they are trellised and pruned begin to enter the domain of the personal, the realm of the winemaker's vision. The elements of terroir that are most difficult to evaluate are those based in culture and history. In France, wines have been made for a thousand years; some vineyards have been in nearly continuous production for hundreds of years. While such long-term influences are not part of the relatively short Napa Valley experience, the historical and cultural context is nonetheless very much a part of today's terroir.

The winegrowers and winemakers are perhaps the most fascinating aspect of terroir, complex systems in and of themselves. Their role is akin to that of the physicist in an experiment—the source of the vision, the builder of the apparatus, the director of the process. Quantum mechanics recognizes, however, that the experimenter can never be separated from the experiment—introducing himself or herself into the system changes the context of the experiment from the pure vision of

AVAs IN THE NAPA REGION

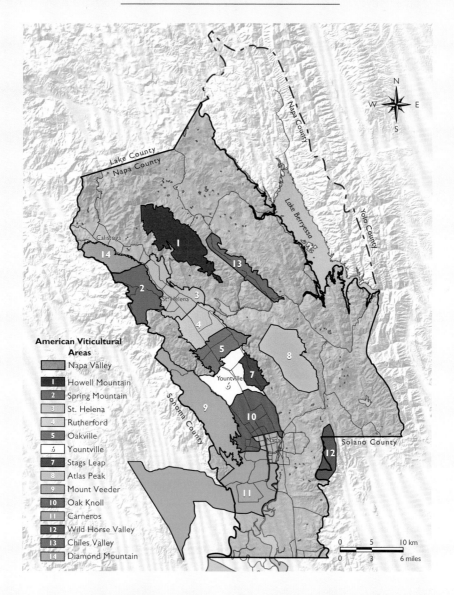

American Viticultural Areas

- Napa Valley
- **1** Howell Mountain
- **2** Spring Mountain
- **3** St. Helena
- **4** Rutherford
- **5** Oakville
- **6** Yountville
- **7** Stags Leap
- **8** Atlas Peak
- **9** Mount Veeder
- **10** Oak Knoll
- **11** Carneros
- **12** Wild Horse Valley
- **13** Chiles Valley
- **14** Diamond Mountain

The Napa region contains multiple American Viticultural Areas (AVAs). The accompanying map outlines Napa County, the Napa Valley AVA, and fourteen smaller AVAs in the region.

The Napa Valley AVA covers an area far larger than the region we think of as the Napa Valley. The valley is about thirty miles long and, at most, three miles wide, and runs from Carneros in the south to Calistoga in the north. The AVA extends well beyond these limits; it is about forty miles long and twenty-one miles wide and includes Chiles Valley, Pope Valley, Wooden Valley, part of Wild Horse Valley, and several smaller named depressions as well as the Napa Valley. And Napa County is bigger yet, extending to the east past the boundary of the Napa Valley AVA. The Napa Valley AVA includes

(continued)

(continued)

each of the fourteen smaller AVAs, which can be considered subappellations within the larger unit.

The U.S. Bureau of Alcohol, Tobacco, and Firearms set up the AVA system in 1978. An individual or a group can apply for an AVA designation for an area that has some physical or historical distinction. (The designation is not an indicator of the quality of the wine made in the AVA.)

Defining the boundary of an AVA can become a political tussle. If the proposed name has some type of cachet—an association over the years with high-quality wines, for example—owners of properties around the edges of the area will lobby vigorously to be included. As a result, some boundaries reflect marketing purposes rather than natural physical realities. By law, boundaries must be drawn on the basis of features visible on maps that are specifically defined in the regulations; the standard generally is a large-scale topographic map from the U.S. Geological Survey. Because the regulations state, however, that AVA boundaries cannot cut existing properties, the outlines of an AVA might be drawn at a political marker such as a road or a town line.

The political nature of defining AVAs has led to some boundaries that do not seem to make much geologic, geographic, or enological sense. In a recent conversation, Tim Mondavi clarified some results of the process that we had found particularly unusual. The boundaries of several of the AVAs that cover the central part of the valley—the Yountville, Oakville, Rutherford, and St. Helena AVAs—run from one side of the valley to the other. Each of these AVAs includes a variety of areas that are geologically and geographically distinct. Mondavi's explanation focused on the relationship of these boundaries to climatic variation. He noted that temperatures within the valley generally increase from south to north and

(continued)

the experimenter to a system that includes his or her influence. So, too, with the winegrower and winemaker, without whom there is no wine and no expression of terroir. Starting with a vision, they activate the links that connect Earth with vine and fruit, guide the transformation of fruit into wine, oversee its maturation, and only then present the liquid that completes the circle, connecting us with the Earth from which the wine arose.

The Napa Valley began its modern rise to prominence in the eyes of the wine world through a surprising event: the legendary 1976 blind tasting of French and American wines in Paris, arranged as a marketing ploy by English wine merchant Steven Spurrier. In that tasting, Warren Winiarski's Stag's Leap Wine Cellars 1973 Cabernet Sauvignon was judged the best of the reds. It won out over four prominent French Châteaux, including Mouton Rothschild (second), and five other American wines. (A Chateau Montelena Chardonnay was picked as the best of the whites, favored even over Bâtard Montrachet, a legendary white Burgundy.) This event changed everything. In 1966, when Winiarski was working at the new and architecturally startling Robert Mondavi Winery, Napa was home to only nineteen other wineries; today, the Napa Valley nurtures more than 280 establishments, many producing wines that are recognized throughout the world. The Napa Valley attracts more than five million visitors each year; it is, in every sense, a world-class producer of fine wine.

The 1976 Paris tasting alone would not have led to the continued evolution that followed. In our view, the combined attributes that underlie

the winemaker's dance—a commitment to
quality, an openness to experience, a willingness
to experiment, and a trust in diverse ways of
knowing—were key. Some of the more apparent aspects of the dance—the fundamentals of
grape growing and winemaking—are well
known, though they evolve with time and experience. Others are less obvious: the influence
of sediments and soils on grapes and wine, for
example, and the balance between the winemaker's hand and the effects of physical terroir.

(continued)

that the boundaries reflect that overall pattern.
He added that he had always perceived the original boundaries as first approximations and expressed the opinion that greater understanding
of the factors affecting variation in grape and
wine quality and character might well lead to
modification of these original boundaries.

The geologic character of the valley and the dynamic history that lies hidden within
its landscapes, sediments, and soils are integral parts of the dance, however far removed
they might seem. And so are the character and personality of the winemaker, that particular balance of spirit and intellect, analysis and intuition, linearity and randomness,
risk and security. Personal style is as influential in the work of making wine as it is in
business, the arts, or science.

In this book, we examine all these elements of terroir to understand how they
are connected by the different rhythms and styles of the winemaker's dance. We'll
look first at the physical aspects of terroir—the evolution of the land, the character
of the bedrock foundation, the nature of sediment and soil, and the relationship between landscape and climate. From that beginning, we'll enter the vineyard, seeing
how variation in physical terroir affects the overall character and quality of grapes
and how winegrowers respond to this interaction. From there, we'll travel to the
winery, once the place where great wine was made, now more often the site of efforts
to preserve the quality that arrives from the vineyard. Winegrowers and winemakers appear throughout the book, and we devote one chapter to the winemaker's dance
as reflected in the words of the men and women who exemplify the idea. We'll end
with a short examination of fad and fashion in the wine business, a critical issue in
today's wine world.

We address the central issue of the relationship between terroir and wine character in a variety of ways throughout the book. From our perspective, the information necessary to make precise statements concerning this relationship, particularly
involving specific wines from specific sites, is ordinarily not available. The variables
(site, substrate, climate, sun exposure, rootstock, clone, trellis, pruning, fertilization,
irrigation, and all that happens in the winery) are many, and their specific effects are
not well substantiated. For us, the available evidence shows clearly that terroir and

wine character are closely related. How else, for example, could those tasters with super-sensitive palates, the Masters of Wine and others who can consistently identify blind-tasted wines down to vineyard and year, do what they do?

For those of us with less sensitive palates, we liken the association of terroir with wine to the notion of provenance for a piece of art. Knowing something about the history of a painting and the social milieu in which it was created adds to its interest and value. Vermeer surely is made more fascinating by the mystery surrounding his life and work, just as Gauguin's decision to leave the world of commerce and spend the latter part of his life in the South Seas becomes a part of his mystique. A Renoir owned originally by a Flemish aristocrat, inherited by a Dutch owner who perished in the Holocaust, stolen by Goering, and then rediscovered decades later and returned to the family of the rightful owner holds something abstract but powerful that sets it apart. So, too, with wine.

Knowing something of the terroir, in all its aspects, from which a wine arises adds a vibrant dimension to the experience of wine. Our goal is to engage these notions and to examine the elements of winegrowing and winemaking—Earth, vines, and people—in a way that will provide avenues for your own exploration of these ideas and associations. Along the way, we hope that you will learn, if you haven't done so already, to trust your own taste.

❖❖❖ *one* ❖❖❖

BIRTH OF A VALLEY

FLYING FROM DENVER to San Francisco at thirty-five thousand feet, you see below, west of the Rocky Mountains, a vast desert cut through by sublinear mountain ranges. This geologic province, known as the Great Basin, extends from the Utah-Colorado border west for several hundred miles. Seared brown flats, with the remains of lakes long ago dried up, separate mountain heights and discourage most human activity. Anonymous dirt roads that seem to come from nowhere end in small clusters of buildings. It is a land that breeds paranoid fantasies of men in black uniforms, of UFOs crashing and being hidden by the government, a land some think inhabited by space aliens.

Patterns on the ground, abstractions in a brown-on-brown palette, record the water flow from snowmelt and rare rainstorms. Mesmerized by mile on mile of this scrolling canvas, you might be jolted by the sudden appearance of steep forest-clad slopes. They rise abruptly, cut by deep canyons, topped by bald gray knobs that roll away north and south into the distance. In the low sun of early morning or late afternoon, curving knife-edge ridges stand out, linking one sharp peak with another. These are the walls of glacial cirques, high-altitude bowls carved when the mountains were host to year-round ice and extensive alpine glaciers. These mountains, the Sierra Nevada, are the cause of the desert that fills the land to the east. Moisture-laden air rises up the gentle western face of the mountains, cooling as it goes, dropping most of its cargo of water on the heights and leaving little for the other side. The desert lies in the rain shadow of the Sierra, and a broad shadow it is.

Crossing the Sierra and moving on toward San Francisco, you may note the long western gradient of the mountains, carved by deep canyons that drain snowmelt and rain. These canyons have the U-shaped form that comes from scouring by valley glaciers; one is the canyon of Yosemite, its cliffs known as American icons.

Gradually the forests give way to scrub growth, and the gentle slope of the mountains merges with the floor of the Central Valley. This great trough runs the length of central California, from Bakersfield in the south to Red Bluff in the north, drained by the San Joaquin River in its southern part, the Sacramento in the north. The valley floor is a quilt of farms, one of the most productive agricultural regions in the world. If not for water from Sierra snows, stored for summer irrigation, this too would be a desert, caught in the rain shadow of the Coast Ranges.

Those hills, farther west and rising to more than four thousand feet, form the western boundary of the Central Valley and the western margin of the continent. The relatively affordable suburbs of the Bay Area swarm along the eastern flanks of these hills, while the cities and more upscale suburbs hug the shores of San Francisco Bay.

If you're flying into Oakland or taking a northern approach to the San Francisco airport, you might notice a couple of valleys that begin at the northern tip of San Francisco Bay. The smaller one to the west is Sonoma; the other is the Napa Valley. Depending on visibility, you might even be able to discern Napa's two parts, a wider southern portion and a narrow northern extension. The valley is the result of a long and complex series of events that tell the tale of how the western margin of North America was formed, a land that was not here 145 million years ago. The story of terroir in Napa begins that far back, when the foundations of the valley began to take shape.

SHAPING THE FOUNDATION

If you had flown over the Sierra 145 million years ago, the picture spread beneath you would have been vastly different, looking more like the Aleutian coast of Alaska, where flight patterns are often interrupted by volcanic activity. Your plane might have had to dodge thick plumes of ash, for the Sierra Nevada of that time consisted of a string of volcanoes that extended the length of the current range. These volcanoes formed from magma that rose as the Farallon plate descended beneath North America. Today's Cascades are the northern and most recent extension of this ancient Sierran volcanism.

The coast was only a few miles to the west of the volcanic range, perhaps like the Peruvian or Chilean coast of today, where the mountains rise steeply out of the Pacific Ocean, climbing to twenty thousand feet within thirty miles of the shore. Scaling a Sierran peak of that day would have been a more difficult and dangerous task, but the view would have been impressive. You would have seen a group of volcanic is-

FIGURE 1. The Pacific coast of North America 145 million years ago. The Farallon plate slides beneath North America, creating a range of volcanic mountains, the precursors to the Sierra Nevada. A group of undersea mountains, some exposed as islands, approaches the coast.

lands much like the Philippines or Indonesia some distance offshore. These islands, borne on the Farallon tectonic plate, were inexorably approaching the coast. Within the next 5 million years, they would slam into North America and slide below its surface, crushed between the two plates and smeared onto the continent, beginning the creation of all of California west of the Sierra Nevada.

During subduction, in which plates or continental masses meet, one slides beneath the other, descending into the mantle, the distinct layer immediately below the Earth's relatively thin crust. On continents, the crust averages about forty miles in thickness; on the ocean basins, about ten (Figure 1). While this difference sounds large, on the scale of Earth it becomes imperceptible, like the variations in thickness in the skin of an inflated birthday balloon. The mantle that lies below the crust is rock under intense pressure and at progressively higher temperatures toward the core, the metallic center of the planet (see Figure 3). Composed of nickel and iron, the outer layer of the core is liquid, while its innermost portion is a solid nearly as hot as the surface of the sun.

As the lower plate slides down into the mantle, friction between the plates heats the rock, while entrained water lowers its melting point. At a depth of about sixty miles, the rock begins to melt. The molten magma rises through the mantle as small blobs and strings, driven by differences in temperature and density. This material rises until its density, lowered by cooling, matches that of the surrounding rock. There it

Geologists work, at best, with limited and indirect data, trying to read a history that is recorded in a nonhuman language with a grammar and syntax made readable only through observation and progressive approximation. Perhaps reading the rocks is a bit like translating Mayan pictographs or Egyptian hieroglyphics, though at least we know those forms are of human origin. In addition, many of the processes geologists attempt to understand, such as subduction, cannot be immediately observed and move at a pace so different from our experience that we can only imagine it. The reconstruction of Earth history is like attempting to reconstruct the daily life and relationships of that early hominid Lucy, whom we know only from scattered fragments of bone. We do the best we can with what we have, but it's merely an approximation of the way things might have been.

accumulates, forming magma chambers some thousands of feet beneath the surface. Eventually the surface above begins to wheeze and crack under the pressure of the rising magma, which erupts either with an explosive roar, as Mount St. Helens did, or more gently, with lava flowing onto the ground in the style of Hawaiian volcanoes such as Mauna Loa. The difference lies in the composition of the fluid—with more silica, the major component of Earth's crust, the magma becomes more viscous and less likely to flow, with a greater tendency to explode suddenly.

The volcanic islands that slid beneath western North America so many millions of years ago are preserved in ocean crust rocks that lie within the foothills of the Sierra. No longer readily identifiable as islands, they exist today as isolated fragments that have been smeared out against the edge of the continent. Imagine the Philippine Islands approaching the Chinese mainland, closing the South China Sea, and then slowly sliding beneath the coast of China, crushed between the Pacific and Eurasian plates, and you'll have a picture of what was happening in California.

Given the scale of this event—an island mass colliding with a continent—the effects were far-reaching. The molding of the volcanic arc into the underpinnings of North America, a bit like squashing a piece of red clay onto the edge of a slab of green, changed the character of plate movement. The position of plates on the globe would remain unusually stable for the next 80 million years, during the period that stretched from 140 million years ago to about 60 million years ago. But at the beginning of this period, some 5 million years after the islands disappeared beneath North America, the subduction zone that marked the western boundary of North America suddenly and mysteriously jumped far to the west, trapping a chunk of ocean crust and adding it to the North American plate. This chunk, now known as the Coast Range ophiolite, forms the foundation for all the other materials that later came together to form the land we call California.

We might say, in summary, that the real history of California began about 140 million years ago. At that time, the physical, geologic, and natural western boundary of North America lay some distance west of the actual coastline, beneath the waters of the Pacific Ocean. At this continental edge, the Farallon plate slid beneath North America, creating a range of volcanoes along the coast that were the precursors of today's Sierra Nevada. About this same time, a set of volcanic islands on the Farallon plate was sliding beneath North America.

As the early Sierran volcanoes built up layer after layer of lava and ash, they slowly took on the volcanic shapes we know so well—the perfection of a Mount Fuji, for example, or the magnificence of a Mount Rainier. Gradually, their weight began to depress the crust, creating a deep trough that extended the length of the range. West of the trough, on the edge of the North American plate, a bulge developed in the sea floor. This upwarp in the crust was linked to the formation of the trough—as one part of the crust is depressed, the adjacent one warps up. You can illustrate this by pressing the edge of your hand into a folded towel, forming a trough; the towel will rise on each side, forming a double bulge. (This process is far more important than it might seem from this brief description. Crustal bulges, which are associated with zones of mountain building throughout the world, contain a considerable portion of the oil and gas that have been trapped within the crust.)

You may wonder at the notion of Earth's crust bowing down under an added weight—after all, rocks are hard and unyielding, and we perceive the crust as rigid and fixed. In reality, however, the crust is quite flexible, and it floats, more or less, on the denser mantle below. Think of a steel reinforcing rod used to strengthen concrete. In short segments, the rod is rigid, impossible to bend. But in lengths of twenty feet and more, it bends under its own weight. Rocks are similar: in larger masses, they become malleable. Traveling through mountainous country—the Alps of Europe or the Appalachians and Rockies of North America, for example—you may notice layers of rock that are bent and broken, often in fantastic shapes (Figure 2). These forms reflect the immense forces that accompany the process of continents colliding, which creates pressures and temperatures that cause rocks to flow while changing their mineral composition. As the rocks cool and the pressure is eased, they become rigid and brittle. Although in Napa you won't see folded rocks quite like those shown in Figure 2, you can find rocks tilted up on edge—layers once horizontal that are now sitting vertically—along the Silverado Trail. Similar rock geometries, though not as steep, occur throughout the Vaca and Mayacamas Mountains.

FIGURE 2. Folded rocks in the Tian Shan Mountains of western China. When under pressure, rocks slowly bend and fold, sometimes in complex shapes.

THE GREAT VALLEY SEQUENCE AND THE FRANCISCAN FORMATION

Beginning 140 million years ago, then, and continuing for 80 million years, volcanic ash and lava erupted from the Sierra Nevada volcanoes. Red-hot ash and rock roared down their sides in pyroclastic flows at velocities up to two hundred miles per hour. Massive thunderstorms flooded the mountains, saturating the soft ash and rock that accumulated on their flanks and forming volcanic mudflows (lahars). We have seen these processes in relatively recent years, particularly at Mount St. Helens in 1980, when pyroclastic flows tumbled down the mountainside and lahars clogged the local rivers with mud and forest debris.

During these volcanic eons in the Sierra, rain and snow fell, rivers ran, the seasons followed one another much as they do today. Beset by weathering processes, solid rocks slowly rotted into smaller particles, which were eroded by water and carried into streams. The streams moved them from the mountains to the shore, storing the sediment temporarily in beaches, marshes, and offshore bars. As material piled up near the shore, periodic events—large storms, earthquakes, tidal waves—shook some of the accumulation loose and transported it in giant undersea mudflows into the deep axis of the trough. Here, layers of sand and silt slowly accumulated, each layer representing one of these catastrophic events.

The slurries that deposited these layers are known as turbidity currents. Scientists understand them well in part because they still occur in the deep sea. Turbidity currents were first discovered some decades ago when a series of undersea cables broke in an unusual nonrandom pattern, starting near the coast and progressing farther out to sea. Investigators determined that the cables had been cut in sequence by a strong undersea current carrying a heavy load of sediment. Geologists have now identified the remains of such currents throughout the long history of Earth and in many places, including the Napa Valley.

Volcanic edifices, composed as they are of layers of soft ash, the rubble of lava flows, and other loose debris, do not last long at Earth's surface, at least in comparison to other geologic features—one hundred thousand years is ancient for a volcano. As volcanic activity died out in the Sierra, the volcanoes were worn away by weathering and erosion that exposed their roots, the huge granite masses called batholiths that, when molten, had fed the volcanic activity. The most photogenic of these masses are the fabled faces of El Capitan and Half Dome in Yosemite National Park. Beneath these bodies, ancient ocean crust and pre-Sierran volcanic rocks lay at the foot of the mountains. These, too, contributed material to the sediments that accumulated in the adjacent basin.

For 80 million years, the boulders, gravel, sand, and clay derived from the Sierra and delivered to the trough at the foot of the mountains piled up to a thickness of about fifty thousand feet. Mind you, this is the present thickness of the pile—the depth of water in the basin itself was never more than perhaps a few thousand feet. As the weight of sediment increased, the crust slowly subsided, making space for additional geologic debris. Now solid rock, this accumulation of sandstone and shale is known as the Great Valley sequence. Slices of it, torn from the parent accumulation by the forces of tectonic faulting, form one of the primary bedrock components of the Napa Valley.

The sandstones of the Great Valley sequence are mostly arkose, a rock made up of light-colored, silica-based minerals with a high content of potassium, sodium, and calcium. The rocks are mainly shades of brown and tan, reflecting their mineral makeup. The character of the rocks in this great pile changed a bit with time, reflecting broad sea-level changes and events in the history of the Sierra, but the story of the Great Valley sequence is notably straightforward and well understood.

During this same time, the Pacific Ocean, stretching west of the crustal bulge, contained all the features that we find in modern ocean basins: extinct, undersea volcanoes with flat, eroded tops (seamounts); island arcs like the Aleutians, the Philippines, or the Indonesian archipelago; and deep-water sediments derived in part from erosion of these other features. These ocean sediments included thinly bedded cherts, rocks of pure amorphous silica derived from the shells of minute organisms that slowly rain onto the sea floor, corpses of the immensely prolific populations of tiny radiolaria that inhabit the surface of world oceans. Pure cherts only form far from land; they accumulate so slowly that delivery of dust, mud, or sand will dilute their concentration. A fraction of an inch of chert will take one hundred years to accumu-

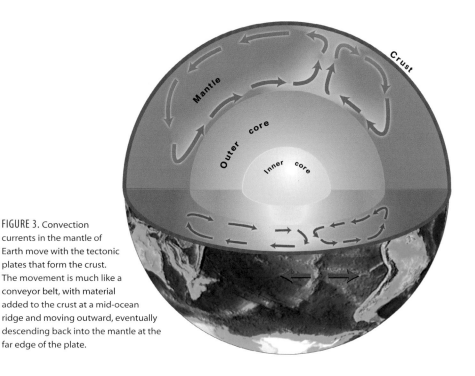

FIGURE 3. Convection currents in the mantle of Earth move with the tectonic plates that form the crust. The movement is much like a conveyor belt, with material added to the crust at a mid-ocean ridge and moving outward, eventually descending back into the mantle at the far edge of the plate.

late; a three-foot thickness represents approximately 1 million years. Cherts occur in Napa north of Lake Hennessey.

During the 80 million years of Great Valley sequence accumulation, up to seven thousand miles of Pacific Ocean crust disappeared beneath North America. Think of it: the equivalent of the entire width of today's Pacific Ocean basin sliding below North America, where it was assimilated into the mantle. As this crust disappeared, new material was added at the other side of the plate, much as new crust is appended today at the mid-ocean ridges that represent plate boundaries. Picture a conveyor belt moving at a rate of a few centimeters each year. Rock is added at the spreading ridge on one end and slides outward, away from the ridge (Figure 3). At the other edge of the belt, the plate slides beneath a continent or an oceanic island arc, returning to the mantle from which it originally arose.

Visualize that plate descending for 80 million years beneath the continent, carrying with it seamounts, volcanic island arcs, chunks of ocean crust, and a variety of sediments, some derived from erosion of adjacent land, some formed within the ocean itself. As the plate slides beneath the crustal bulge, rocks and sediments are literally scraped off and plastered onto the continent. In a crude analogy, put yourself in a kitchen cleaning up after dinner. Imagine a large spatula (North America) sliding

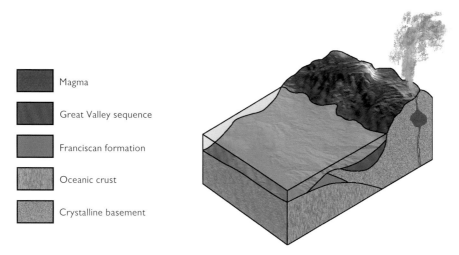

Magma

Great Valley sequence

Franciscan formation

Oceanic crust

Crystalline basement

FIGURE 4. The Napa region about 90 million years ago. The weight of the growing volcanic mountains formed a deep trough along their length, with a crustal bulge west of the trough at the geologic edge of the continent. Sediments of the Great Valley sequence accumulated in the trough, while the components of the Franciscan formation were added to the continent at its edge. The crystalline basement represents the continental rocks that existed before the formation of the volcanic mountains.

over a dinner plate (the ocean crust) and beneath the leftovers (the ocean floor material) to scrape them off. The result is a conglomeration of stuff, food in this case, mashed together and smashed onto the spatula. Material from the sea floor was smashed onto the edge of North America in much the same way.

This geologic flotsam and jetsam is known as the Franciscan formation. This complex rock unit underlies much of coastal California and is one of the major bedrock components of the Napa Valley region. The Franciscan formed off the coast during the same period in which the Great Valley sequence was accumulating in the trough adjacent to the Sierra Nevada. The two rock units developed contemporaneously under quite different environmental circumstances (Figure 4).

The importance of this history was surely a mystery to Chris Howell when he arrived at Cain Vineyards high on Spring Mountain in 1990. But he has been farming these vineyards and making wine from the grapes long enough now to know well the challenges of growing fruit on the Franciscan formation—dealing with the difficult chemistry of Franciscan sediments; working with the instability of Franciscan rocks on steep, terraced slopes; and understanding these odd rocks and the soils that form on them. Howell is sure that the characteristics of the Franciscan that make it difficult to work also provide the elements for a wine of particular distinc-

FIGURE 5. Franciscan mélange at Cain Vineyards, with a large chunk of ocean crust about twenty-five feet high, called a knocker, standing out against the smooth slopes that form on finer-grained sediments. Smaller knockers are found in the undeveloped patches within the vineyard.

tion, one that truly reflects place. And that's what makes the Franciscan formation so interesting.

The Franciscan formation, overall, is a heterogeneous and puzzling set of materials. It includes serpentinites—rocks containing chemical elements, particularly nickel, that are toxic to grapes. And it tends to be high in magnesium, which requires special awareness and care on the part of the winegrower, as it affects the uptake of potassium, an element vital to good fruit. Individual rock components of the Franciscan are readily identifiable in terms of their origin—an individual outcrop might be recognizable as an ancient seamount or deep sea fan, for example—but their relationship to one another is often unclear. The mechanics that brought together the components of the Franciscan formation remain something of a mystery.

When geologists can't explain the parts, they invent a term to embrace the whole. Most of the Franciscan in the Napa Valley area consists of just such a material, known as mélange, a chaotic mixture of ocean floor sediment and chunks of ocean crust. As you drive through the Coast Ranges, you can see deposits of Franciscan mélange scattered through the hills. The less resistant sea floor sediments form smooth, soft-looking, rolling hills, punctuated by sharp, irregular masses of rock often tens of feet in diameter that dot the hills like so many raisins in a rice pudding (Figure 5). These are chunks of ocean crust, harder and more resistant than the surrounding sediments, which wash away with greater ease.

Let's recap the geologic events we've been describing. For about 80 million years, the geography of California featured a volcanic mountain range that shed sediments into a trough at the western edge of North America, forming the Great Valley sequence, a diverse accumulation of sand and mud, now transformed into sandstone and shale. West of this trough, at the far edge of the continent, lay a crustal bulge. There, the Farallon plate continued to slide beneath North America, adding to the continent the complex materials of the Franciscan formation, scraped from the ocean plate. Subduction of the Farallon plate occurred in fits and starts; during certain periods, compressive forces affected the continent all the way to Colorado. By dating the timing of events such as uplift, mountain building, and volcanic activity, geologists have assembled a reasonably clear history of this process, in which periods of dormancy gave way to episodes of mountain building, all reflecting the stuttering impact of subduction at the western margin of North America.

Then, about 60 million years ago, things changed drastically. Ranges of volcanic mountains began to appear progressively eastward from the Sierra Nevada, eventually reaching Colorado. The region of mountain building, the result of compression associated with active subduction, also moved east, as far as South Dakota, where the Black Hills stand in stark witness to the process. The cause of this change is not immediately apparent, but it probably involved a sudden alteration in the angle of subduction. "Sudden," of course, is a relative term—the change occurred over some tens or hundreds of thousands of years, the equivalent of a quarter or so of the total history of the human race, but a blink for the planet. The effects were far ranging: instead of descending steeply below North America, the Farallon plate flattened considerably, probably because the younger, more buoyant, incoming crust sank more slowly into the mantle. Thus the point at which the subducting plate reached a depth of sixty miles—the depth at which melting begins—moved steadily eastward. The volcanic arc marched along with it, the rocks at the surface reflecting this history.

THE SAN ANDREAS SYSTEM AND THE NAPA VOLCANICS

Some 25 million years ago, a critical event in the history of California occurred, which haunts us still: the San Andreas fault system was born. The mechanics of its development are complex, but the pattern is easy to discern. The movement of three plates—the Farallon plate, the Pacific plate, and the North American plate—brought them together at a point on the coast that geologists describe as a triple junction, a place where three different entities converge. The particular geometry of this meeting created a transition on the coast from subduction (one plate sliding beneath an-

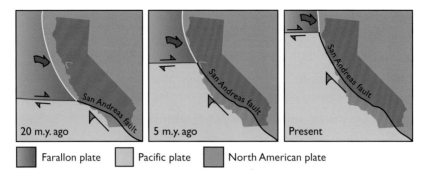

FIGURE 6. The meeting of the Farallon, Pacific, and North American plates created a triple junction that moved up the coast, forming the San Andreas fault. Complex movement of the plates continues to extend the fault system to the north.

other) to translation, in which one plate slides past the other horizontally, or laterally. This is the motion of the San Andreas fault and its related faults—the Hayward, the Rogers Creek, and the various others that splay from the San Andreas and affect much of the length of coastal California (Figure 6). As the three plates continued to move, the triple junction traveled up the coast, with the fault following along. The moving triple junction, in effect, cut into the Earth's crust just as a scalpel slices the skin, separating California into two parts, east and west of the complex system of faults.

The transition from subduction to lateral movement was accompanied by an advancing conflagration of fiery lava eruptions and outpourings of ash and gas that skipped up the coast along with the triple junction, beginning about 24 million years ago in southern California. The volcanic centers are separated from one another—after the fireworks died off at one location, and after the triple junction had traveled some distance, another would appear farther north but with no pattern other than the association with the triple junction. At each volcanic location, a thick covering of ash and lava would blanket the region for many square miles over a period of a few million years. Older volcanic accumulations were sliced up and offset by the faults of the growing San Andreas system, making the bedrock geology increasingly complex, a jigsaw puzzle of displaced fragments.

And then, approximately 7 million years ago, the volcanism reached Napa, at that time an area of considerably less relief than today. As in regions to the south, volcanic rocks would cover hundreds of square miles with a thick veneer of Napa volcanics (the name we use here for what are officially known as Sonoma Volcanics) over the next 5 million years or so (Figure 7). They formed the top layer of a sand-

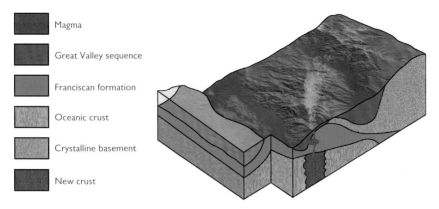

Magma

Great Valley sequence

Franciscan formation

Oceanic crust

Crystalline basement

New crust

FIGURE 7. The Napa region 5 million years ago during the eruption of the Napa volcanics, which eventually covered several hundred square miles with layers of diverse volcanic rocks.

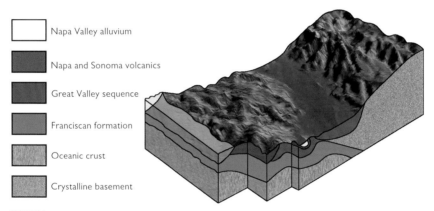

Napa Valley alluvium

Napa and Sonoma volcanics

Great Valley sequence

Franciscan formation

Oceanic crust

Crystalline basement

FIGURE 8. Formation of the Coast Ranges defined the topography that we see today. Napa is one of a host of valleys defined by the uplifted hills.

wich, with oceanic crust the bottom layer, and the Franciscan formation and the Great Valley sequence serving as the fill (Figure 8).

As you drive up Highway 29 from Napa north into the valley on a beautiful fall or winter day when the air is clear and crisp, the sharp outline of Mount St. Helena looms ahead. It seems to stand alone, framed by the Mayacamas Mountains on the west and the Vaca Mountains on the east. Mount St. Helena is nearly symmetrical, with the steep sides and truncated top of a classic volcano. Similarly, as you drive along the Silverado Trail in the late afternoon, after the sun has sunk behind the Mayacamas Mountains, the blue-black profile of Mount St. John, with the same symmetrical form, dominates the western sky. Everyone in the region "knows" that these two mountains were the source of the volcanic rocks that underlie so many of Napa's vineyards. But the truth is that not a single volcanic eruption burst forth from either peak. Mount St. John and Mount Veeder are made up of the sedimentary rocks of the Franciscan formation and the Great Valley sequence, respectively; and Mount St. Helena, while formed of volcanic rock, is not a volcano.

Rather than creating edifices like Mount Fuji, the Napa volcanics erupted from great elongate cracks in Earth's crust, and they must have been terrifying. These were not gentle outpourings of lava that flowed along relatively contained, and avoidable, pathways like those you can approach in Hawaii or on Mount Etna. Instead, these were violent explosions of volcanic rock, ash, and gas that burst high into the atmosphere, darkening the sun and creating their own thunderous weather. Any life in the area would have been engulfed by deathly hot rock and dust, much as the victims of the Mount St. Helens explosion were. The aligned trees at the Petrified Forest west of Calistoga, laid side by side like the downed trees at Mount St. Helens, are a mute remnant of a powerful lateral blast. Also near Calistoga, the Palisades—the prominent cliff-forming rock that caps the Vaca Mountains in this area—are made of ignimbrite, coarse-grained volcanic rocks created by large eruptive blasts in which ash and coarser fragments are thrown high into the air and fall quickly back to Earth. The coarser fragments land first, forming a flow that thickens as the material moves down gullies. The thickness acts as insulation, and the high internal temperatures of the flows cause shards of glass, cooled somewhat and solidified in the atmosphere, to remelt. As this material cools once again, it welds the coarser volcanic fragments together into hard, resistant beds like those that hold up these cliffs.

Explosive eruptions, the roar of pyroclastic flows, the rumble and grinding of lahars—all were part of the landscape during the few million years in which the Napa volcanics were forming. Violent thunder and lightning accompanied the eruptions, with torrential rains forming thick mudflows from the loose ash and other accumulated debris. But the volcanic activity was not continuous. Ric Forman's vineyard and caves on Howell Mountain, and the area near the crest of Old Howell Mountain Road, for example, contain river gravel composed mainly of Franciscan and Great Valley rocks layered within the Napa volcanics. While the name "Napa volcanics" may suggest a monolithic deposit, in truth these rocks are strikingly diverse, including tuff (volcanic ash) of various chemical and mineralogical compositions, lava flows, pyroclastic deposits, volcanic mudflows, intrusive (noneruptive) rocks, and sedimentary rocks of volcanic origin.

In addition to lateral motion, movement along the San Andreas fault also contained an element of push and pull, compression and tension. At the fault's inception, the northward-drifting Pacific plate was also moving slightly west. This pull on the crust created depressions, or basins, which filled with sediment eroded from adjacent highlands. These basins include the Southern San Joaquin Basin, the Santa Maria Basin, the Los Angeles Basin, and even the ancestral San Francisco Bay. Cold waters of the Pacific filled these quiet, oxygen-deprived depressions with rich populations of marine algae preserved in thick, organic-rich bottom deposits. This organic gunk was later transformed into some of the richest oil deposits in the world (measured not in total amount but in the volume of oil per cubic yard of rock). Similar basins formed in the area of San Diego, Bakersfield, Santa Barbara, and on up the coastal region of California. But no such basin appeared in the Napa Valley region—had it done so, the valley today might well be filled with oil derricks and pumps rather than vineyards.

Evidence does suggest that a small, ancestral Napa Valley formed at about this time, providing space for the sediments of the Glen Ellen formation. Modest mountains to the east shed gravels that accumulated above sea level, the debris spreading over a broad plain. Gravels and chert-rich sediments accumulated in lakes, in rivers, and on flood plains, along with thick deposits of nonmarine clays, the sediments delivered by streams and rivers draining the hills nearby. These materials make up the Glen Ellen, which underlies much of the Carneros region, providing a substrate unlike anything else in the Napa Valley AVA.

About 3 million years ago, the Pacific plate once again changed direction, now pushing the two sides of the San Andreas fault toward each other, creating a bit of compression. It was only a small force, perhaps 5 or 10 percent of the total movement along the fault, one kilometer of compression for every ten kilometers of lateral movement. But it was enough to create the California Coast Ranges and the ridges that define Napa. Slices of rock were stacked atop one another to form the Vaca Mountains, a crustal wrinkle formed the Mayacamas Mountains, and the downwarp that separated the two ranges defined the Napa Valley (Figure 9). During a respite in this process, a flat erosion surface called a pediment formed at the base of the Vaca Mountains, later to be uplifted as the Vacas rose.

The folding and faulting began in the east and progressed westward. The ranges east of the Napa Valley are more complex than those to the west, indicating a longer period of deformation. The geometry can be mind-boggling: elongate slices of crust concurrently folded and stacked, rocks of different kinds mixed higgledy-piggledy. Think of one of those highway pileups that happen in dense fog, dozens of cars and trailer trucks strewn over the road, crushed against and on top of one another,

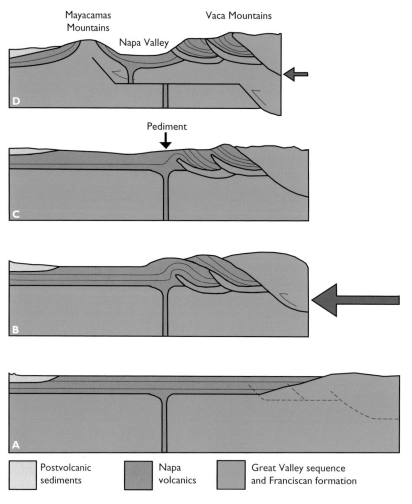

Mayacamas Mountains

Vaca Mountains

Napa Valley

D

Pediment

C

B

A

| Postvolcanic sediments | Napa volcanics | Great Valley sequence and Franciscan formation |

FIGURE 9. The architectural evolution of the Napa Valley. The Napa volcanics covered a relatively flat expanse of land under which lay the rocks of the Great Valley sequence and the Franciscan formation (A). Within the past 3 million years or so, compression associated with the San Andreas fault began deforming the rocks, first in the east (B). A period of erosion followed, which lowered the mountain front and formed a pediment at its foot (indicated by the vertical arrow) (C). Renewed deformation lifted the Vaca Mountains to their present height and created the Mayacamas Mountains (D).

squeezed, bent, piled in a haphazard mass. In the geologic case, the only way to understand the architecture is through detailed geologic mapping—the equivalent of working out the sequence of events in one of those fog disasters. Such work is being refined for the Napa region as we write these words. (We will discuss geologic maps further in chapter 2.)

The stage for the winemaker's dance in Napa Valley continues to change and evolve even today. Anyone who assumed stability and security for this tidy little paradise had their illusions dashed by the earthquake that shook the Mayacamas Mountains in 2001, rattling crockery and tumbling chimneys. And the slow and incremental processes that turn solid rock into the soft sediments that form the substrate for vines continue moment to moment.

The attitude of winemakers to these materials—the bedrock, sediments, and soils that are the foundations of wine—has also evolved, from a kind of superior disinterest during the 1980s to a deeply involved concern today. In the following chapters, we will examine this change and its implications. But first we need to look more closely at the foundations themselves, both to provide greater understanding and to correct some misperceptions.

two

THE UNDERPINNINGS OF TERROIR

LATER IN THIS BOOK (chapter 3), we make a distinction that is basic to investigating and understanding the connection between physical terroir and wine character. That distinction is between soils, which are produced by soil-forming processes such as leaching of chemical elements by acid water and the work of bacteria and other microorganisms, and the materials on which soils form, which are created by more general geologic processes such as those that build alluvial fans and river deposits. One person to whom we described this notion suggested, perhaps jokingly, that we were committing "agricultural heresy" by intimating that geology is more fundamental than soils. For most crops, it probably isn't; for grapes, we think that it is. This means also that winegrowers need to understand their land in a broader context than that provided by soil analysis alone, however important that may be to growing grapes.

The present chapter sets the stage for that discussion by describing the underpinnings of the Napa region, the bedrock and the sediments derived from it, which are the materials on which soils develop. To understand the distribution of these materials, we'll rely on a variety of maps. For many people, the language of maps is as confusing as Sanskrit. But maps, especially the types we use in this book, are a primary tool in understanding Earth and how it took shape.

In attempting to establish the history of an area, geologists first look for patterns, for fabric, for some sense of order in what often seems a chaotic mix of elements both on the ground and on maps. Such patterns are a feature of all types of maps; ordinary road maps, for example, commonly reveal topography as surely as a topographic map does. The checkerboard pattern of roads on the plains of Colorado evokes the flatness of the land, while the irregularly curving roads in the adjacent mountains reflect the irregularity of the slopes (Figure 10). Similar patterns are re-

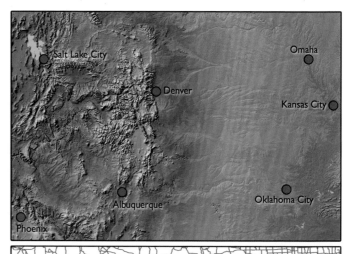

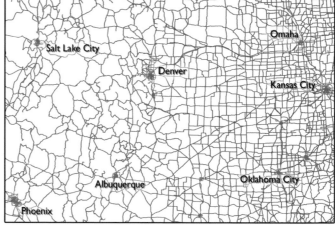

FIGURE 10. The upper portion is a digital elevation model (DEM) of an area extending from the flat plains of Kansas and eastern Colorado across the Rocky Mountains to Salt Lake City. The pattern of roads seen in the lower portion reflects the two types of topography.

vealed on historical maps, economic maps, population maps—it's all in knowing how to read the information.

Most of the maps in this book are based on a digital elevation model (DEM). The DEM is made by placing a grid of points on a conventional topographic map and digitally recording an elevation that represents an average between that point and each of its neighbors. On a topographic map, each contour line connects points of the same elevation. Every point on the two-hundred-foot contour is two hundred feet above sea level. The elevation difference between adjacent contours commonly depends on the map scale; it might be twenty, fifty, or one hundred feet (or meters), for example. All the points on each contour are that number of feet, or meters, vertically above and below the two adjacent contours.

Once you understand the nature of a topographic contour, you can begin to per-

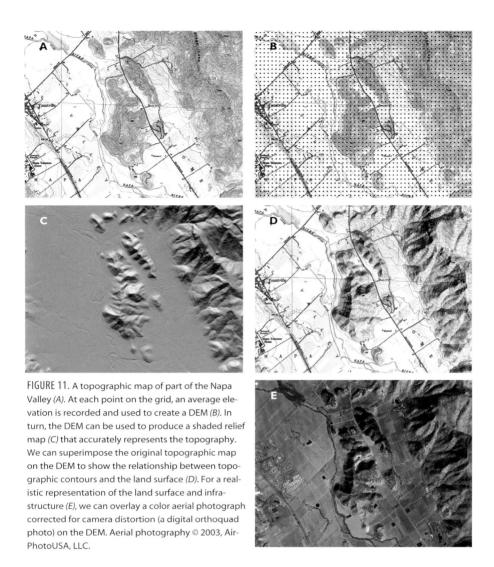

FIGURE 11. A topographic map of part of the Napa Valley *(A)*. At each point on the grid, an average elevation is recorded and used to create a DEM *(B)*. In turn, the DEM can be used to produce a shaded relief map *(C)* that accurately represents the topography. We can superimpose the original topographic map on the DEM to show the relationship between topographic contours and the land surface *(D)*. For a realistic representation of the land surface and infrastructure *(E)*, we can overlay a color aerial photograph corrected for camera distortion (a digital orthoquad photo) on the DEM. Aerial photography © 2003, AirPhotoUSA, LLC.

ceive the map as a three-dimensional surface. Where contour lines are close together, the elevation is changing rapidly, indicating a steep slope. Where the lines are far apart, the slope is gentle or flattening out. A shaded relief map—a three-dimensional representation of Earth's surface, here constructed from the digital data—makes this description more vivid. By superimposing the original topographic map on the shaded relief model, the relationship between contour lines and the actual form of Earth's surface becomes clear (Figure 11).

We'll use various informational overlays on the DEMs throughout our discussion. The most common overlay is a digital orthoquad photo (DOQ), an aerial photograph corrected for the distortion of a camera lens. The DOQs used in this book are natural-color aerial photographs taken in 2002. The vineyards and infrastructure shown on these maps represent quite accurately what you see on the ground. We can use these maps to view any part of the valley from any angle and any elevation, a flexibility that allows fresh perspectives.

For an investigation of terroir, however, our interest lies primarily in what exists below the surface. In the early 1990s, the general view was that soil provided support for vines and storage for water; if one treated the vines reasonably well, provided the necessary water, dusted with sulfur to prevent or kill powdery mildew, and kept an eye out for bugs, the grapes would be fine. After all, wine was made in the winery, and the vineyards were simply the source of raw material. But times change, people learn, ideas and approaches evolve. Now dirt is king, and those who best understand what underlies the land—the bedrock, sediments, and soil—might also be growing the best grapes. In this new light, the distribution of different kinds of Earth materials becomes of prime interest to winegrowers, winemakers, and wine enthusiasts—not to mention geologists—who are interested in exploring the interaction of terroir and wine.

BEDROCK

We begin with bedrock, the solid rock that is the foundation for everything else. It is the underpinning that supports the mountains and extends beneath the flat valley floor and from which we read the history of the region. In much of the Napa Valley AVA, on the mountain slopes and ridges, bedrock is at or near the surface, covered by perhaps a few inches of loose material or by accumulations of forest debris. In some places, it forms impressive cliffs that tower over the valley (Figure 12).

Tom Burgess remembers planting his vineyard on the steep slopes of Howell Mountain by cracking the bedrock with dynamite to make room for vine roots. Ric Forman used a thousand sticks of dynamite in his upper vineyard to break and dislodge the volcanic rock that covered a layer of river gravel. When Jan Krupp developed the 650 acres of Stagecoach Vineyards in the region of Atlas Peak, he ripped an estimated half million tons of boulders, many twelve feet or more in diameter, from what he then considered very rocky soil. In other words, in the hills, bedrock is close to the surface and very much a factor in planting and growing grapes.

The loose material that lies atop the bedrock, usually just a thin cover in the hills but a thicker layer in the valleys, is created as weathering processes break down the bedrock. Water, made slightly acidic by contact with organic material, works its way

FIGURE 12. The cliffs of the palisades that loom above the Stags Leap District.

stealthily along tiny cracks, fractures, and grain boundaries, slowly dissolving minerals and loosening fragments. Solid rock is transformed, slowly but continuously, into loose particles—boulders, gravel, sand, silt, and clay.

Water and gravity transport this loose stuff down stream courses into the valley below, where it mixes with other material carried, in this case, by the Napa River. Slowly, the valley fills with these sediments that are constantly reworked by the river as it meanders, eventually creating a flat flood plain. Each of the valleys—Napa, Chiles, Pope, Wooden—has been filled in this way, by erosion of weathered materials from the surrounding hills. The chemical and mineral composition of the sediments in the valleys thus reflects the bedrock in those hills.

Geologic maps record the distribution of different types of rock, together with descriptions of its character and orientation (horizontal, vertical, at an angle). Although the geologic map of the Napa region (Figure 13) looks as if someone had splotched color on the DEM with all the skill of a kindergartner using poster paint, a closer look reveals a more sophisticated story. Even though the information on this map has been simplified from the much larger original, it is nonetheless obvious that the bedrock of the region shows considerable diversity. One of the map's most distinctive features is the general northwest-southeast orientation of color patterns. This reflects the structural trend—the orientation of the various geologic elements that form the bedrock. "Geologic structure" is the formal jargon for what we will call the rock architecture, the geometric relationships between the various rock units—

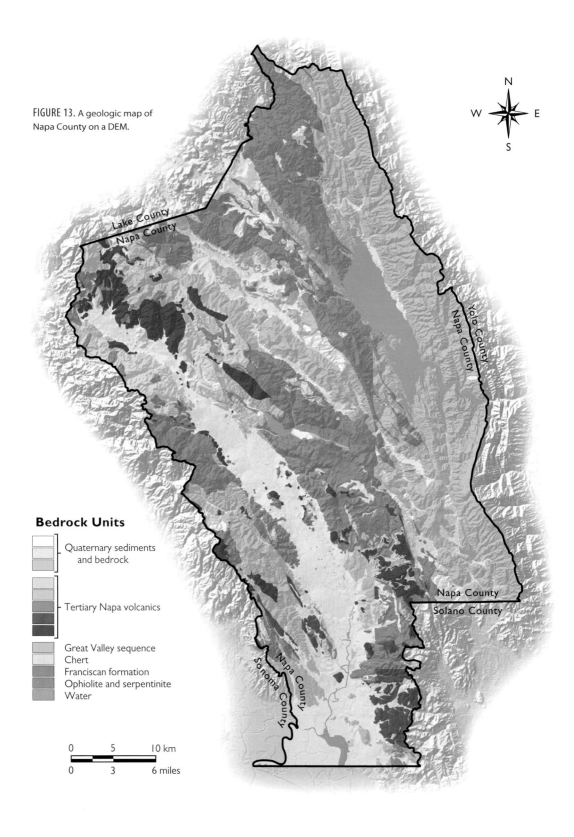

FIGURE 13. A geologic map of Napa County on a DEM.

Bedrock Units

Quaternary sediments and bedrock

Tertiary Napa volcanics

Great Valley sequence
Chert
Franciscan formation
Ophiolite and serpentinite
Water

Lake County
Napa County

Yolo County
Napa County

Napa County
Solano County

Sonoma County
Napa County

0   5   10 km
0   3   6 miles

FIGURE 14. A cross section of flat-lying rocks seen in areas of the western United States such as the Grand Canyon. Geologists call this "layer-cake" geology.

Franciscan formation, Great Valley sequence, Napa volcanics—that underlie the region.

To picture this architecture more clearly, geologists rely on cross sections, slices through the uppermost part of Earth's crust. Picture a slice of cake, with all its layers lying atop one another evenly. In an area that has been geologically stable for the past few hundred million years—the region around the Grand Canyon, for example—a cross section looks remarkably like such a piece of cake, with layers of rocks stacked in an orderly fashion (Figure 14). In areas of mountain building, a geologic cross section looks more like a tiramisu or a trifle, one that has been jiggled a bit or compressed, the layers broken apart, cake mixing with fruit and cream in disorder, though still with a sense of the original components (Figure 15).

Historically, geologic cross sections have been the most economically important element in the process of mapping the distribution of geologic units, providing a view, however subjective, of the regions beneath the surface that

THE FIRST GEOLOGIC MAP

Few people recognize how profoundly important geologic maps have been in the history of human affairs since 1815, when William Smith drew and colored by hand the first such map of a large area. An important pioneer in establishing geology as a science, Smith began as a yeoman surveyor, canal digger, and drainer of marshes in England in the late eighteenth and early nineteenth centuries. In his early twenties, Smith was charged with mapping the distribution of coal beds for a wealthy landowner in England's coal country. Smith was impressed by the miners' ability to recognize each coal seam from its visual character and the apparent content—the fossil plants, for example—of each seam as well as the look and feel of the coal itself.

He began to recognize a regularity beyond these observations, a predictable repetition of strata in which the coal seams are found. In pit after pit, Smith became familiar with this sequence and then began to wonder whether such repetitive sequences might also be found in the strata above and below.

Serendipitously, at about this time canals began to snake through the coal country, providing a cheap and efficient means of transporting the heavy product to the rail lines that would distribute it. Smith was hired to lay out and supervise the cutting of a number of these canals.

In carving the canals, Smith recognized the strata he had first seen in the coal pits and other layers above and below. He collected fossils from these layers and arranged them in order of occurrence, from lower to uppermost, associating each with the rock layer from which it had been plucked. As he worked throughout the south of England, making similar observations farther and farther afield, Smith began to envision the revolutionary possibility of knowing what exists beneath the landscapes that meet

(continued)

(continued)

our eyes, what lies within and beneath the hills and valleys through which we move daily.

Imagine the perceptual breakthrough this notion represented. By simply observing and recording what existed at the surface, together with its attitude—the angular relationship between any rock layer and an imaginary horizontal plane—one could predict what lay below the surface. By putting this information on a two-dimensional map, one might even provide a key to the materials that are found underneath a large area—a county, perhaps, or even an entire country.

And this is just what Smith did. Beginning with a small map of the distribution of strata around the city of Bath, he progressed, albeit slowly and with many a turn of fate (including a stay in debtors prison), toward the work that would establish him as the founder of stratigraphic geology: the great geologic map of England, eight feet six inches high by six feet two inches wide, the precursor of tens of thousands of geologic maps that have followed. Simon Winchester describes the significance of this achievement in his book *The Map That Changed the World: William Smith and the Birth of Modern Geology* (New York: HarperCollins, 2001).

For at least a century and a half, virtually anyone trying to work out the history of a piece of Earth's crust—petroleum geologists looking for oil, hydrogeologists searching for water, mining geologists prospecting for gold—made maps this way, by observing what lies at the surface and recording this information on topographic maps and in aerial photographs. While certain aspects of the science became progressively more "scientific" and less subject to personal interpretation, picturing what was going on beneath the landscape continued to rely on the ability of individual geologists to observe the surface, record it on maps, and then project it into depth.

FIGURE 15. A cross section of folded and faulted strata in an area of high deformation.

might contain mineral wealth. These diagrams come in three levels of detail and accuracy: cartoons or drawings constrained only slightly by the facts; diagrams that are tied more closely to rocks exposed at the surface; and balanced cross sections, a quantitative methodology based on rock properties and our knowledge of how rocks bend and break. Balanced cross sections are especially useful in areas where the rocks have been pushed around by the forces that move Earth's crustal plates and are consequently highly deformed.

In California, particularly in the Coast Ranges, the rocks have indeed been deformed, pushed together by movement along the San Andreas fault system, which runs northwest-southeast, parallel to the structural trend of the rocks. Wrinkles in the crust—the hills and valleys that reflect folded and faulted rocks beneath—generally form perpendicular to the forces that create them. If you push a rug from one end, folds will form parallel to the end you're pushing, perpendicular to the force. If you push from the corner, the folds will cross the rug at a 45-degree angle. Compression associated with the

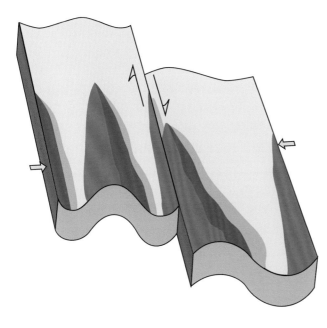

FIGURE 16. Movement along the San Andreas fault system is mostly lateral, with one plate sliding past the other horizontally. A small component perpendicular to the fault squeezed the plates together, causing wrinkles and folds in the crust.

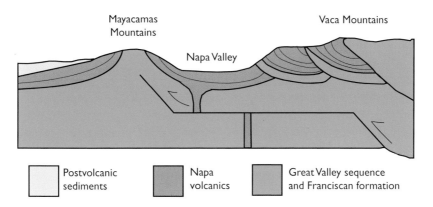

| | Postvolcanic sediments | | Napa volcanics | | Great Valley sequence and Franciscan formation |

FIGURE 17. The Mayacamas Mountains are formed by an upwarp, or anticline; the Napa Valley by a downwarp, or syncline; and the Vaca Mountains by a shingled stack of rock slices.

San Andreas system was directed perpendicular to the fault trend, leading to folds that parallel the fault (Figure 16).

A cross section of the Napa region (Figure 17) indicates that the Mayacamas Mountains are an elongate upwarp, or anticline, a fold in which the beds on opposite sides dip away from each other. This geometry puts the youngest beds on the outside of the fold. The Napa Valley is a downwarp, or syncline, in which the beds on opposite sides generally dip toward each other, the youngest beds lying in the middle. Other valleys in the region have a similar origin, as downwarps in the crust. The geometry on the northeast side of the Napa Valley is more complex. There, a series of rock slices, each hundreds of feet thick, bounded by faults and dipping to the northeast, are stacked like so many shingles.

Throughout their length, the Vaca Mountains consist of primarily one geologic formation, the Napa volcanics. These rocks also cover the Mayacamas Mountains north of St. Helena. They occur as a thin band along the base of these mountains from south of St. Helena to the Yountville hills, and as a thicker band from there to just north of the city of Napa. They reappear as a thin band at the foot of the mountains in the Carneros District. Most of the hills and knobs that dot the valley floor are made up of Napa volcanics, which are the dominant rock type in the area bounded by the Mayacamas and Vaca Mountains, the heart of the Napa Valley AVA.

Wineries that produce from grapes grown on volcanic soils often imply that these soils provide some special quality to the grapes and wine. The dominance of volcanic rocks, however, likely has no particular significance. Throughout the world, great wines are made from grapes grown on rocks as disparate as limestone and granite; volcanic rocks are just part of the mix. But winegrowers in Napa have commonly overlooked one aspect of the Napa volcanics that, in fact, is of considerable importance: the degree to which they vary in character.

These rocks run the gamut of volcanic lithologies, including tuffs, lava flows, mudflows, pyroclastic flows, and stream deposits made up of volcanic particles. Each has a different texture and structure, and each breaks down into somewhat different granular by-products. Airflow tuffs may weather in place to soft beds of clay, whereas the harder welded tuffs that resist erosion form cliffs and ledges. Stream deposits composed of boulders and pebbles from both volcanic and sedimentary sources differ from hard beds of frozen lava. And although the chemical composition of these rocks is grossly similar, local variation in the balance of chemical elements may well influence the character of grapes grown on diverse types of parent volcanic material. The general term "volcanics" risks masking the true nature of these complex rocks and their contribution to the most fundamental character of the Napa region: the diversity of ground and climate that creates local microenvironments.

While volcanic rocks may be the primary bedrock components of the Napa Valley region, Franciscan mélange and Great Valley sequence rocks have been equal contributors to Napa Valley terroir in position and prestige, if not in volume. Franciscan rocks cover the central Mayacamas Mountains from Oakville to St. Helena. Few wineries are located in the Mayacamas Mountains on Franciscan formation rocks (Cain and Long Meadow Ranch are the exceptions), but this stretch of bedrock feeds

FIGURE 18. Ribbon cherts along Highway 128 north of Lake Hennessey. The cherts are composed of the minute shells of radiolaria, shown here at a magnification of about 150×.

debris to a portion of the valley that is redolent with the aroma of great wines produced over many vintages, particularly on the Rutherford Bench, at the foot of the mountains west of the town of Rutherford. The vineyards of Georges de Latour, Inglenook (now part of Niebaum-Coppola), and BV, together with a variety of small but prestigious growers, have thrived in this area.

Rocks from the Franciscan formation also appear in a broad band north of Lake Hennessey, underlying the highlands that mark the southwestern border of Chiles Valley. Ribbon cherts are found along the road leading north from the east end of the lake (Figure 18). These rocks, composed mainly of the shells of radiolaria, accumulate as gel-like substances on the floors of deep ocean basins. Under pressure, these gels slowly compress. As they do, clay minerals segregate from the silica-rich gel and concentrate as thin layers that form the ribbon-like character seen in these outcrops.

You might wonder about the presence of Great Valley sequence rocks in the Mayacamas Mountains, far west of the Central Valley—the trough in which they

FIGURE 19. An outcrop of the Great Valley sequence near the top of Oakville Grade. The rocks are fine-grained sandstones cut by a multitude of fractures.

accumulated. Originally, the Great Valley sequence was deposited as a fifty-thousand-foot-thick pile of strata that extended continuously for several hundred miles. Subsequently, the forces exerted by the San Andreas fault bent, broke, and shifted the western extremities of this immense pile. Great Valley sequence rocks that now lie west of the San Joaquin and Sacramento Valleys exist as displaced masses, slices, and layers of rock, separate from one another, shuffled together with rocks of the Franciscan formation and the Napa volcanics like cards at a blackjack table.

From Oakville south, Great Valley sequence rocks form the surface of the Mayacamas Mountains, except for a fringe of Napa volcanics at their base. Mount Veeder supports a number of wineries (Hess Collection, Mount Veeder, Mayacamas) and growers, but the rocks here have also fed some historically rich wine ground in the valley, including the Oakville Bench, home to the great To Kalon Vineyard, now owned mostly by Mondavi; Martha's Vineyard, just south of To Kalon; and John Daniel's property, Napanook, now Dominus. Fine-grained sandstones of the Great Valley sequence are exposed in outcrops at the top of Oakville Grade and down the western side (Figure 19). The bedding here is diffuse—myriad fractures break the rock into a pebbly-looking surface. Individual beds of Great Valley sandstone, a foot or two thick, formed almost instantaneously as mud slurries (turbidity currents) flowed into the deep ocean basin that fronted the Sierra Nevada volcanic arc. Each of these beds represents, literally, a few hours of time.

Great Valley sequence rocks account for much of the bedrock surface in the northeastern half of the Napa Valley AVA. They are found along the northern boundary of Chiles Valley and beneath the hills that are the southern boundary of Pope Valley, where they also appear along the lower edge of the northern border. In addition, the

Napa Valley AVA contains other small areas of Great Valley sequence rocks, including part of the hill occupied by the Pine Ridge and Silverado wineries in the Stags Leap District, as well as the hill on the opposite side of the Silverado Trail. (The knob at Stag's Leap Wine Cellars, however, is a volcanic plug, part of the Napa volcanics.)

The rock serpentinite—its ominous name foreshadowing its equally dark presence—also exerts an important influence on Napa Valley terroir. The mottled green sheen of the mineral serpentine resembles that of a serpent; serpentinite, a rock dominated by serpentine, has the bite of its namesake, for its high-nickel and high-magnesium chemistry is deadly to grapevines. Serpentinite forms when high-temperature water alters ocean crust rocks. The only major body of serpentinite that intrudes on premier grape-growing land in the Napa Valley region lies at the edge of the Mayacamas Mountains south of St. Helena, in the area of Zinfandel Lane. This region is drained by Bale Slough, long known as difficult ground on which to grow grapes. Within the Franciscan mélange of the Mayacamas Mountains, serpentinite does occur in small scattered patches. A wide band of serpentinite runs from south of Lake Berryessa to the northern boundary of the AVA, and a thin band extends along the southwestern boundary of Chiles Valley. The Lake Hennessey area contains three small patches of serpentinite, one along the southern margin of the lake, interbedded with ribbon chert.

THE VALLEY FILL

Bedrock in its various manifestations is the parent material for all the sediments and soils of the valley. Some geologists believe that the present valley fill has been accumulating since the mountains rose, about a million years ago, but that event has not yet been dated accurately. We argue that the story is more complex, involving fluctuations in sea level and their impact on the Napa region, particularly on the age of the valley fill. We can begin to examine some of these processes in the vineyards of Volker Eisele.

Eisele has been working eighty acres of vineyards in Chiles Valley for some thirty years, selling grapes and, more recently, making wine—mainly Cabernet Sauvignon, though he grows a broad variety of both red and white grapes.

Chiles Valley, at an elevation of about eight hundred feet, is not an easy place to grow high-quality grapes. Cool temperatures and the narrow profile of the valley, which shades the edges of the vineyards, make full ripening difficult. These conditions are of little concern to Eisele, as he has no interest in producing the powerful fruit-driven wines from extremely ripe grapes that are the height of wine fashion today. Rather, Volker Eisele Cabernets are more restrained, elegant wines that keep drawing one's attention and curiosity rather than providing information and satisfaction with the first mouthful or two. They are good wines for food.

But Eisele does have one difficult problem here in the mountains: the "hungry" character of the water that flows out of the hills and across his vineyards. Several years ago, severe gashes appeared in the vineyards, the result of rains so abundant that water sheeted down the hills and eroded deep channels when it hit soft ground.

Eisele put in extra drainage and began a program of planting native grass cover crops in every other row in an attempt to break up the flow of water and decrease its cutting power. These tactics have slowed the erosion, but they have also lowered grape yields: competition from the grasses for water and nutrients has dropped his production by 40 percent, a yield that will not sustain the vineyards economically. The situation illustrates not only the constantly changeable life of farming but also the way the energy of water works continuously to balance erosion and deposition. These actions are expressed in the concept of a stream profile, a notion that has much to do with the history of the Napa Valley and its terroir.

The profile of a stream or river is a side view of its course from headwaters to mouth—steep in the hills, flatter in the lower reaches, like an elongated ski jump. The profile reflects the tendency of a watercourse to reach a dynamic equilibrium between potential and kinetic energy.

When water evaporates from a lake or the ocean, water vapor rises, carried by currents of warm air. As it rises, it gains potential energy, the energy of place. It is like a bobsled at the top of a run, full of the potential stored in its position, the accumulation of the energy exerted to raise it. When the sled starts down, potential energy is transformed into kinetic energy, the energy of movement. At the bottom of the run, kinetic energy is dissipated through friction and heat from the sled's brakes and the heels of the riders digging into the ice to stop the sled. So too with water and water vapor: when water vapor rises, accumulates potential energy, and is carried over a mountain ridge, the vapor cools, condenses, and drops as rain. Potential energy is converted into kinetic energy. On the mountain, the kinetic energy of many drops comes together in rivulets and streams. If the energy of a stream is great enough— if it is "hungry," as hydrologists say—it will eat away at the loose sediment and solid rock on the mountain slope and carry the resulting debris into the valley below. When the stream reaches the valley floor, the velocity decreases rapidly, the kinetic energy dissipates, and the water is satiated and drops its load.

By eroding in the hills and depositing at its mouth, the watercourse builds an ever-changing profile that balances erosion and deposition. The profile is "graded"—

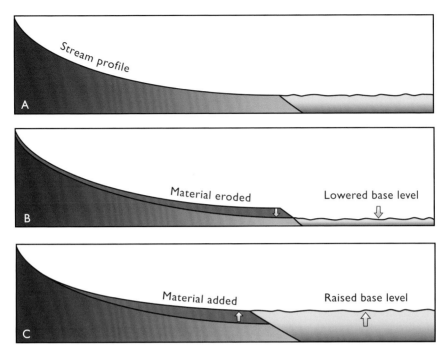

FIGURE 20. Streams tend to adjust their gradient, or profile, to the level of the body of water into which they flow (A). If that base level is lowered, the stream gains energy and erodes its bed, down and headward (B). If the base level rises, the bed of the stream builds up (C).

adjusted—to the elevation of the stream mouth. Change that elevation or change the volume of water, and you change the equilibrium of the stream, which then adjusts its profile. Picture, for example, a river flowing into a lake formed by a beaver dam. Remove the dam, creating a new base level, and the stream profile is now too steep. The base level to which the flow is adjusted moves to the next lower body of water or the valley floor, and the stream suddenly has more potential energy and can carry more sediment. It becomes hungry and eats its way down and back into the headwaters, forming a new profile adjusted to the lower base level. Alternatively, if the base level is raised, the potential energy drops, the stream is overfed, and sediment builds up along its lower reaches (Figure 20).

At the height of the last ice age, when much of Earth's supply of water was frozen in continental glaciers, sea level was some 350 feet lower than it is today. The coastline of northern California lay near the Farallon Islands. From about 125,000 to 15,000 years ago, sea level rose and fell, but it never came close to what we see today (Figure 21). San Francisco Bay was dry, except for the Sacramento River, which roared through a complex and perhaps verdant system of valleys. The Napa River

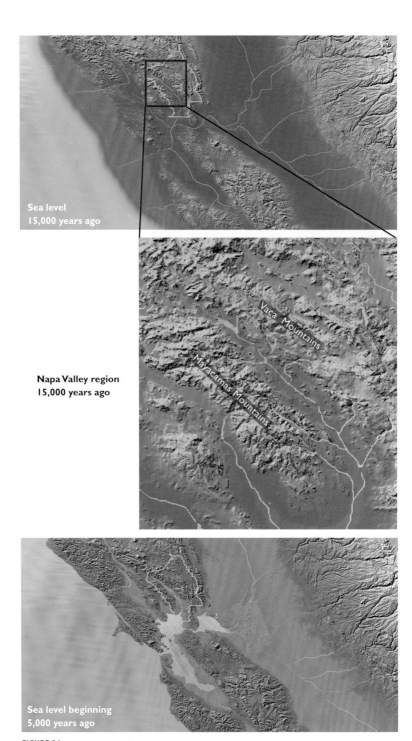

**Sea level
15,000 years ago**

**Napa Valley region
15,000 years ago**

Vaca Mountains

Mayacamas Mountains

**Sea level beginning
5,000 years ago**

FIGURE 21. Sea level 15,000 years ago was about 350 feet lower than it is today. At that time, the Napa Valley was being eroded by fast-moving streams and the Napa River. By 5,000 years ago, sea level had risen to its current level. Since then, San Francisco Bay has been partially filled, mainly by the influx of sediment from hydraulic gold mining in the Sierra Nevada and by recent commercial development.

was a tributary to the Sacramento, entering it somewhere in what is now San Pablo Bay. When a tributary stream enters the trunk, or main, stream, the tributary velocity decreases abruptly, and the stream rapidly drops its load.

If you've ever rafted the Grand Canyon, you've directly experienced the results of this process. In the canyon, you spend much time bouncing along on choppy water, marveling at the immensity of the cleft, reveling in the brilliant color of the rocks, watching the birds wheel and float overhead. Then suddenly you notice that the water has turned still, with a mirrorlike surface. You see a thin white line ahead and hear a subtle but growing roar as the water starts tumbling over the edge of an obstruction, rushing below in one of the many rapids that line the river. Side streams, eroding aggressively back into their headwaters, have dumped coarse gravel and boulders at their mouths, material that the river cannot shift. These small deltas have slowly built their way across the river, forming natural dams that pool the river behind them. This becomes the base level for the tributary stream, and the Colorado River becomes a series of rapids punctuated by mini-lakes formed by the natural dams.

The Napa and Sacramento Rivers met at an elevation of perhaps a couple hundred feet below today's sea level. The profile of the Napa River was steeper then; it was actively seeking a more stable energy profile by eroding headward, rushing through its valley, allowing little accumulation of loose fill. Similarly, tributaries to the Napa River—Dry Creek, Sage Creek, Rector Creek, Milliken Creek, and other smaller streams—were also filled by hungry water cutting its way back into the mountains, eroding the surprisingly deep canyons and smaller stream courses that drain the hills. Try to imagine the huge amount of rock that was worn away and moved by water to form Rector Canyon and the very large Hennessey drainage. The cutting of Rector Canyon alone eroded some two cubic kilometers of rock, all of it carried into the Napa Valley (Figure 22). This volume is difficult to grasp, even if we visualize it as 8 trillion barrels of wine or eighty times the 2001 world wine production, but perhaps these measures provide a more human context.

Most of the sediment appears to have been swept from the valley by the Napa River while sea level was low, sometime between 125,000 and 10,000 years ago. If this is true, most of the eroded sediment lies somewhere between San Pablo Bay and the Pacific Ocean floor. One of the important corollaries of this notion is the idea that today's valley fill accumulated over the past 10,000 to 15,000 years, a geologic instant, too short a time for the creation of mature soil profiles.

Erosion of the mountain slopes, together with the formation of the hills and valleys by major Earth movements, created faceted hillsides of diverse elevation and orientation to the compass—and thus to the sun (Figure 23). The importance? Every

FIGURE 22. The depth of Rector Canyon (and the size of the Hennessey drainage to the north, not shown here) indicate that water eroded a massive amount of material from the Vaca Mountains. The small size of the alluvial fans at the mouths of these drainages suggests that most of the material was transported out of the valley when sea level stood lower than it does today. Aerial photography © 2003, AirPhotoUSA, LLC.

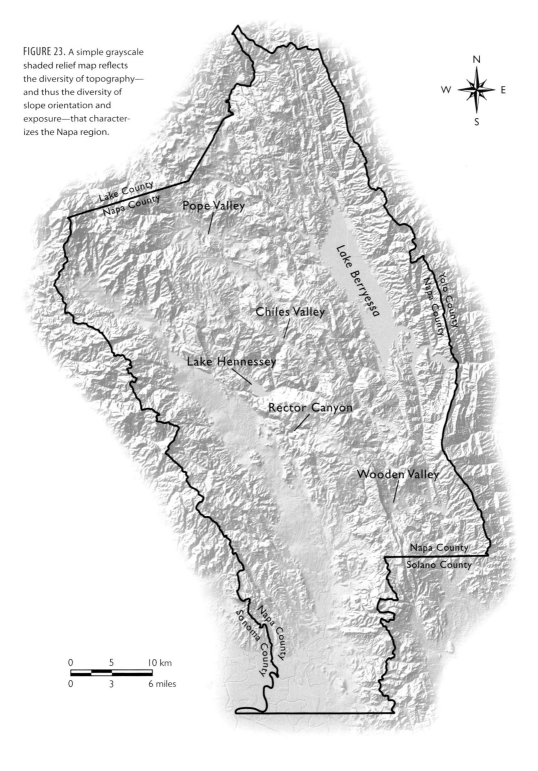

FIGURE 23. A simple grayscale shaded relief map reflects the diversity of topography—and thus the diversity of slope orientation and exposure—that characterizes the Napa region.

Lake County
Napa County

Pope Valley

Chiles Valley

Lake Hennessey

Rector Canyon

Lake Berryessa

Yolo County
Napa County

Wooden Valley

Napa County
Solano County

Napa County
Sonoma County

N
W   E
S

0   5   10 km
0   3   6 miles

DIAMOND CREEK VINEYARDS

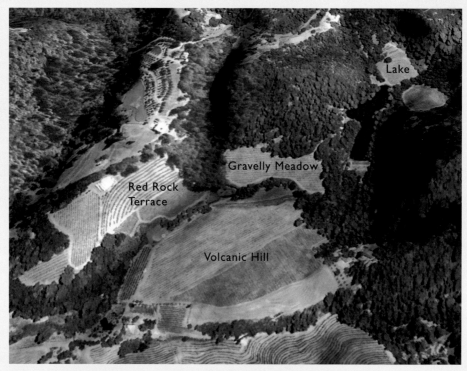

Diamond Creek Vineyards. Aerial photography © 2003, AirPhotoUSA, LLC.

Diamond Creek Vineyards, a mile or so up Diamond Mountain Road on the west side of the Napa Valley near Calistoga, is a classic example of microenvironments and their potential. While clearing thick brush from twenty acres at the heart of his ninety-seven-acre parcel in the bottom of narrow Diamond Creek, Al Brounstein began to sense that he had something special: three distinct types of ground on which to grow grapes. He decided to keep the fruit from these three vineyards separate, thinking that perhaps each had the potential to produce distinctive wine. If site affects grape character, he reasoned, it would surely be obvious here, even though the vineyards were so close together.

Volcanic Hill, shown in the accompanying aerial view, is a gentle, rolling slope, facing southwest, with a surface of gray dust as fine as cake flour that lies over a base of volcanic tuff. Across the way, facing northeast, the steep slope of Red Rock Terrace is covered by bright red residual sediments, the color coming from lava flows rich in iron, now deeply terraced to support the vine rows. Up the creek beyond a small island in the lake, behind a row of trees, lie the vines of Gravelly Meadow, a gentle slope that rises from the stream to the woods, its surface covered by coarse river gravel. Some years after planting these three, Brounstein developed a fourth vineyard, Lake, farther back on his property. From this three-quarters of an acre, he makes a highly prized wine only in certain years.

Each of the three main vineyards has a particular geologic character and differs from the others in slope, orientation and exposure to the sun, and temperature profile. And each indeed produces a distinctive wine that Broun-

(continued)

FIGURE 24. Variation of the soil color in vineyards reflects changes in sediment, soil, and/or the underlying bedrock.

change in slope orientation, in steepness, in elevation adds to the diversity of microenvironments available for winegrowers to explore the expression of terroir within the Napa Valley.

A microenvironment is a location distinguished from its neighbors by a different combination of bedrock, sediment, soil, topography, and climate—in other words, by a different physical terroir. Some variations are clearly visible: surface color, for example, can reveal diverse sediments or soils in a vineyard (Figure 24). Others are more subtle and not easily discerned: a cooler or warmer section of a vineyard, local differences in clay content, the quality of drainage across a property, the patterns of wind flow. The specific impact of any one of these factors on the character of grapes grown within the microenvironment is difficult to establish, though many winegrowers are well aware of variation in quality and character within their vineyard blocks. When Jan Krupp planted Stagecoach Vineyards, he mapped out one hundred blocks based on soil character. Over time, he will almost

(continued)

stein equates with three of the great wines of Bordeaux—Haut Brion, Latour, and Margaux—from which the original budwood may have come, smuggled in through Mexico, transported into California by small plane. In the early days of Diamond Creek, many wondered whether the highly tannic and tight character of these mountain wines would temper quickly enough to let the fruit shine through before it disappeared forever. There was no need for concern, however; the wines have aged extremely well, for twenty years and more, often maintaining bright and youthful character well into maturity.

Brounstein likens Red Rock Terrace to Château Margaux, calling it the softest of the three wines. Volcanic Hill, hard and austere in its youth, according to Brounstein, but long-lived, is his Château Latour. He equates Gravelly Meadow with Haut Brion, a very earthy wine. But palates differ: James Laube describes Volcanic Hill as "usually the earthiest and most tannic" of the three, Red Rock Terrace as "elegant and refined," and Gravelly Meadow as tending "toward more herb and mineral flavors."

surely find variation within these blocks, reflective of local environmental differences. It would be interesting to know the number of microenvironments encompassed within Napa, but the daunting tasks of defining them precisely and substantiating their differences stymie any attempt to count them.

THE LAY OF THE LAND

Topography strongly influences terroir through its connections with sediment distribution, soil character, temperature, rainfall, fog, and drainage. Topographic variation in the hills is apparent, but the valley, flat as it may seem, has its own special character. The main body of the Napa Valley, from Carneros to St. Helena, has a sense of spaciousness, an openness that is welcoming and comfortable, perhaps because it is bounded by the surrounding hills.

Looking east from the top of Oakville Grade, you see a swath of green that extends from the Stags Leap District in the south to near St. Helena in the north. Mount St. Helena stands out as a northern sentinel. You can also pick out wineries scattered over the valley floor, noting their relationship to one another and perhaps understanding something about the character of the AVAs in which they reside. Opus One is a modern Mayan pyramid, a sacrificial altar to the Gods of Wine. Across the valley, tiny vehicles travel the Silverado Trail, and landmarks such as flat-topped Haystack Mountain, Rector Dam, Backus Vineyard, Stagecoach Vineyards, and Dalla Valle lie in the hills above (Figure 25). You might even note the flat surfaces that cut into the distant hills, three levels of them, all sloping gently north.

On the valley floor, driving north on Highway 29 and passing St. Helena, you cross a threshold into a different world. It's almost as if a giant vise has squeezed and twisted the valley, narrowing it and changing its direction. The road, which tracks nearly flat along straight segments of the broad valley south of the town, now begins to wind around the lower ridges of the Mayacamas Mountains and cruise up and down slopes of the hills. The valley is linked here more directly to the ridges, forming a transition zone between the mountains on each side. The slopes along which the road travels are alluvial fans, piles of debris deposited at the foot of the hills by streams cutting back into their headwaters. At Dutch Henry Creek, on the east side, the valley floor merges with the wide mouth of the canyon, further obscuring the distinction between valley and ridge. As you look across the valley, the short distance creates an intimacy that does not exist south of St. Helena.

Fifteen thousand years ago, the scene was quite different. The valley floor was more rugged than today's, and several hundred feet deeper. The knobs and hills were

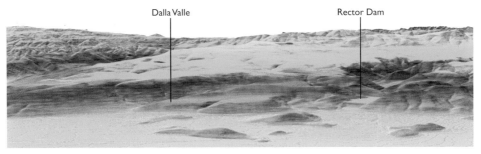

FIGURE 25. The panorama from the top of Oakville Grade looking toward the Vaca Mountains. Note the flat, subhorizontal surfaces that cut across the face of the hills, sloping slightly from upper right to lower left. The DEM below the photo accentuates these flat surfaces.

more impressive, standing higher off the deeper floor. The Napa River rushed around the hills, with significant rapids when it ran heavy with water. The river's steep course and high velocity kept the valley mostly free of sediment. A variety of wildlife inhabited the area—large camels, big cats, a stray mastodon or two, wolves, and black bears that stood ten feet tall. It was a wild land, devoid of the order and security of patterned ground. And while it was surely a place of great beauty, as for growing grapes—well, the thought undoubtedly never crossed the minds of the earliest humans who passed through here about twelve thousand years ago, three thousand years after the maximum extent of continental glaciation.

Fifteen thousand years ago, the vast ice sheets that covered much of North America had reached their southern limit; as melting began, the ice fronts retreated northward, and sea level began to rise at a rate of about one centimeter per year—a nearly imperceptible pace that nonetheless led to enormous changes as the centuries passed. Approximately ten thousand years ago, San Francisco Bay began to fill with water; five thousand years ago, sea level reached its current position. As sea level rose, base level followed. River gradients flattened, and water velocity decreased—the rivers could no longer carry sediment into the ocean realm. Mud and sand that had been carried away from the continent began to accumulate in San Francisco Bay and the surrounding valleys. Cobbles and sand, delivered from the hills and dropped closer to the source, spread

FIGURE 26. The view looking northwest from above the southern end of the Stags Leap District, showing the line of knobs and hills that extends north from the district as far as St. Helena. The Yountville Hills appear in the upper left corner. Aerial photography © 2003, AirPhotoUSA, LLC.

out as deltalike fans. During floods, the Napa River topped its banks, depositing its load of finer sediment—sand and mud—on the valley floor. Gradually, the river built a flood plain, which grew by increments, burying the base of the knobs and hills that now rise through the fill, slowly creating today's broad, productive valley floor.

These knobs and hills appear to be ordinary features (Figure 26), but they are set apart by their occupants and their origin. Robert Mondavi lives atop one hill, with his son Michael occupying a small knoll to the south. Warren and Barbara Winiarski's home caps a nearby knob. Pine Ridge Winery nestles in the cleft of an adjacent hill, with Silverado Vineyards on its northern flank. Other hills and knobs are capped by

FIGURE 27. Nested megaslides in the Vaca Mountains, outlined by arcuate ridges behind the Stags Leap District. Aerial photography © 2003, AirPhotoUSA, LLC.

opulent mansions or less obtrusive Napa Valley ranch houses of decades past. The Yountville Hills are the largest of these features north of the city of Napa; the smallest are a couple of knolls that lie bumped up against the base of the Mayacamas Mountains. Alta Heights is the most prominent of a group in the Coombsville region east of Napa. John Kongsgaard makes Chardonnay from grapes grown in the vineyard behind his mother's house on the northeast side of these hills.

To us, the knobs and hills have been perplexing geologic and topographic features. We first thought they might be remnants of erosion, pieces of once-continuous bodies of rock that were cut out by the Napa River, like mesas in the Arizona desert partially buried by river debris. But this idea does not fit with what we know of the geologic architecture—the geometry doesn't work. Nor does the notion that they are wrinkles on the larger structural fold, the syncline that forms the valley. We had spent some time puzzling over the knobs and hills, to no avail, until one day we saw the region in a new light.

While examining a perspective view of a shaded relief map with a DOQ overlay, we noticed three arc-shaped surfaces expressed by high ridges with steeply tilted western faces (Figure 27). Here, in the Vaca Mountains, we saw a geometry that looked surprisingly like the landslides that David had been studying throughout the world. The ridges and their western slopes have the form of displacement surfaces— the curved, lower boundaries on which blocks of earth slip downward during land-

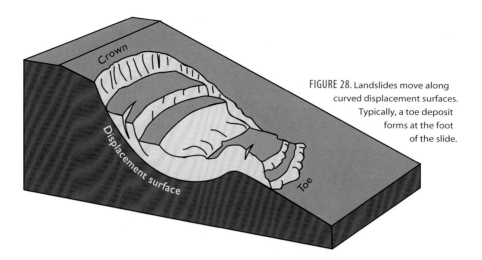

FIGURE 28. Landslides move along curved displacement surfaces. Typically, a toe deposit forms at the foot of the slide.

slides (Figure 28). We did not believe that these features in the Vaca Mountains were landslides per se; after all, the largest, from where it disappears beneath valley fill in the south to the same point in the north, is about ten miles long. But certainly they appeared to be surfaces along which movement had occurred, the movement of large blocks of rock sliding down toward the valley floor.

We quickly made a connection with the knobs and hills in the valley. When strata or blocks of rock slide, they move along surfaces that curve back toward the point of least resistance, the surface where rock meets air, punching out a pile of material at their toe. In Napa, the knobs and hills seem to fit geometrically within the projected confines of the displacement surfaces—that is, they appear to be the leading edges of these large slides (Figure 29). What's more, the upper surfaces of the slide blocks tilt back into the displacement surfaces, just as one would expect from observing landslides and other displacement blocks (Figure 30). David's colleagues at the U.S. Geological Survey agreed that this hypothesis was reasonable, given the available data. We concluded, then, that the knobs and hills are piles of debris, the toe deposits that represent the up-thrown leading edge of slabs of strata from the western slopes of the Vaca Mountains. Later, in a quarry in the Yountville Hills, we saw rocks standing vertically, apparently thrust up by the force of the sliding blocks, offering further support for this somewhat outlandish notion (Figure 31).

This idea of great blocks shifting downslope and punching up hills at their toe, displacing millions of tons of rock, lies so far outside our experience that it is difficult to grasp, but the geologic picture is simple enough. The Vaca Mountains, forced up by plate tectonic movement and compression along the San Andreas fault system, rose to such a height that the rocks were unable to maintain their structural integrity.

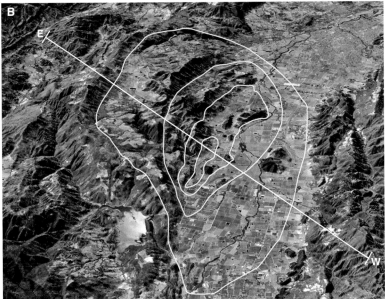

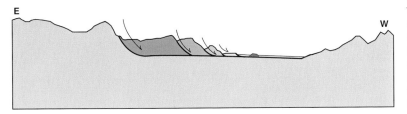

FIGURE 29. The view looking south from above St. Helena shows nested curved ridges that mark the displacement surfaces along which the megaslides moved (A). In this scenario, the hills and knobs are the toe deposits of the megaslides. This hypothetical cross section (B) demonstrates how the slide and the knobs may be linked along displacement surfaces. Aerial photography © 2003, AirPhotoUSA, LLC.

FIGURE 30. The view northwest up Soda Canyon. The slide block lies to the left; the slide surface, gullied by subsequent erosion, lies to the right. The top of the slide block tilts back into the slide surface, a typical feature of landslides of all sizes. Aerial photography © 2003, AirPhotoUSA, LLC.

FIGURE 31. A quarry in the Yountville Hills with vertical bedding and contact between two massive rock units. A person standing on the slope in the upper right indicates the scale.

FIGURE 32. The flat surfaces that step down the Vaca Mountains formed when a segment of the valley floor that included a pediment was uplifted and then displaced downward by sliding. Stagecoach and Atlas Peak Vineyards lie on the upper surface, Oakville Ranch on the next lower, and Dalla Valle, Showket, upper Backus, and Vine Cliff on the lowest. The view is from the northwest. Aerial photography © 2003, AirPhotoUSA, LLC.

The higher the mountains rose, the more gravity worked to bring them down. Simply put, the pile just got too high. It's like building a skyscraper: if its height exceeds the strength of the steel girders that hold it up, it comes crashing down. Once the first break occurred, along some preexisting plane of weakness, the movement continued until the redistribution of mass reached an equilibrium, with the rock mass spread out into a more stable pile.

This mechanism also provided an explanation for the flat surfaces we had seen in the Vaca Mountains as we looked across from Oakville Grade (Figure 32). We had found these surfaces as puzzling as the knobs and hills. Flat surfaces don't form in mountains, where water runs downslope, cutting gullies and valleys, creating a landscape that is anything but flat. Flat surfaces reflect a base level of erosion, a surface cut by a trunk stream adjusting its valley to a regional base or by waves along a lake shore or ocean coast—not by water draining from mountainous country. So how were they created here in the Vaca Mountains?

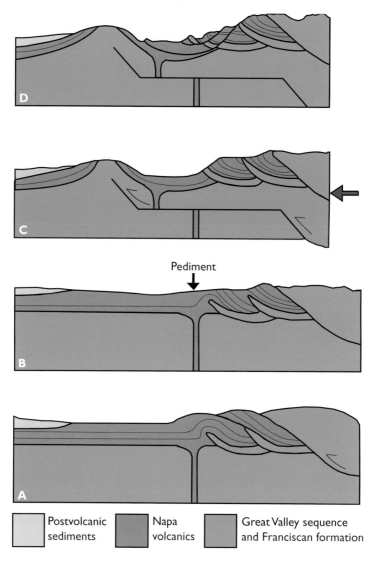

FIGURE 33. The complex origin of the flat surfaces in the Vaca Mountains. After uplift of the Vacas (A), erosion formed a nearly flat surface, or pediment (B). Further uplift raised the Vacas and the pediment (C) to a height that exceeded the strength of the rocks, which broke along a series of displacement surfaces, forming the megaslides (D).

The possible answers are few: flat erosion surfaces form as river terraces, on coastal plains, or along the shores of large lakes. In this case, the surfaces clearly cut across the tilted Napa volcanics, so they must have been shaped during the initial stages of uplift of the Vaca Mountains. Imagine streams and rivers flowing westward, away from a slowly rising mountain front (Figure 33). The flat surfaces de-

FIGURE 34. A view of the "cup and saucer" area of Coombsville, east of the city of Napa. The horseshoe-shaped ridge outlines the displacement surface. The hill in the center right, known as Alta Heights, is the toe deposit of this displacement. The Napa River runs between Alta Heights and the city of Napa. Aerial photography © 2003, AirPhotoUSA, LLC.

veloped as a gently sloping rock surface—a pediment—bordered to the east by the rising slopes of the Vacas. The erosion surface appears to signal a lull in the ongoing process of deformation. On a dynamic coast, however, with crustal plates in continual motion, little is quiet for long. Eventually, the forces of compression began to act on the crust again, uplifting first the Vaca Mountains and then, as the process progressed westward, the Mayacamas. As the Vacas went up, they took the flat surface with them, raising it intact to their highest reach. When the crash came, the Vacas collapsed along the displacement surfaces, with blocks and crustal slivers sliding down toward the open valley. The ancient erosion surface moved down as well, on the backs of these slides, creating the stepped flats and the knobs and hills on the valley floor.

We first recognized the displacement surfaces east of the Stags Leap District, the three nested surfaces that appear on the shaded relief map shown in Figure 27 (page 53). A fourth, apparently unrelated, is located east of the city of Napa, where Alta Heights and the smaller hills nearby are the toe deposits of a displacement that slid along a surface indicated by the half-circle ridge to the east (Figure 34). This region, known as Coombsville, is home to Caldwell Vineyards, Perry Vineyards, Stag's Leap Wine Cellars' Arcadia Vineyard, and various smaller operations. Ken Bernards makes Pinot Noir at Whitford in this area, buying grapes from a number of growers with very small plots, a practice closer, perhaps, to the Burgundian land tradition than to the trend in the main part of Napa toward mergers and consolidation in large corporations.

When geologists first noticed this "cup and saucer" feature, they believed it to be a caldera, the remnant of a volcano that had collapsed inward after a large eruption, forming a circular depression. But the deformation that folded volcanic rocks throughout the Napa region would also have affected the outline of any caldera, and here we see no such result. Also, the layers of tuff in Alta Heights are uniformly tilted to the east, not the jumble of collapsed strata one would expect after a caldera eruption. Alta Heights and its companion hills, then, appear to be chunks of strata that slid down from the mountains that today are the backdrop for the Arcadia, Caldwell, and Perry vineyards.

THE TOURS

---◆◆◆---

part one

YOU'VE COME TO NAPA, MOSTLY TO VISIT WINERIES AND TASTE THEIR PRODUCTS. As you drive up Highway 29 or the Silverado Trail, you note the wineries you pass, make plans to visit some of them, and start thinking about where to eat lunch. You stop at the Oakville Grocery for picnic supplies, jostling through the crowd at this trendy place. The sun is shining, you're with your friends, and you're having a great time. You take a Mondavi tour, or maybe you belly up to one of the tasting bars to get the sales hype along with your ounce and a half of the "blockbuster vintage that's filled with cherry and raspberry and jammy black currant with a hint of Asian spice and violets on top of toasty oak with a touch of vanilla." As you drive on to another winery, the countryside slips by scarcely noticed, except for its general beauty.

In the midst of all this abundance and sheer pleasure, we'd like to give you something else to do. We've included two guided tours of the valley, which provide a visual connection to some of the features and places discussed in this book. (One is presented here; the second follows chapter 5.) Although we hope that our descriptions in the text are informative, nothing replaces actually seeing the "real thing" on the ground. A firsthand glimpse, combined with a little knowledge, can make Napa's features much more than just a hill, or a rock beside the road, or another steep and beautiful ridge.

If you undertake these trips, be sure to drive slowly and carefully, pay attention to the traffic, and shut off your radio. Pull over when you want to take an extended look; relax and let your eyes range across the landscape.

An expanded, downloadable version of the Tours is available at www.ucpress.edu/winemaker/. There you may also send us comments and questions that arise from the tours or the book; we'll try to provide an answer.

HIGHWAY 29, CARNEROS TO CALISTOGA

Traveling north from San Francisco, you enter the Napa Valley from the southwest, through the Carneros AVA, on Route 12. (For a map of the American Viticultural Areas in the Napa region, see page 7.) This road runs through the center of the AVA, which is one of two Napa Valley viticultural districts that straddle county borders. The western two-thirds of the Carneros AVA lies in Sonoma County, the eastern one-third in Napa. (Wild Horse Valley, mostly in Solano County on the east, has two small extensions into the Napa Valley AVA.) Coming into Napa from the southeast, on Routes 12 and 29, you traverse about three miles of the eastern portion of the Carneros AVA after crossing the Napa River.

The southern reaches of this AVA rise gently from the sloughs and marshes that mark the northern shore of San Pablo Bay. Its central section is characterized by rolling hills covered by Chardonnay and Pinot Noir. Its northern regions, which are warmer than its southern parts, climb the southern slopes of the Mayacamas Mountains. The Glen Ellen formation underlies much of the Carneros region, making it geologically distinct from the rest of the Napa Valley AVA. The Glen Ellen is a series of sandstones, siltstones, and clay deposits formed mainly in alluvial fans, rivers, and lakes.

Carneros is an interesting and complex region with a unique viticultural and winemaking history. The climate here, strongly influenced by the waters of San Pablo Bay to the south and the inflow of ocean air from the Pacific to the west, is cooler and foggier than the rest of the Napa Valley AVA. Long considered suitable mainly for Chardonnay and Pinot Noir, Carneros became a center for these grapes and for sparkling wine. More recently, Merlot has begun to thrive in the region's cooler climate and clay-rich soils. In the northern part of Carneros, in the foothills of the Mayacamas Mountains, a small region has temperatures warm enough to ripen Cabernet Sauvignon, the favored grape of most of the Napa Valley AVA (Figure 35). Our focus in this book is on the part of the Napa Valley AVA that grows this grape, the source of the region's worldwide reputation. If you are interested in exploring Carneros in detail, we recommend following *Carneros: Travels Along the Napa-Sonoma Edge,* a field guide by Eileen Campbell, published by the Carneros Quality Alliance (available directly from the CQA or in local wineries).

At the eastern edge of Carneros, Highway 121 meets Highway 29, the main thoroughfare that runs north on the west side of the Napa Valley. For several miles north of this intersection, Highway 29 travels through the western side of the city of Napa. Gradually, the urban sprawl fades

FIGURE 35. Looking south from Truchard Vineyards across the rolling hills of northeastern Carneros to the flat landscape adjacent to San Pablo Bay.

FIGURE 36. The view east from Highway 29 south of Yountville, toward the Vaca Mountains, which rise behind the Stags Leap District.

and vineyards border the road. You are now driving through the Oak Knoll AVA, which begins at Trancas Avenue in Napa and ends in Yountville. Much of this AVA lies on a very large alluvial fan that extends from the mouth of Dry Creek. (Chapter 3 describes the origin of alluvial fans.) This deposit, which covers much of the width of the valley, stretches from just north of Napa to slightly south of the Veterans Hospital in Yountville.

Highway 29 runs along the western edge of the valley throughout its length. In the distance to the east (to the right, if you are going north) lie the Vaca Mountains (Figure 36). To the west

FIGURE 37. The Maya-camas Mountains from Highway 29 south of Yountville. In their southern reaches, shown here, the crest of the Mayacamas slopes gently to the south.

FIGURE 38. Dominus, originally John Daniel's Napanook, is located west of Highway 29 at Yountville. The vineyard can be seen in the center of the image, outlined by boundaries that diverge toward the hills. The winery, a gray rectangle, appears in the lower center. Aerial photography © 2003, AirPhotoUSA, LLC.

are the Mayacamas (Figure 37). Near the second exit for the town of Yountville, look to the left for a glimpse of the gray, minimalist winery building at Dominus. This vineyard was called Napanook when it was owned by John Daniel Jr., a legendary Napa figure of the 1940s and 1950s (Figure 38).

North of the Yountville Hills, after you pass Brix and Mustards Grill on the left, the valley opens to its widest extent. The vineyards on the left, at the foot of the Mayacamas, lie on a series of alluvial fans that edge the west side of the valley. Paradigm is located here, with Far Niente's historic winery providing the focal point for this area. The winery was originally constructed as a gravity-flow facility in 1885 and then restored in the early 1980s by Gil Nickel, who owned it until his death in 2003. The winery is known for its Cabernet Sauvignon and Chardonnay.

Harlan Estate, which produces one of the valley's most intense and expensive wines ($235 a bottle), tops the low ridge behind Far Niente. Harlan overlooks Martha's Vineyard, hidden from sight at the base of the hill (Figure 39). Martha's Vineyard achieved renown when Joseph Heitz began bottling it in the mid-1960s as a single vineyard wine, which became known as a wine of exceptional balance and intensity with a notable mint character. Oakville Grade intersects Highway 29 north of Far Niente's vineyards. Near the top of the grade, informal paths lead to the best panorama on the west side of the valley.

The valley remains wide and open all the way to St. Helena (Figure 40). It stretches along the lower reaches of the alluvial fans that extend, deltalike, from the mouths of streams that drain the Mayacamas Mountains (Figure 41). The road subtly reflects the topography of these fans, although

FIGURE 39. Harlan Estate's main vineyards blanket the top of a ridge that is separated from the main mass of the Mayacamas Mountains by a small, deep valley.

FIGURE 40. The southern part of the Napa Valley is open and spacious. This is the view looking northeast toward the Vaca Mountains from Highway 29 just north of Oakville Grocery.

FIGURE 41. Looking from the top of the Opus One winery westward toward the apex of the Oakville alluvial fan (A). The fan slopes outward from the mountain front in all directions, but so gently that the slope is difficult to discern. (B) Aerial view of Oakville fan with Robert Mondavi Winery at lower center. Aerial photography © 2003, AirPhotoUSA, LLC.

this may be difficult to perceive in the midst of weekend or commuter traffic. Early Saturday or Sunday morning, before eight o'clock, is the best time to see these features. Past Oakville Grade, Highway 29 ascends gently onto the Oakville Bench, which is actually two coalescing alluvial fans. As you pass the Oakville Grocery, Opus One appears on your right and the northern end of To Kalon Vineyard on the left. If you look to the left up one of the vineyard roads that extend all the way to the hills, you may detect a slight upward slope, the gentle surface of the alluvial fan.

The vineyards of Opus One and Robert Mondavi Winery are perhaps the best examples in the valley of closely spaced, severely hedged vines (described in chapter 5). Opus One is a partnership between Robert Mondavi and the late Baron Philippe de Rothschild, owner of Château Mouton Rothschild and other well-known wine properties. The spacing and hedging in these vineyards are more common in Bordeaux than in Napa. As you pass the Robert Mondavi Winery, the road slopes slightly downward, reflecting the northern slope of the alluvial fan.

Just past the Beaulieu Vineyard sign, the road begins to climb again, onto another fan, which crests at Manley Lane. This alternation of gentle upslope and down continues to St. Helena. At Rutherford, Niebaum Lane leads to Niebaum-Coppola, which includes the original Inglenook winery and vineyard founded by Gustave Niebaum in the 1880s. Niebaum-Coppola produces wine of several levels of quality and price, but it is perhaps best known for its flagship wine, Rubicon, a red blend made from grapes grown in the vineyards that produced Inglenook's best wines in the past (Figure 42).

FIGURE 42. The vineyards of Niebaum-Coppola, west of the town of Rutherford, incorporate the original property of Gustave Niebaum and the famous Inglenook winery. Aerial photography © 2003, AirPhotoUSA, LLC.

FIGURE 43. North of St. Helena, the valley narrows and bends to the west. Aerial photography © 2003, AirPhotoUSA, LLC.

North of St. Helena, the valley narrows and changes orientation, from northwest-south-east to more nearly east-west (Figure 43). The road rises through town and peaks at Madrona Avenue. A few blocks down Madrona, surrounded by housing development, lies Spottswoode, one of Napa's classic vineyards (Figure 44). Established in 1882, Spottswoode has been the property of the Novak family since 1972. The vineyard, managed by Napa native David Abreu, is located near the apex of the Sulfur Creek alluvial fan. Spottswoode grows organically and produces a classically rich and elegant Cabernet Sauvignon and one of the most highly regarded Sauvignon Blancs in the valley.

A couple of blocks north of Madrona lies the historic Rhine House, now the hospitality center for Beringer Vineyards. Founded in 1876, Beringer is the oldest continuously operating winery in the Napa Valley. To the north of Beringer, you pass the imposing rock walls of Greystone Cellars on the left, now home to the Napa branch of the Culinary Institute of America (CIA), whose dining

FIGURE 44. The location of Spottswoode Vineyard, on Madrona Avenue in the middle of residential St. Helena, illustrates the intermingling of winegrowing and development in the Napa Valley. Aerial photography © 2003, AirPhotoUSA, LLC.

rooms are open to the public. Past the CIA, north of the Victorian offices of St. Clement on the left, a series of small vineyards occupies the slopes, including Grace Family Vineyards, identified by its original one-acre plot fronting a gray Victorian house. Wine from this small property, first made as a family hobby, was a success from the initial vintage in the late 1970s. The Grace family uses the vineyard and its wines to promote a wide variety of charitable work with children.

Farther north, the road continues to rise and descend along the slopes of alluvial fans, which are smaller, steeper, and more noticeable than those to the south. As you look to the east (to the right, if you are going north), the fans slope distinctly downward into the flat valley at their feet (Figure 45). Through most of this northern segment of the valley, the hills, separated by only a narrow strip of flat land, tend to dominate the view. The exception lies at Dutch Henry Canyon (north of Larkmead Lane, looking east toward the Vaca Mountains), where the broad mouth of the canyon merges with the valley (Figure 46). North of Dutch Henry lies the narrowest part of

FIGURE 45. The steep slope of a small alluvial fan in the northern part of the Napa Valley.

the valley, a ridge capped by the stark white buildings of the Sterling winery (Figure 47). Past this ridge, Diamond Mountain rises to the left, with Diamond Mountain Road intersecting Highway 29 north of the Sterling hill. Diamond Creek Vineyards (pictured on page 48) was one of the first properties developed here in the modern era.

At Calistoga, Highway 29 turns north into town, while Route 128 continues west, taking you first to Petrified Forest Road and then to Tubbs Lane. Petrified Forest Road heads over the Mayacamas ridge into Sonoma County and leads to the Petrified Forest for which it is named, a remnant of a lateral volcanic blast during the period of eruption of the Napa volcanics. On Tubbs Lane, in the northwestern extremity of the Napa Valley, lie both the gateway to the geysers— a remnant of volcanic activity—and Chateau Montelena Winery (Figure 48). Alfred Tubbs

FIGURE 46. Looking east from Highway 29 toward Dutch Henry Canyon. An alluvial fan slopes steeply to the flat valley floor, which is the thin green area between the trees at the bottom of the vineyard and the hills in the distance.

FIGURE 47. Sterling winery sits atop a ridge at the narrowest point of the Napa Valley.

founded Chateau Montelena in 1882. James Barrett restored the winery and replanted the vineyards in the early 1970s. The 1973 Chateau Montelena Chardonnay, made by Mike Grgich (now proprietor of Grgich Hills), was deemed best of the white wines in the 1976 Paris tasting (see page 8). Montelena's Cabernet Sauvignon has been one of Napa's most consistent and highly acclaimed wines for the past thirty years.

FIGURE 48. Chateau Montelena, one of Napa's best-known wineries, lies in the northwestern tip of the valley, off Tubbs Lane. Aerial photography © 2003, AirPhotoUSA, LLC.

❖ ❖ ❖ three ❖ ❖ ❖

GREAT WINE BEGINS WITH DIRT

NOT MANY YEARS AGO, winemakers regarded vineyard earth as secondary at best—wine was made in the winery, and grapes were just a commodity. Today, however, Cathy Corison makes wine only from grapes grown on Bale gravelly loam. David Abreu loves Akin Series soils, with their deep red iron stain. Steve Rogstad of Cuvaison avows that "the soil is always knowable, the climate uncertain." Tony Soter is increasingly focused on wines from specific plots, for both Cabernet Sauvignon and Pinot Noir. The Mondavis now produce some wines whose labels feature the district designation more prominently than the grape variety. The prices of "cult" wines—Harlan Estate, Screaming Eagle, Eisele, Grace Family, Bryant, Shafer Hillside, Dalla Valle Maya, Colgin—which are produced mostly from small properties with limited production, are escalating; and ambitious new candidates such as Barnett, Showket, Sawyer, and Merus are crowding them, showcasing handmade wines from select locations.

Winegrowers throughout the valley are matching rootstocks to soils, choosing which varieties to plant based on soil content, building great wine from the ground up. Vineyard designations are appearing on wine labels along with varietal names, promoting an identification with the land on which the grapes were grown. Grape growers and winemakers are adjusting farming techniques to substrate variation in vineyards and keeping grape lots separate to better create wines that reflect the heritage of site and soil. Suddenly, it seems, location is everything, and soil is king.

This new focus for Napa winegrowers is at the heart of a restructuring of purpose, arising from the recognition that Napa can produce world-class wine of great diversity and character. The valley's reputation, particularly for Cabernet Sauvignon, has grown steadily since 1976, the year of the famous Paris tasting described in the introduction. The character of Napa wines has also changed over this period. The intensely tannic, heavily oaked wines of the 1970s and early 1980s gave way to a search for complexity and balance in the mid-1980s and early 1990s, which in turn bowed to the current focus on intensely ripe, supple, and approachable wines—the "New World," or "International," style. This style itself may evolve, though its widespread acceptance suggests that this emphasis on accessibility and the hedonistic side of wine will not diminish soon. Napa winegrowers, then, have come to an interesting and important crossroads, one with an ironic twist.

Not long ago, a decade or two at best, a number of critics began to comment that all Napa Cabernet tasted the same. Paul Frank, owner of Gemstone Vineyard, remembers being inspired by an article in a British wine magazine in the late 1980s: "The article began in a very complimentary vein but went on to say that, unlike Bordeaux, where one would never mistake this for that, all California [Cabernet Sauvignon] wines tasted the same, as if they had come from the same vineyard. I was very indignant . . . and thought this statement was entirely untrue. But when I got over my outrage, I began to think that while generally I could not buy into the notion, I could see the seed of truth. At that time, most of the budwood came from Davis. It was heat-treated, certified, all from the same clone, planted on the same rootstock, trellised the same, farmed the same. If all these aspects were similar, perhaps there was some kernel of truth in the article. When we designed Gemstone, we decided to break all established conventions and see what would happen."

About the same time, John Caldwell was starting a nursery with clonal material from France, and winegrowers were beginning to reconsider the role of substrate and soil in making great wine. The stage was being set to capitalize on Napa's great diversity of microenvironments, a characteristic unmatched by any other first-rank wine region in the world. Together with recent experimentation in trellising and new viticulture and winemaking technology, these attributes provide winegrowers in Napa with a unique opportunity to explore character, nuance, and style within the context of high quality.

And here lies the irony: at the same time, other forces are moving winegrowers in the opposite direction, toward a style of wine that blurs character differences, negates nuance, and honors power and intensity above all. Winemaker Philippe Melka considers this a crucial issue: "We work now with the future of winemaking. Technology is going in the right direction, improving the wine, but there is a negative side—wines are less distinct than they once were or could be. Why? Winemaking and viticulture are moving in the same direction: concentrate as much as you can. Lower the yields, expose the fruit, thin the crops, push maturation, pick much later. . . . In winemaking, push everything, macerate at higher temperatures, use stronger yeast that will resist higher alcohol, macerate longer. . . . Now some are pushing the edge with micro-oxidation to accelerate aging.

"All these technologies can be useful, but the danger always is to overdo and homogenize the wines. Site—terroir—is important because this is the only element that does not change; it provides the stable factors. This is all we really have to [help us] differentiate, to put character into the wines. If we use extreme technology, all this is lost. The character is changed."

This confrontation between diversity of character, on the one hand, and power and intensity, on the other, is occurring in large part because the "Gods of Wine"— the most influential wine critics, Robert Parker and James Laube for California, and Parker worldwide—generally reserve their highest kudos for powerful, intense wines, which tend to mask character and overshadow their subtle and often most enticing aspects. The technology of which Melka speaks is the direct road to high marks from Parker and the *Wine Spectator*.

We do not intend to belittle the services that Parker and the *Wine Spectator* have provided to the public. Over the past twenty-five years, Parker's approach to evaluating wines has freed the process from the grip of history and established reputation, placing wines on a more equal, though no less subjective, footing. Both Parker and the *Wine Spectator* have been a source of accessible and reliable information and have played a leading role in revealing new and interesting wine regions around the world.

The downside is that the personal tastes of the Gods of Wine are reflected in their reviews. They clearly favor "blockbuster" wines—fruity, rich wines that fill the mouth with flavor and drink well in their youth. Parker and the *Wine Spectator* are not shy about this preference. And their enormous influence on buyers encourages the industry to emphasize this style of wine. Consequently, consumers now stand to lose access to a broad diversity of style and character that arose as new wine regions around the world were brought to light.

In our view, the key to long-term excellence and continued international attention for the Napa region lies not in the ability to produce wine of a particular style, for the style in favor will surely change. Rather, it lies in Napa's potential to produce wines of great quality and diverse character within, and in addition to, the stylistic tendencies of the time. To lose sight of this is for Napa to lose its integrity as a region of unique and varied attributes. It risks having the region fall into the grab bag of places that, by not honoring their intrinsic possibilities—their terroir, if you will— stand with the good rather than the great.

We will expand on this view in succeeding chapters; here, our intent is to provide the foundation for that perspective by looking at the stuff in which the grapes are grown—the sediments and soils of the Napa region.

WHY DISCUSS DIRT?

Few of us are truly interested in the dirt beneath our feet—soil is understandably on the periphery of our awareness. For all except the real gardeners among us, soil is just the stuff we wipe off our shoes after walking in the garden, or along a trail, or in a park on a wet day. Yet soil is one of the most valuable resources in the world, the foundation for our physical well-being and a source of considerable wealth. In it grow the crops that feed and nourish us, the trees that provide lumber for buildings and furniture, the plants and flowers that grace our gardens and offer the comfort of natural beauty. Without soil, our lives would be quite barren.

In those areas of the world where deserts have expanded into previously rich and productive land, we see the effects of losing soil—in sub-Saharan Africa, in northern and western China, in the Middle East. During the 1930s, people in the Oklahoma dust bowl painfully learned what it means for soil to disappear, to simply dry up and blow away, making farming impossible. The dust-bowl refugees, as Woody Guthrie called the Oklahoma emigrants of the time, knew that soil is life and that without it we tread the thin edge of starvation and disaster.

The Napa Valley, where vineyard land—which, remember, is agricultural land—sold for more than one hundred thousand dollars an acre in 2002, is about as far from dust-bowl Oklahoma as the imagination allows. But don't take the willingness of some to pay large sums for farm property as a measure of our general knowledge of, or interest in, matters of the land. As our national affluence grows (albeit in fits and starts), our connection with the soil fades. Most of us know little about how soil forms, where it comes from, how it nourishes and supports plants—and few care to learn. But for those who enjoy wine, especially fine wine that reflects the influence of terroir, knowing something about soils and how they affect grapes and wines should be part of what we bring to the table.

Without such an understanding, how do we make sense of statements that attempt to relate wine quality and character to the environments in which the grapes were grown? Unless you have some knowledge of soils, climate, rainfall, and the inclusive concept of terroir, the poetic prose that slides off the pens of wine writers and fills winery brochures can slip past your hype detector as smoothly as the most delicate oyster slides past your tonsils. Even a small amount of information can help you to evaluate wine writing, providing a fresh perspective based on personal understanding rather than the opinions and assumptions of others.

What does this knowledge mean for you as a consumer? A few examples:

• When you see "Rutherford" or "Oakville" or "St. Helena" on a bottle, you will know that these subappellations cover a diversity of geologic ground and reveal only a limited amount about the character of the wine. You will want to know, for example, where in the AVA the grapes were grown and perhaps even something about the substrate that supported them.

• You should be better able to tell whether a vineyard designation has significance or whether it is just window dressing. You might discover that you want to know more than simply the name of the vineyard.

• When people talk or write about terroir, you can quickly discern whether they know whereof they speak or whether they are only repeating something they have heard elsewhere. You will be better able to evaluate the usefulness of descriptions offered by wine writers, winemakers, and wine sellers.

• Above all, through informed exploration, you will learn to trust your own taste, without relying on the palates or opinions of others. You will also be able to figure out whether your local wine merchants really do know what they're talking about or whether they're using the lazy sell, relying on Parker, Laube, and the others whose small shelf cards carry their numerical opinions.

THE PURPLE PROSE OF WINE

"The red soils here are deep and thick, and the 1999 Stoller Vineyard Pinot expresses its redness with a medley of red fruit, red raspberry scents and a coarse wild strawberry and red cherry flavor. Even red spices come to mind; sumac, cinnamon" ("The Guide to Tasting Wine," *Wine and Spirits*, Fall 2002, special issue, p. 42).

This description and the many like it that characterize much of the writing in wine magazines illustrate the confusion and difficulties involved in talking and writing about terroir. Tasting wine is surely a multidimensional experience, first of the senses and then of the mind and imagination. And wine writers are surely among the most imaginative and creative practitioners of the literary arts. A swirl in the glass, a glint of color, a mouthful of flavor sets their imaginative juices flowing in a way that we more lowly communicators can only envy. The color of soil is connected to the color of wine, the color of the fruit, and even to the colors of imagined spices. But note that the spices "come to mind"—leaving us to wonder whether they also come to the palate or whether the words reflect thoughts triggered by the eye rather than the mouth. This passage seems to have little real connection with terroir, with place. Rather, the experience reflects a creative mind searching for connections between wine characteristics and soil color.

Wine is multidimensional in part because it embodies so many influences, all the complex aspects of its history that are wrapped up so succinctly in the word "terroir." It is simple to state that the characteristics of a wine reflect the soils and rocks, but it requires much greater effort to establish the reality of such a relationship. In addition, our individual experience of wine varies immensely. One of us took part for a couple of years in a tasting panel held by

(continued)

(continued)

Cooks Illustrated magazine in which ten or twelve people would gather once a month to evaluate a group of wines. Usually, half were professionals in the wine industry, and half were amateurs. The most interesting part of the experience was the constant variation in taste—the professionals almost never agreed with one another about which wines they preferred, nor did the amateurs.

The bottom line: take wine writers' descriptions with a large grain of salt, particularly when they make pronouncements about wine and terroir. If you're truly interested in terroir, put together some structured tastings to explore for yourself how different wines reflect the land on which they were grown. Be skeptical about what you read and what others tell you, and trust your own taste—it's the best arbiter around.

OF SEDIMENT AND SOIL

The *American Heritage Dictionary* defines soil as the loose material at the surface of Earth, a vague description at best. With this in mind, beach sand becomes soil, as does a pile of rock rubble below a steep mountain face. To most of us, however, soil is the brown, crumbly stuff of gardens, farms, and forests; the material in which we grow houseplants and mushrooms; the dirt that's scraped off the surface before a backhoe digs a hole for a house foundation.

Soil, actually, is something of a slippery concept, a chimera, with no substance in and of itself. Soil always forms by transforming an existing substance—that is, it does not exist in its own right, as beach sand or bedrock does, but instead needs a substrate. Soils are created when weathering processes alter bedrock or sediments that lie at the surface of Earth. Over time, these processes penetrate deeper into the substrate, and a soil profile develops, extending from the surface down to fresh bedrock or sediment. Depending on the age of the soil and on the climatic conditions, a soil may range from a few inches to several feet in thickness. The break between the soil and the sediment or rock can be sharp or gradational. This distinction, between soil and the material on which it forms—a distinction not made in agricultural circles—is fundamental to many of the notions we present in succeeding chapters.

Soil scientists refer to the sediment or bedrock from which soil is created as the "parent material." This phrase is a bit of a misnomer, however, as "parent" suggests the creation of an offspring, something new. But the formation of soil involves decay, a process more akin to aging than to parenting. And, to make the issue even more complex, soil scientists tend to employ the dictionary description of "soil," often using the term to indicate all the loose material above bedrock. This designation, however, masks genetic characteristics that can be used to understand, and even predict, the distribution of different types of substrate in vineyards, information that has an impact on planting and picking decisions. And here lies the major difference between geologists and soil scientists: geologists are concerned with understanding the creation of the original materials, whereas soil scientists describe and classify the transformed product. A geologic map provides information that allows you to read a story, whereas a soils map simply records the distribution of soil types.

It has not always been this way. Hans Jenny, a famous soil scientist in the early twentieth century, argued strongly, and unsuccessfully, before Congress that the Soil Conservation Corps should become part of the U.S. Geological Survey. He was concerned that if the corps was subsumed under the Department of Agriculture, it would lose its focus on science and research and become concerned only with agricultural issues. And so it did, though not rapidly. The 1938 *Soil Survey of the Napa Area* has substantial geologic underpinnings; the 1978 *Soil Survey of Napa County* was designed to respond to a much broader variety of needs and lost its geologic focus along the way. (Both surveys are referenced in the bibliography.) The change was more formally recognized in 1980, when the methodology of soil classification changed from one that had some geologic input to one that focused more on control of soils by climatic factors.

Bedrock and the sediments derived from it, however, are the parent materials of soil, and geologic factors are the primary influence on soil character, at least in youthful soils, which are the kind we find in the Napa region. Mature soils take tens of thousands—even hundreds of thousands—of years to develop fully, which means that the materials on and from which they form must be relatively stable. Soils are not created on active beaches, for example, where the sediment is continually shifted by waves and tides. But if the beach is stabilized with grass, soil-forming processes begin to change the deposits through the addition of organic matter and through the same chemical weathering and biological mechanisms that promote decay and breakdown of rock. To understand terroir and its effect on wine quality, character, and diversity, we must look both at the soils and at the substrate on which they form. We'll begin with the latter.

Most of the rock and sediment exposed on continents originate in granite, rocks that are rich in silica, with a high content of quartz and major contributions from silica-based minerals high in calcium, sodium, and potassium. The ocean floor is quite different, composed of basalt, which contains silicate minerals rich in iron and magnesium, with little or no quartz. Granites and basalts are formed at the high temperatures and pressures of Earth's interior. At the lower temperatures found on Earth's surface, they become unstable and vulnerable to weathering, a bit like Rocky Road ice cream taken from the refrigerator. At the warmer temperature of a bowl, the frozen dessert breaks down into its component parts—cream (with dissolved sugar), nuts, and marshmallows. With granite and basalt, the process is considerably more complex, of course, but rocks also break down into their component parts—the mineral grains that make up the original rock.

Water is the key, together with acids produced by plant decay. Seeping into cracks and along tight crystal boundaries, these substances eat away at the edges of mineral grains. Some elements go into solution and are carried away by water—what's left is changed, chemically and in mineral form. Depending on the initial materials, clay minerals (tiny grains with a layered structure like mica) and quartz are the ultimate products of deep weathering, all that remains after many thousands of years. The rate of this weathering depends largely on climate: in the heat of the tropics, chemical processes proceed much more rapidly than they do in the cold of the arctic. Mechanical processes also hasten the decay and breakdown of solid rock, with water again one of the primary instruments. In climates with a wide temperature range, rocks are broken apart by continual freezing and thawing as water expands and contracts (think about dealing with frozen and split pipes in the winter).

In short, solid rock exposed at the surface breaks down into smaller particles, and its mineral and chemical composition changes. The granular product ranges in size from large blocks to fine clays. Most of it is in between—boulders, cobbles, gravel, sand, and silt, as geologists term material that is the size of grapefruits, lemons, large blueberries, seeds, and gritty dust, respectively. Silt ground between the teeth is gritty and abrasive, whereas clay is smooth, in part because of its layered crystal form, which allows it to be used as filler in toothpaste.

Gravity is working all the time, drawing everything downward. As particles loosen, they fall off the parent rock and accumulate in place or are carried downslope by water. Geologists call the material that stays in place "colluvium"; here, we use the term "residual materials." In some cases, rocks weather totally in place, transforming from solid rock to soft sediment with no movement of solid material, only water and chemical compounds.

We found an extraordinary example of this phenomenon at Stagecoach Vineyards, high in the Vaca Mountains adjacent to the Atlas Peak AVA. When Jan Krupp developed Stagecoach, he found what he believed were soils up to sixteen feet thick, with boulders as large as twelve to fifteen feet in diameter (Figure 49). We found these facts difficult to reconcile—thick soils at the head of Rector Canyon, an area of significant erosion and otherwise thin soils, associated with an extraordinary accumulation of boulders, which one would expect to find at the base of an eroding cliff. One of David's volcanologist colleagues, however, identified the boulders as core stones, which had been formed in place by the weathering of an originally solid layer of lava.

The core stones began to develop as rock layers cracked in response to the release

FIGURE 49. Although core stones in Stagecoach Vineyards appear to be boulders, they were actually formed by weathering along fractures in a once-continuous layer of rock. Water percolating through the fractures creates weathering rinds that round the edges, mimicking boulders that have been rounded by water.

of confining pressure as they were exposed at the surface of Earth, through the removal of overlying materials and uplift by mountain-building forces. Water percolated along the cracks and began to alter the mineral composition in a thin surface layer (Figure 50). As time passed, the altered rim thickened (Figure 51), leaving separate solid cores surrounded by the softer products of alteration. In time, all evidence of solid rock disappeared, and the material took on the soft and crumbly character of a soil. The sixteen feet of soil that Krupp found at Stagecoach is residual bedrock material developed in this way.

Residual bedrock materials do not commonly have the thickness that Krupp reports at Stagecoach. More often, most of the debris of weathering moves downslope, ending up in the valley. There it is distributed by water in a somewhat predictable way, which is instrumental in creating a variety of characteristics of local terroir—variation within a vineyard and from one vineyard to the next.

Much of the rock debris moves from the highlands during driving rainstorms, when sheet floods pick up loose material and transport it into streams that run wild for brief periods, carrying the debris downslope. Larger materials—cobbles and gravel—roll along the bottom of the stream bed, while the smaller particles are suspended in the flow. The mid-size materials, fine gravel and coarse sand, are bounced

FIGURE 50. A core stone with a broken edge showing the altered surface material (orange at the surface, white just below) and the fresh rock (gray with white crystal specks).

FIGURE 51. Boulders formed by concentric weathering along fracture surfaces of a once-continuous lava flow. Concentric weathering rinds around the layers illustrate varying degrees of decay, increasing away from the cores, the last remains of the original rock. This material can be traced upward into a soil zone and downward into progressively fresher rock.

along the bottom in a kind of transition zone between the bed load and the suspended load. How various particle sizes move depends mainly on stream velocity. At higher velocity, more sediment is in suspension, and bigger blocks can be rolled and tumbled along the bed.

The energy of fast-moving water can carry along a substantial quantity of material. When the water leaves the mountains and hits the nearly flat valley floor, the velocity drops rapidly, and with it the ability to transport rock debris. The great deltas at the mouths of the Mississippi, the Nile, and the Niger have been created in the same way, on a grand scale. The huge volume of water in these rivers carries an enormous amount of sediment both as suspended load and as bed load. When the river hits the sea, the water fans out, its velocity decreases, and sediment begins to drop. Over time, a fan-shaped deposit builds up, with its apex at the mouth of the river.

On land, the result is much the same: an alluvial fan is created. In the Napa Valley, alluvial fans line the base of the Mayacamas Mountains; the local term is "bench," as in the Oakville Bench or the Rutherford Bench. As you travel up Highway 29 between Oakville and Rutherford, north of the Oakville Grocery and south of the Robert Mondavi Winery, you might want to stop and look up the rows of vines in To Kalon Vineyard, one of the historically great sites for grapes in the Napa Valley. You won't see a bench, but you might note that the land rises ever so slightly as it approaches the Mayacamas Mountains. This rise is the topographic expression of the broad Oakville alluvial fan as it thins out onto the valley floor.

In thinking about alluvial fans and vineyards, it's useful to know some detail about how the fans form. When the stream leaves its mountain cleft and pours out onto the valley floor, it drops most of its sediment load along a path in and adjacent to the stream course. Over time, the deposits build up to form a small ridge, with the stream flowing down its center. But water does not like to be restricted, and it is relentless in seeking the path of least resistance. Sooner or later, during a period of high flow on the alluvial fan, the water will break through the banks that constrain it and find a new, more efficient path. Over time, as the stream moves from one course to another, back and forth across the ground that surrounds the mouth of the stream, it builds a stack of fanlike shapes (Figure 52).

This process also creates a variety of sedimentary deposits. As the water moves down the fan, its velocity decreases. Sediments drop out along the way, the coarsest at the base of the mountains, the finer down the fan. The result is a general size gradient from coarsest at the top to finest at the toe. We can identify an upper, a middle, and a lower segment of the fan on the basis of grain size in the sediments of

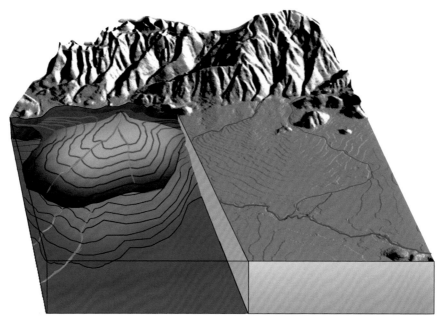

FIGURE 52. Alluvial fans are created at the mouth of a stream where the stream enters a river valley. Stream velocity decreases rapidly, and the coarser sediment is dropped near the mountain front; finer material is carried farther out onto the fan. Over time, the stream follows successive paths down the surface, building up a fan-shaped pattern. Eventually, successive fans form in the same area. The blue pattern on the left side of the diagram represents an earlier and more extensive fan; overlaying it is a later fan, shown in red. The right side of the diagram illustrates the gently sloping surface of a modern fan south of St. Helena.

each zone (Figure 53). The stream, however, is also changing position across the fan. Along any single path, the coarsest material drops in or near the stream channel, with finer material spreading out during periods of flood. So we end up with a complex pattern of variation in texture and structure of the sediments down the fan, across the fan, and in depth vertically through the fan deposit.

How do these processes relate to growing grapes? Depending on rootstock, vine roots can penetrate thirty feet or more below the surface, though they are usually concentrated within the upper ten or twelve feet. For a soil study of a vineyard, a backhoe digs at most one pit per acre, to a depth of about six feet. (By law, a worker cannot enter a pit that extends above his or her head.) An acre is about 44,000 square feet (if it's square, that measures about 210 feet on a side). The sedimentary deposits, however, vary on a scale of a few feet, laterally and vertically. What you see in the backhoe pit here may be quite different from what you see there, ten feet away. And while the upper six feet might be filled with gravel, the next ten feet down could contain a lot of clay or a mixture of gravel and clay.

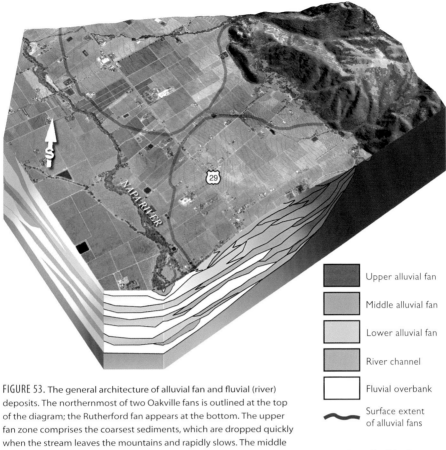

Upper alluvial fan

Middle alluvial fan

Lower alluvial fan

River channel

Fluvial overbank

Surface extent
of alluvial fans

FIGURE 53. The general architecture of alluvial fan and fluvial (river) deposits. The northernmost of two Oakville fans is outlined at the top of the diagram; the Rutherford fan appears at the bottom. The upper fan zone comprises the coarsest sediments, which are dropped quickly when the stream leaves the mountains and rapidly slows. The middle zone contains a mix of coarse and fine debris, while the lower reaches are composed mainly of the finer materials carried farthest by water with diminishing velocity. The lower fan sediments interfinger with channel deposits of the trunk stream and flood plain sediments. (The arrangement of these units below the surface is highly generalized in this figure.) The fluvial environment is an interlayered mix of coarser channel deposits and broadly distributed, finer-grained, overbank sediments deposited during floods. Aerial photography © 2003, AirPhotoUSA, LLC.

John Livingston told us of seeing vine roots that followed gravel bands—old stream channels—twenty feet below the surface in a large foundation pit at Frog's Leap Winery, indicating clearly that variations in substrate character can have a strong influence on how vines grow. And how vines grow influences how grapes taste. Planting a vineyard is thus a bit of a crapshoot. You can always replant on the basis of what you learn from the first try, but that's an expensive method, which perhaps also affects your reputation for sagacity. But if you understand the processes that formed the sedimentary deposits in which you're planting, you can make predictions about the variation and enhance the odds of success.

Beyond the toe of the fan, water and sediment enter the fluvial regime, a realm dominated by the hydraulic forces of the river. At this stage of its history, the Napa River has developed a flood plain, a broad, flat valley floor built up by the accumulation of fine-grained sediment—mainly silt and clay—during thousands of episodes of overbank flood. The river meanders back and forth across this plain on its way to San Pablo Bay, undercutting its banks, reworking sediments already deposited, and incorporating new material from tributary streams.

Through much of its course, the Napa River hugs the eastern edge of the valley, pushed there by the alluvial fans extending out from the western hills. Coarser sediment accumulates in the stream channel, with the finer-grained material either moving downstream to San Pablo Bay or lingering behind on the flood plain. The fine-grained sediment is mostly mineral debris, but it also contains much organic material delivered by side streams and the caving of the riverbank. Flood plain deposits and the finer-grained, peripheral parts of alluvial fans, then, tend to have high organic content, accounting in part for their agricultural vigor. These deposits are also deep, commonly containing intermixed layers of clay minerals that hold water.

Growing vines on these soils is a bit like trying to nourish a child on unlimited quantities of peanut butter, ice cream, and candy. The vines grow wildly in all directions, out of balance and with little concern for future generations—represented by the fruit and its seeds. They provide an interesting challenge for the grape grower, just as that child might be something of a trial to his or her parents. The sediments in these areas of the valley are not known for producing grapes suitable for the finest wines, though some winegrowers maintain that new vineyard techniques can coax high-quality grapes even from these marginal areas.

The tendency of stream channels to cut through a piece of land has been the bane of farmers for centuries. Imagine planting a vineyard along a riverbank and losing a significant chunk of it to bank erosion. Rivers erode on the outer side of meander bends, where the velocity is highest, and deposit material on the inside bend, where the water is often very still. At Rudd Estate, at the intersection of Oakville Crossroad and the Silverado Trail, north of Rector Reservoir, the owners have lined a watercourse with large blocks of rock, up to several feet in diameter, in an attempt to stabilize the stream. Runoff from heavy rains in 2003 moved many of the carefully placed blocks ten feet or more from their original position and deposited boulders and gravel from upstream in the stream bed. Finer sediment accumulated in the lower parts of the vineyard, around vine roots and other obstructions that slowed the flow of water. At Frog's Leap, John Williams has planted willows on slump blocks that have caved from the bank next to one of his Rutherford vineyards, in the hope of reducing erosion. Eventually, however, the water always wins.

A NEW FRAMEWORK

Bedrock, residual sediment that stays in place, alluvial fans, fluvial (river) deposits— these are the materials on which soil-forming processes work. The differences among these deposits are so fundamental to the work of growing grapes that we have given them a collective name: earth process units, or EPUs. We can map three types of EPUs in the Napa Valley:

- residual EPUs, which lie mainly in the hills

- alluvial EPUs, which encompass the alluvial fans

- fluvial EPUs, which comprise the deposits of the Napa River

These units, shown in Figure 54, provide a new framework for examining the relationships between ground and grape, place and quality.

From the perspective of terroir, one of the most striking characteristics of the EPU map is the concentration of alluvial fans on the west side of the Napa Valley, where they form an almost unbroken band from west of Napa to north of St. Helena. In the narrower northern segment of the valley, fans are less continuous, but the difference between fluvial and fan environments here is also less marked. Because much of the finer material contained in sediments in the upper reaches of the Napa River has been winnowed out, it's difficult to distinguish fluvial deposits from adjacent fan material. Along Larkmead Lane, for example, coarse, cobbly sediment lies on the surface across the width of the valley, except immediately adjacent to the river.

On the eastern side of the valley, discontinuous small fans lie at the mouths of some large drainages. The Hennessey drainage is fifteen miles long, nearly half the length of the valley, yet the Hennessey fan is poorly developed, more a swath of sediment that angles down the valley than a true fan. Similarly, Rector Canyon cuts deeply into the Vaca Mountains, yet the Rector fan is about one-quarter the size of the St. Helena fan. These drainages were cut at a lower stand of sea level, when the Napa River and its tributary streams were adjusting to a base level in today's San Pablo Bay. The material eroded from the Hennessey and Rector drainages was never stored in

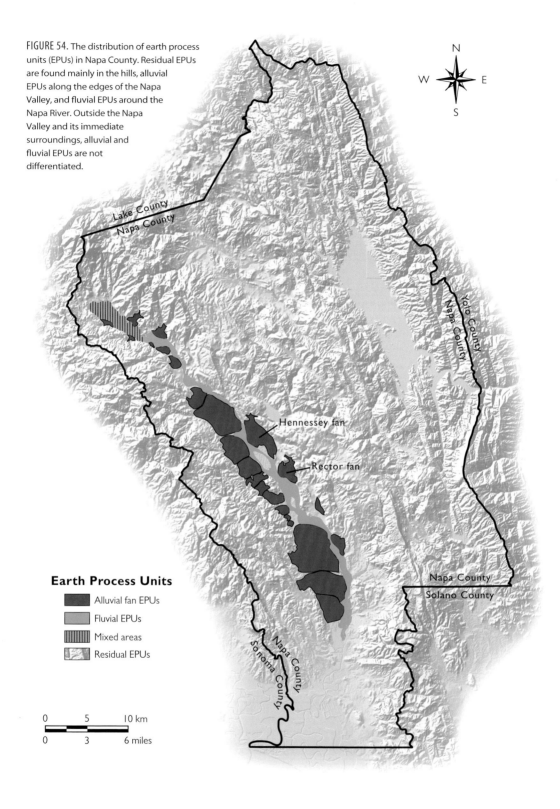

FIGURE 54. The distribution of earth process units (EPUs) in Napa County. Residual EPUs are found mainly in the hills, alluvial EPUs along the edges of the Napa Valley, and fluvial EPUs around the Napa River. Outside the Napa Valley and its immediate surroundings, alluvial and fluvial EPUs are not differentiated.

Lake County
Napa County

Yolo County
Napa County

Hennessey fan

Rector fan

Napa County
Solano County

Napa County
Sonoma County

Earth Process Units

Alluvial fan EPUs

Fluvial EPUs

Mixed areas

Residual EPUs

0   5   10 km

0   3   6 miles

N
W   E
S

the Napa Valley, and thus these streams never developed large alluvial fans. The alluvial fans on the western side of the valley appear to have formed later, while the Napa River was adjusting to a rising base level and filling its valley with sediment.

In addition, the valley appears to be asymmetric. The 2001 earthquake in the Mayacamas Mountains demonstrated that the western part of the range is moving up and the eastern part is moving down. In the Vaca Mountains, older, uplifted alluvial fans suggest that the western side of this range is rising. These movements would give the Napa Valley a slight westward tilt, creating a depression on the west side that would provide space in which sediments could accumulate as alluvial fans. Because no similar space exists on the east side, most of the material eroded from the Vaca Mountains is transported down the Napa River.

The composition of alluvial and fluvial EPUs reflects the source of their sediment. Streams and rivers drain specific areas called watersheds. The continental divide that runs down the Rocky Mountains defines the two major watersheds of the United States. A drop of water falling on the east side of the divide drains eventually into the Mississippi and then into the Gulf of Mexico; a drop falling on the west side ends up in the Pacific Ocean or the Gulf of California. The same is true for streams of all sizes. The watershed defines an area in which every drop of rain that falls has a common destiny.

A single stream usually feeds an alluvial fan; the chemical and mineral composition of the fan reflects the composition of the bedrock in its watershed, just as the DNA of a child can identify a parent. The watershed of the Napa Valley, however, drains all the bedrock surrounding the valley. Sediment delivered to the river from tributary streams is mixed by the river, homogenized like sand, gravel, and portland cement in a cement mixer. The sediments of the river at any point, then, mirror the overall composition of the rocks in the hills above that location. The sediments of the alluvial fans are tied to the more specific composition of a particular piece of territory in the Mayacamas or Vaca Mountains.

This map of the distribution of EPUs (see Figure 54) is a fundamental new tool in the exploration of wine and place, usable by winegrowers and wine drinkers alike. We will explore this map and its implications in more detail toward the end of this chapter, but first we need to delve further into the world of soil.

A CLOSER LOOK AT SOIL

Soil scientist Paul Anamosa is standing in a backhoe pit on a piece of Lee Hudson's land in the Carneros AVA. After digging a chunk of sediment from the wall of the pit, he has sprayed it with water and is working it in his hand. A little more water, a little more pressure, and he begins to mold the sediment between his fingers. This squish test is designed to get a feel, literally, for the range of grain sizes that make up the material. Feeling grit, he knows that the sediment contains sand or silt along with the smooth, silky clay. He can discern the grain size—sand is coarser, silt finer—and the amount by feel, and he terms this a silty clay. He checks the dark reddish-brown color against a book of defined tones. He estimates the percentage of "non-soil" material—gravel and cobbles, perhaps some manganese concretions.

When Anamosa first entered the pit, he looked at the exposed layers and gauged the depth of each change, an assessment that was not clear-cut, for the layers are transitional and the boundaries a bit blurry. Now he's examining each layer while his assistant makes notes. It's apparent that two people are needed on this job, since the hands of the person in the pit are slick with mud.

Anamosa is describing a soil profile, the vertical series of changes that result from soil-forming processes. Soil profiles vary, but their overall character is common (Figure 55). The O, or top, layer is a zone rich in organic material, humus from rotted accumulations of plant debris, the material we wipe from our shoes. This, together with the next lower zone, the A layer, is the part of the profile that is alive with a vast ecosystem of animals and plants ranging in size from burrowing rodents—moles and voles—to minute bacteria. It is claimed that a single handful of soil—the stuff of the O and A layers—contains about the same number of bacteria as there are humans on Earth. The bacteria break down dead plant tissue, making its chemical components available to other organisms and plants. The lifespans of the bacteria vary from a few hours to a few weeks, depending on the species. Their tiny bodies disintegrate to give up ammonia and nitrates to the soil, compounds that provide nitrogen to plants.

If the grape grower has been kind to the land, attempting to keep a natural balance while developing it for grapes, earthworms will be working through the O and A layers. They are the soil restorers, who ingest the material of these layers, pass it through their bodies, and send it out the other end enriched in nutrients and bound together by earthworm goo. This adds structure to the soil, making it crumbly and loose, giving it "tilth," in the organic farming vernacular. On the other hand, if the grape grower loads the vineyard with herbicides and pesticides, everything changes—the bacteria die, the earthworms move elsewhere, the soil community becomes impoverished, and the plants and soil become increasingly dependent on artificial input from the farmer.

The complex community of the O and A layers is a kind of mini-terroir within the terroir, and just as difficult to comprehend. As with terroir, the key is not to try

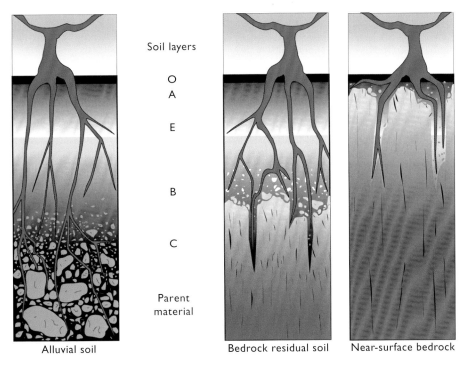

Soil layers

O
A

E

B

C

Parent
material

Alluvial soil   Bedrock residual soil   Near-surface bedrock

FIGURE 55. Generalized soil profiles. The O layer consists primarily of decomposed organic matter such as grass, leaves, and twigs. In the A layer, percolating water leaches chemical elements and carries them, along with very fine clay minerals, into the B layer, where they accumulate. The B layer is gradational with the rock beneath, in the C layer. The E layer is a zone of extreme depletion.

to understand this biological community but rather to sense how the vineyard is working, to ask whether you are doing anything to harm the soil ecosystem. If it is treated with care and respect, the community will achieve a natural balance for its environment, which now includes you and your grapevines. Accommodation, not dominance, is the goal. More and more Napa Valley winegrowers recognize this aim and are rethinking vineyard practices, cutting back on poisons, using integrated pest management, and exploring organic agriculture, with some even applying biodynamics. Many believe that these explorations are the path to the long-term health of the soil and the industry.

In younger soils, organic material from the O layer mixes with mineral matter in the rocks and sediments beneath, forming the A layer. As water percolates through the A layer, it dissolves mineral elements, forming a depleted zone known as the E layer. In fully mature soils, the A and E layers are like an orange sucked dry of its juices—most of the chemical and mineral elements useful to plants have been removed. This extreme state takes many thousands of years to evolve in most climates.

The mineral elements that are dissolved from the E layer end up in the B layer as chemical compounds that cannot be utilized by plants. In some cases, hardpan is created, a solid layer that roots cannot penetrate. Below the B layer, the soil merges with unweathered bedrock or sediments.

The pit in which Anamosa is standing is a little over six feet deep—he's quite literally in over his head, breaking the Occupational Safety and Health Administration regulations. He doesn't need to worry, though, because the profiles in these pits are heavy with clays, gummy sediment that holds together pretty well until it becomes saturated with water and gets very slippery. Here on Hudson's land, the soil is moist but not wet, and Anamosa hops into and out of seven or eight pits with no hint of disaster.

In one, he's chipping at a layer with a shale hammer—one end a hammerhead, the other a flat pick—sometimes picking at it with a knife, testing how the soil breaks up, how strongly the particles adhere to one another. These characteristics control root penetration. Roots easily penetrate blocky soils; are stopped by massive, highly compacted ones; and grow downward along prism boundaries in prismatic soils. Anamosa ends his examination of each layer by chipping a sample into a plastic bag for physical and chemical analysis. The results will come to Lee Hudson as a report providing an overview of soil variation, graphic illustrations of what was found in each pit, and recommendations for planting and soil amendments.

Of all the features Anamosa has been recording, texture and structure are the most important, as both are related to drainage, water retention, and root penetration. Texture refers to the size of the grains that make up the deposit and their relative percentages. In general, the coarser the grain size, the better the drainage. Clays, in contrast, tend to hold water in their mineral structure and, in quantity, impede water movement. Vines, as they say, don't like wet feet; so a thick clay layer relatively near the surface is not good news. Just the right amount of clay, however, stores water and feeds it to plant roots over time without keeping them soaked.

A combination of coarse-textured, well-drained sediment with just enough clay to store some water is perhaps the best material available for growing grapes, especially Cabernet varieties. A mixture of sediments such as this—complexly interlayered coarse- and fine-grained material—is most likely to form on an alluvial fan and to be found within the boundaries of the alluvial EPUs, not here in Carneros. These pits Anamosa has been describing are typical of the Carneros AVA, heavy with clay deposits. Originally the home of distinguished Chardonnay and Pinot Noir, Carneros has more recently become known for fine Merlot, a grape that seems to accommodate to clay soils and to the cooler Carneros climate better than Cabernet does.

Clay minerals are also important holders of nutrients such as calcium, potassium, magnesium, and sodium, as well as the micronutrients copper, zinc, boron, manganese, and perhaps a host of others we have not yet assessed. As water dissolves small amounts of these elements, it carries them from the A layer into the B layer, where they combine with others to form compounds that hold them tightly, making them unavailable to the vines. Clays, however, adsorb the minerals as cations (negatively charged particles), uncombined with other elements, releasing them into ground water through exchange processes that allow vine roots to access these important nutrients. Given the opportunity, vines are binge drinkers and eaters: they'll take all they can get while it's available and grow wildly as a result. A water and nutrient supply metered out by clay minerals reduces their ability to overindulge and overdevelop.

Large area soil surveys, such as those conducted in Napa County and reported in 1938 (Figure 56) and 1978 (Figure 57), are quite different from Anamosa's work. Napa winemakers consider the 1938 map a work of art. It is much sought after and difficult to obtain, and the descriptions that accompany it are based on an unusual appreciation of geology. The 1978 survey (digitized and revised in 1999) was undertaken to serve a broader set of purposes, ranging from agricultural concerns to the

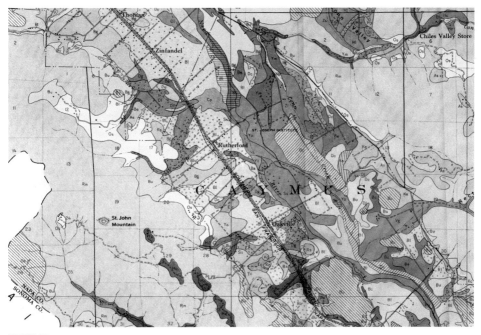

FIGURE 56. The 1938 soils map, detailing a part of Napa Valley extending from St. Helena in the north to the Yountville Hills in the south. (Source: E. J. Carpenter and Stanley W. Cosby, *Soil Survey of the Napa Area, California,* Series 1933, no. 13 [Washington, D.C.: U.S. Department of Agriculture, Bureau of Chemistry and Soils, January 1938]).

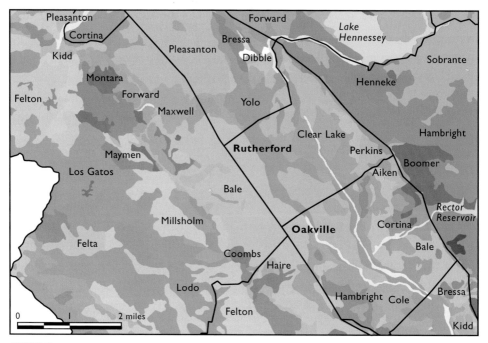

FIGURE 57. The 1978 soils map (digitized and revised in 1999), covering approximately the same area as Figure 56. (Source: G. Lambert and J. Kashiwaga, *Soil Survey of Napa County, California* [Washington, D.C.: U.S. Department of Agriculture, Soil Conservation Service, 1978]. The 1999 revised map is available online at www.ftw.nrcs.usda.gov/ssur_data.html.)

availability of building materials to recreation, which makes the interpretation of its data a bit difficult.

Large area surveys need more data than backhoe pits can provide. Instead, surveyors use a large screw, about five feet long, with a flat spiral blade about eight inches across that is rotated into the ground. As it descends, soil and sediment rise up the blade, allowing the operator to sample at least the upper five feet of loose material. The basic data of the soil survey come from the hundreds, perhaps thousands, of auger holes pocking Napa County, enhanced by laboratory analysis of auger samples and some backhoe pits. Unfortunately, no record of the location or description of the auger holes exists, so correlation with any later work is impossible. Lost information is a bit ghostly—its image is available in maps and general descriptions, but the rich detail of the physical samples from specific locales floats in the ether, unavailable to the winegrowers and scientists who could use it in the context of today's greater focus on place.

As soil scientists dot the land with auger holes, they record the soil type at each location, attributing it to an identified Soil Series or describing a new one. They also document the information on aerial photographs or topographic maps. Slowly, a picture emerges of areas covered by specific soils. The investigators also observe the vegetation, particularly plant communities that are limited to specific substrates. In the Napa region, for example, ghost (gray-needle) pines grow on serpentinite. Back in the office, this information is added to the map, which notes the distribution of vegetation.

The 1978 *Soil Survey of Napa County* recognized thirty-five Soil Series in the Napa Valley AVA and eighty-two "mappable units"—Soil Series modified by slope inclination—though only thirteen of the Soil Series cover any significant area within the subappellations.

WINE AND TERROIR: SOME LIMITATIONS

The existence of such detailed maps from years past implies that knowledge of sediments and soils has been integral to winegrowing in Napa for some time. Would that it were so.

Science and technology have been increasingly important aspects of winemaking since the mid-twentieth century, when Maynard Amerine of the University of California at Davis began insisting that an understanding of plant physiology and wine chemistry was essential to making great, or even good, wine. His work and influence were perhaps more important than those of any other individual in the rapid ascent of both California and Napa in the world of wine. But scientific study has focused mainly above the soil surface or on soil type; little attention has been paid to the geologic architecture of vineyards, the textural and structural components that result from geologic processes. At a time when talk of location and terroir rolls off the Napa tongue as smoothly as wine pours from its bottle, one might be surprised by the lack of understanding of what exists beneath the thin surface of vineyards. And while winegrowers and winemakers speak freely of terroir and its influence on wine, they offer little other than anecdote, intuition, and the feats of skilled wine tasters to support the connection.

One of the few positive correlations between substrate and wine character is quoted by John Gladstones, an Australian who surprised the wine world a decade ago with a remarkable book titled *Viticulture and Environment* (Adelaide: WineTitles, 1992). Though technical in character, it is filled with comments supporting the notion that wine character and place are indeed related. His most specific reference concerning the relationship between substrate and wine quality is this: "Carbonneau and Casteran . . . in Bordeaux, more recently demonstrated experimentally a difference in wine style which could reasonably be ascribed to soil type. . . . Cabernet

Sauvignon vines grown on a moist sand were 'significantly more balanced and soft or velvety,' whereas those grown on a dry gravelly soil 'significantly possess better aromatic quality, fruit, colour quality and intensity, structure but higher astringency, bitterness and acidity'" (p. 33).

The importance of this science-based observation lies not in the particular descriptions—depending on our palate, we might use different words to describe these same wines—but in the detection of consistent qualities attributable to differences in substrate. We do not suggest that the sought-after but oft-tainted "objectivity" of science is the only measure of credibility. There is much to be said for personal experience, however subjective, as a source of information, particularly when the subject is taste. By the time we read Gladstones's account, Ed Sbragia had already observed that "gravelly soils produce harder wines, while bigger, softer ones come from soils richer in clay." And because we do not know the conditions under which the experiment of Carbonneau and Casteran was undertaken, we cannot vouch for the accuracy of their conclusions.

Carole Meredith lives in the middle of this sometimes contentious juncture between science and experience, held there by her two vocations: professor of viticulture at the University of California at Davis (now retired), and grower of Syrah wines on Mount Veeder with her husband, Steve Lagier. On our visit, Steve met us at the base of the road (then a dirt track) that winds steeply up the slopes of Mount Veeder, where they've lived for better than fifteen years. The farther we went, the steeper and more rutted the road became. After a jarring drive, we finally broke out of the woods into an open space of steep slopes and small, rolling fields at the top of the ridge. Their main vineyard, only a couple of acres, dips steeply eastward away from the deck of a weather-beaten, wood-sided rustic retreat.

We talked in the sun on a clear fall day, looking across the valley over the Yountville Hills toward the Stags Leap District and the ridge of the Vaca Mountains in the distance, taking in the view with a chorus of hummingbirds. The red soils of Stagecoach Vineyards stood out on the upper flats of the Vaca Mountains, and we could see Oakville Estate, Dalla Valle, Backus, and Rudd on the flat surfaces that step down the slope below.

Meredith knows both sides of the terroir issue. By training and primary occupation, she is a scientist, and passionately so. In this role, Meredith argues for objectivity, for the need to support concepts with evidence, for the importance of isolating variables, for the attributes of consistency and repeatability. She speaks of the "myths" of Napa—the beliefs of Napa winegrowers, unsupported by scientific data, concerning the effects of site on wine. She argues vigorously and cogently that the only way to establish the effect of site is to isolate it as the only variable. In other words, winegrowing and winemaking involve numerous processes and decisions, any (or all) of which might influence the character of the product. To test the effect of any one variable—substrate (soil and sediment), for example—you must hold all the others constant while varying only the one under examination.

This, of course, is extraordinarily difficult. It means using the same rootstock, the same grape variety, the same clone. The vines must be planted the same way, pruned the same way, trellised the same way, irrigated the same way. This is all possible, but you must also consider the human factor, recognizing that the experiment will be influenced by the people who undertake it. Then you must also duplicate the aspects of place other than substrate—solar exposure, rainfall, slope angle, aspect, temperature. The problem is obvious.

When Meredith talks of Lagier-Meredith Syrah, however, the tune changes. Suddenly, site becomes everything and emotion reigns. She is not unaware of this dichotomy—you might think from the tone of her conversation that she's even a bit delighted by the inconsistency. As she describes the Syrah, her hard-nosed, intense, show-me-the-data scientific approach to the question of terroir is transformed into a more relaxed, flowing wonderment about the character of this wine that she and Lagier produce and what it reflects. They speak of its distinctiveness, a word they often hear in blind tastings. They describe it as "very complex, very concentrated, with a spiciness not usual in New World Syrah, more like the northern Rhone, but more concentrated due to riper fruit." They talk about the red berry and black pepper flavors, attributing all this to the particularities of site.

While acknowledging clearly that they don't know which specific aspects of the site provide distinct character to the wine, they speculate with some conviction that the primary factor is temperature, the coolness resulting from elevation and proximity to San Francisco Bay. This view springs from the notion that most California Syrah, which is usually grown under warmer conditions, lacks the spiciness and complexity they find characteristic of this east-facing parcel high on Mount Veeder. Meredith feels strongly enough about this to defend the notion that site influences the character of a wine, something that her colleagues at Davis would still dispute. The wine academics are perhaps justifiably skeptical, given the lack of truly scientific data. But Meredith and Lagier bought the land and developed it themselves, planting and nurturing the vines for fifteen years. They now understand, and share, the passion they have seen in others for making wine from grapes grown on your own land.

Our meeting with Meredith and Lagier reminded one of us (Jonathan) of a term paper he wrote in graduate school for a course in mining geology, on the origin of the Witwatersrand gold deposits in South Africa, some of the richest in the world. The arguments were both clear and unresolved: were these accumulations the result of erosion of some mother lode, with the eroded gold carried by and deposited in streams and rivers; or were the gold deposits the result of precipitation from hot, mineral-rich solutions flowing through ancient stream deposits? In the case of the Witwatersrand, the academics—the theoreticians—concluded that the deposits were hydrothermal, formed from hot solutions, whereas the geologists who saw and worked with the deposits every day concluded that they were the result of stream deposition. In this case, both groups consisted of trained scientists, but the more important distinction appeared to be between theoreticians and practitioners.

Attempts to assess the influence of terroir on wine reflect a similar dichotomy, between wine academics and winemakers. Consider the years Lagier and Meredith have spent in their vineyard, preparing, planting, pruning, watching the vines and grapes, harvesting, feeling the sun and rain, walking in the fog, hearing the crunch of ground beneath their feet—and remember that we, and they, are learning every moment. Much of the learning is intuitive, nonanalytical, sensory, and sometimes even subconscious and difficult to express; but it is no less valid, and the understanding that arises from it no less useful, than more easily identified ways of knowing. Meredith knows that her grapes and wine express something unique to that particular site high on Mount Veeder. She will continue to wonder about the cause and hope to find a definitive answer, even while acknowledging the slim chance of that happening. Perhaps it is not such a bad thing to be kept wondering, recognizing that it is simply part of the mystery not only of wine but of life itself.

WINE AND TERROIR: SOME ASSOCIATIONS

The purpose of this book, however, is to illuminate such mysteries as best we can. A vineyard designation on a wine label that suggests the special character of a place means considerably less if it cannot be clearly associated with aspects of terroir that potentially mold the character of the wine. We can use the EPU map presented earlier (Figure 54, page 88), together with informational overlays, to summarize what we have learned so far about provenance and pedigree in Napa—about the relationships among bedrock, sediments, soils, and wine.

Most of the land shown on the EPU map—hilly, dissected by streams, often steep—falls in the category of residual EPUs, covered with residual materials. These EPUs have, at best, a thin cover of sediment over bedrock, except in small protected pockets with thicker accumulations. Soils are sparsely developed, drainage is extreme, nutrients are sparse, and vines are naturally stressed. Here we find the mountain vineyards known for intense, highly concentrated wines that tend to be tight and tannic. These wines are sometimes tough in their youth, but the best of them transform with age into marvelously balanced, even elegant, wines.

Dunn Howell Mountain and the three wines of Diamond Creek Vineyards are the quintessential examples of wine from these residual EPUs. Mayacamas, Mount Veeder, and La Jota are other long-established mountain vineyards with a similar wine-making approach. Constant and Marston, both made by Philippe Melka, seem of similar breed, though perhaps slightly more reflective of today's tendency toward more approachable wines. Harlan lies low on the slopes of the Mayacamas Mountains, just above Martha's Vineyard; it produces one of the most powerful and intense Napa wines, perhaps reflecting its position lower on the slopes, where temperatures are warmer. Some mountain winemakers, von Strasser most overtly, have chosen to use viticulture and winemaking practices that make wines more accessible in their early years. Whether these wines will age as gracefully as the more classical examples from mountain vineyards remains to be seen.

Alluvial EPUs lie at the foot of the mountains, lining the edges of the Napa Valley, some extending well out onto the valley floor. The alluvial EPUs are accumulations of gravel, sand, silt, and clay, arranged in an architecture controlled by the processes of deposition that characterize this geologic regime. Springs sometimes line the break in slope at the base of the hills, as they do at Dominus, where they create a zone of greater agricultural vigor, which encourages excessive vegetative growth in the vines. As Daniel Bosch observes, "Vigor follows drainage." Alluvial sediments vary irregularly in depth—silt or clay might underlie coarse sediment at the surface, or vice versa. Organic content is linked to grain size: finer-grained sediments contain greater amounts of organic material and tend to hold water, characteristics that make them agriculturally more vigorous. Alluvial fan sediments are thick, and most are easily penetrated by roots. Drainage is good, except where they are dominated by clay.

The west side alluvial EPUs contain much of the rich history of Napa wine. Gustave Niebaum made wines here, as did Georges de Latour and John Daniel Jr. The Rutherford fan is home to Niebaum-Coppola (previously Inglenook) and Beaulieu, while the Oakville fan is the home of Robert Mondavi Winery, the fabulous To Kalon Vineyard, and Bella Oaks. Martha's Vineyard lies at the head of a fan south of Oakville Grade. More recent luminaries include Dominus (on a small fan in Yountville), Staglin, Spottswoode, and Abreu (from Madrona Ranch at the foot of Spring Mountain). Cathy Corison has made wine from grapes grown on these fans for some years and now owns a small vineyard south of St. Helena. This list is by no means complete; in particular, it does not include the many growers located on these fans who supply a variety of producers. Wines from the western fans are said to have berrylike fruit, rounded tannins, and a generally softer character than their mountain cousins. These characteristics are in line with the statements from Carbonneau and Casteran reported by Gladstones and quoted earlier in this chapter.

On the east side of the valley, Nathan Fay set the stage for the development in the Stags Leap District; he was followed shortly by Warren Winiarski at Stag's Leap Wine Cellars, John Shafer at Shafer Vineyards, and Bernard Portet at Clos du Val, to name only a few. But even now, few prominent east side vineyards are located on alluvial fans—there is little alluvial fan area on which to plant. Stag's Leap Wine Cellars' Fay and SLV vineyards lie mostly on a small alluvial fan complex. Clos du Val and Chimney Rock are on a larger fan south of Fay and SLV. Screaming Eagle and its relatively new neighbor to the south, Paul Frank's Gemstone Vineyard, are on alluvial fan deposits.

Caymus, situated on flatter land away from the hills, is on Conn Creek, which carried the sediment outwash from the large Hennessey drainage before it was dammed. The northern part of the Rudd Estate vineyards sits on an alluvial fan. Eisele Vineyard is located on a small fan in the northern end of the valley, and Chateau Montelena's most prized vineyards lie on small fans in the northern tip. Other prominent east side vineyards—Backus (Joseph Phelps) and Quintessa, for example—are located either on the lower reaches of the rocky slopes that border the valley or on knolls. We are talking here of the valley and its edges, not the hills above. The limited extent and local character of these eastern fans virtually preclude general comments about the wines produced from them, though the east side, in general, is hotter than the west and seems to exhibit this difference in more aggressive development of tannin.

Fluvial EPUs occupy the remainder of the valley floor, the region adjacent to the Napa River and between the river and the alluvial EPUs. These are the thickest and agriculturally richest of Napa sediments, showing great nutritional vigor, which demands special attention and modified viticulture practices. Few have mastered the skill. While Opus One lies close to the river and grows grapes in part on fluvial deposits, the wine is made from grapes grown both there and elsewhere. We know of no prominent wine that is made exclusively from grapes grown on fluvial EPUs. In general, wines from these EPUs tend to have prominent herbal characteristics.

Adding informational overlays to the EPU map broadens the data available for exploring the relationship of terroir and wine. A watershed map (Figure 58) relates the fans to the stream watersheds that provide them with sediment. A geologic map (Figure 59) reveals the type of bedrock that feeds each fan, offering a general idea

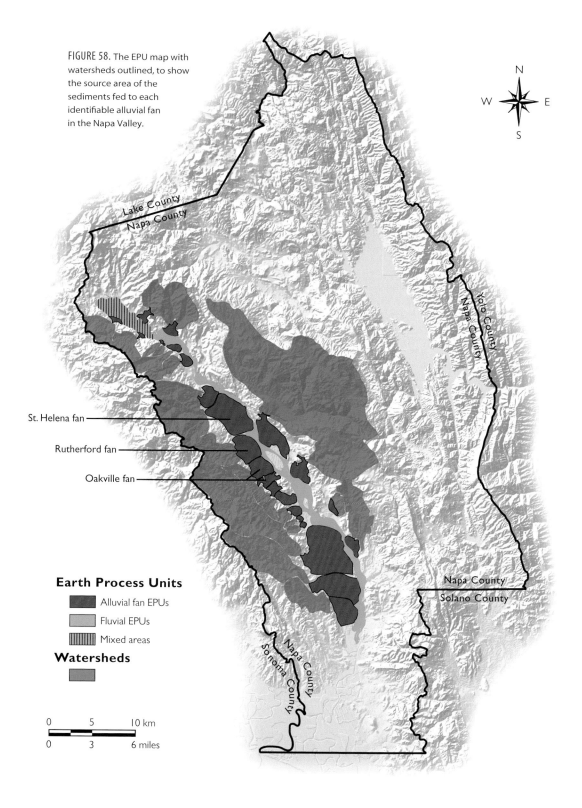

FIGURE 58. The EPU map with watersheds outlined, to show the source area of the sediments fed to each identifiable alluvial fan in the Napa Valley.

Lake County
Napa County

Yolo County
Napa County

St. Helena fan

Rutherford fan

Oakville fan

Napa County
Solano County

Earth Process Units

Alluvial fan EPUs
Fluvial EPUs
Mixed areas

Watersheds

Napa County
Sonoma County

0   5   10 km

0   3   6 miles

N
W   E
S

of the potential mineral and chemical differences between fans. The Rutherford fan, for example, lies at the foot of a canyon that drains an area underlain by rocks of the Franciscan formation, marine sediments with chunks of ocean crust, rich in iron and magnesium minerals. In contrast, the two fans that make up the Oakville Bench lie at the mouths of streams that drain mostly rocks of the Great Valley sequence, marine sediments rich in quartz, with sodium and potassium minerals.

Historically, wines made from these two fan complexes, Rutherford and Oakville, are considered distinctive, though many of us would be hard-pressed to identify the difference. It is tempting to say that any characteristics unique to one or the other reflect the sediments that make up these fan complexes, but no data exist to either support or disprove that notion. Although these fan complexes are adjacent, differences in climate and other factors may be enough to affect the character of the wines from each area. Such variations between fans do occur: based on acid values alone, both Cathy Corison and Frank Leeds can distinguish wines grown on the St. Helena fan from those grown on fans to the south.

Grapes from To Kalon Vineyard used in Robert Mondavi Reserve Cabernet, among the best grapes produced by that winery, come in large part from the upper reaches of the Rutherford fan. These deposits, which lie adjacent to the mountains, tend to have coarser sediments, and thus better drainage, than deposits from farther down the fan, away from the hills. We might even speculate that because of their shared geologic attributes, wines from the upper reaches of the Rutherford and Oakville fans will show greater similarity to one another than they will to wines from regions of the same fan farther from the mountains. This notion could be the basis for an interesting tasting, particularly if it was expanded to include other alluvial fans from both sides of the valley.

The geologic map shows that many of the alluvial fans in the valley have a source in volcanic bedrock. But this commonality does not mean that all these fans are the same and should therefore produce similar wine. Remember that the Napa volcanics exhibit considerable diversity of rock type. Other variables operate as well: for example, topography, temperature, and precipitation in the source areas control weathering and runoff, which in turn feed into the composition and character of the sediments delivered to the fans.

An additional word about EPUs and soils is in order. The sediments that fill the Napa Valley are young, mostly accumulated over the past ten thousand to fifteen thousand years; mature soil profiles are rare in this region. The character of the loose substrate— the materials in which the vines are planted—is controlled primarily by geologic processes, modified in part by human hand through vineyard preparation practices such

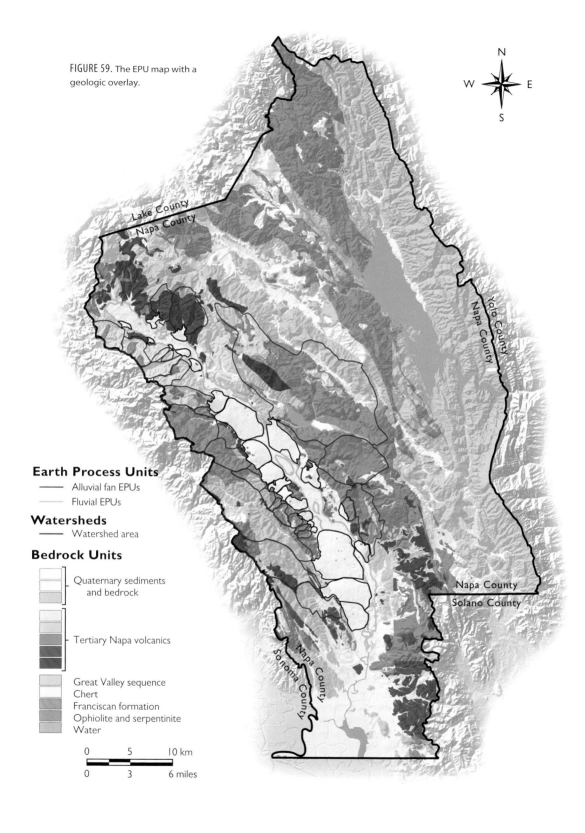

FIGURE 59. The EPU map with a geologic overlay.

N
W   E
S

Earth Process Units
——— Alluvial fan EPUs
——— Fluvial EPUs

Watersheds
——— Watershed area

Bedrock Units

Quaternary sediments and bedrock

Tertiary Napa volcanics

Great Valley sequence
Chert
Franciscan formation
Ophiolite and serpentinite
Water

0   5   10 km
0   3   6 miles

Lake County
Napa County

Yolo County
Napa County

Napa County
Solano County

Napa County
Sonoma County

ORGANIZING A STRUCTURED TASTING

The vineyard-designated and estate-grown wines that might reveal the influence of terroir in Napa tend to be expensive, often $30 to $40 and up. But if you organize a number of interested people and share the cost, you can put a group of these wines together for a reasonable price per person. A single bottle is adequate for twelve to fifteen people at a tasting. If you plan to taste eight wines at an average cost of $70, you can assemble an informative structured tasting for about $40 a person and taste wines that you might otherwise not approach.

Choosing an appropriate group of wines is simply a matter of deciding where to focus your attention. For example, you might compare wines from Rutherford with a group from Oakville. Or you could pick a group of eight wines from the valley ranging from Carneros to Calistoga. Wines from the Mayacamas Mountains could be compared to those from the Vacas. You might taste a flight of wines from different alluvial fans or from areas of different bedrock. You could choose wines from successive properties ranging up the displacement surfaces in the Vaca Mountains. Or you could focus on a group of wines made by a single winemaker.

The tasting at Berkeley mentioned in chapter 8 consisted of eight wines whose origin ranged from one end of the valley to the other: Truchard, from the warmer northern part of Carneros ($38); Caldwell, from the eastern edge of Coombsville ($85); Mondavi Stags Leap District ($50); Stag's Leap Wine Cellars' Fay ($75); Mondavi Oakville ($50); Dalla Valle Napa ($100); Cain Concept ($65); and Chateau Montelena ($125). The total cost was $578; spread among fifteen participants, each would have paid $42.25.

as ripping the upper few feet with steel hooks. In other regions, the balance of influence between sediment (EPUs) and soil is quite different. In some areas of Washington and Oregon, for instance, deep soils have developed on either bedrock or glacial till, and two basic soil types dominate the winegrowing regions. Although we have no knowledge of how this influences the relationship between the physical aspects of terroir and wine character, we can at least say that the condition is in stark contrast to Napa's extreme, and perhaps unique, variation.

Obviously, the deeper we get into the territory of terroir, the less clear the path becomes. Discerning which aspects of a wine reflect the terroir, for example, or which aspects of terroir influence the wine, or sorting out the influence of terroir and the hand of the winemaker—these are complex tasks, requiring a disciplined approach to wine tasting. Wine tastings structured around the notion of terroir can be interesting events in which one's sharpness of perception grows in response to the need for greater, more focused attention.

In reality, the elements of terroir are intimately connected in ways that we might never fully understand—we separate them here only for ease of communication. Nevertheless, it is clear that great wine is not limited to a single Napa terroir, or to any particular sediment or soil. Just as we cannot live on bread alone, however, grapes don't survive only on sediment, soil, and the nutrients they provide—they also need sun and water. In the next chapter, we'll take a look at how these elements feed into the equation. Both are intricately linked with landscape, one of Napa's most arresting features.

❖❖❖ *four* ❖❖❖

THE LAND AND ITS CLIMATE

TOPOGRAPHY IS THE PHYSIOGNOMY of the land, and climate is its expression; they are linked as closely as a face and the emotions it displays. Because they are so familiar, they have also become a context we seldom notice, like the painting hanging for years in the same place or the view we walk by every day. It's not often that our senses become so alive that we notice the shadow on a ridge in the late afternoon that controls sun exposure, see the differences in vegetation that reflect levels of moisture, or become aware of the path of the sun at different times of the year. Obviously, we can't engage you directly with the landscape in this book, but we can focus your eye and mind on a few connections you might otherwise miss.

It's useful to begin with a comparison of Bordeaux and Napa. That two such different places can produce equally classy wine suggests that, whatever specific effects terroir might have on wine character, the range of terroir that can produce great wine is broad. Topographically, these two regions are virtual opposites: Bordeaux displays the smooth, rounded, and subdued topography of an aged landscape, whereas Napa has all the sharp angles, jagged edges, and abrupt slopes of youth. The culture and even the character of the winemakers seem to fit their respective topographies: Bordeaux thrives on cultural uniformity, tradition, and regulation, whereas Napa glories in individualism, experiment, and free expression. But the differences don't end there.

Proximity to the sea is critical to both regions, though for opposite reasons. Without the Gulf Stream, which bathes its six-hundred-mile coastline with the balmy waters of the Caribbean, Bordeaux would be more like Minneapolis, a city whose latitude—45 degrees north—it shares. Without the cold offshore current, Napa would be more like California's Central Valley, oppressively hot. Bordeaux has a maritime climate, Napa a Mediterranean one. In Bordeaux, the prevailing westerly winds sweep over the warm Gulf Stream, picking up moisture and dumping it on land

❖ 105

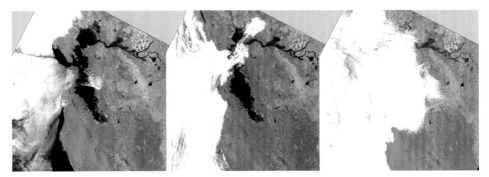

FIGURE 60. Hot air rising from inland valleys draws offshore fog into the Napa Valley during the summer months. The fog travels several pathways—through the Golden Gate and San Francisco Bay, through the Estero Americano gap, down the Russian River, and sometimes over the Mayacamas Mountains. (Source: U.S. Geological Survey.)

FIGURE 61. Napa villas overlooking fog in the valley.

throughout the year; summers are cool and wet, winters stormy and rainy. In Napa, summers are hot and dry, with fog seeping in from the coast to moderate the heat; winters are cool and wet. Napa's climate is more like that of the Languedoc-Roussillon region on the Mediterranean coast in southeast France.

The close link between topography and climate is clearly seen in Napa. The Mayacamas Mountains on the west, for example, keep at bay the cool ocean breezes as well as the summer fog that results when moist, hot air that has swept across the Pacific comes in contact with the cool current offshore (Figure 60). Hot air rising from the Central Valley in the summer draws the offshore fog onto the land in the afternoon (Figure 61). Without the Mayacamas, this fog would pour unobstructed into the Napa Valley, giving it a climatic pattern more like Sonoma. At the same

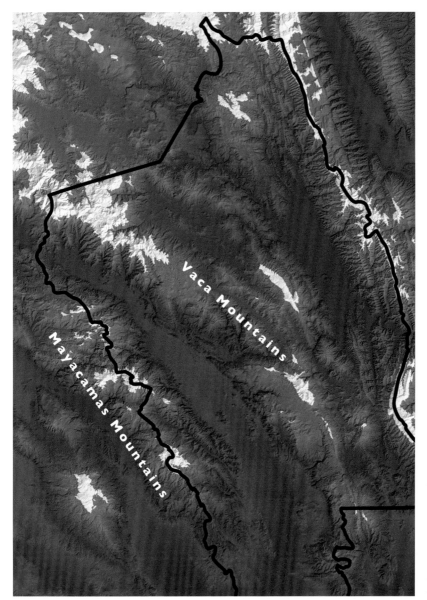

FIGURE 62. Shading all elevations below 2,000 feet reveals that the Mayacamas and Vaca Mountains are of similar height. Mount St. John, the highest peak in the Napa Valley AVA section of the Mayacamas, is about 2,400 feet; Rattlesnake Ridge, the highest in the Vacas, is 2,750 feet. Mount St. Helena is over 4,000 feet, but it lies outside the Napa Valley AVA.

time, the Vaca Mountains and the linear ranges to the east protect Napa from the searing heat of the Central Valley. Without them, Napa would be more like Lodi, a prolific producer of very good high-volume wine. It's as if the cool coastal climate and the hot interior have agreed on a buffer zone between them—the Napa Valley.

Many in Napa assume that the Mayacamas Mountains are higher than the Vacas. We had tacitly accepted this notion until one day when, for some forgotten reason, we shaded out all elevations below 2,000 feet on a map (Figure 62). The few "islands" that poke their heads above such an imaginary sea include Mount Veeder, Mount St. John, and the tops of Diamond and Spring Mountains in the Mayacamas, as well as Atlas Peak and a large part of the Pinnacles ridge in the Vacas. Other than Mount St. Helena, no peak in either range exceeds 2,750 feet in elevation. The Vaca Mountains are, indeed, as lofty as the Mayacamas.

We had also assumed that the Napa Valley rises gently along its length from San Pablo Bay to Calistoga. That may be the perception of those traveling through it, but in fact the southern boundary of the Napa Valley AVA in Carneros lies a few feet above sea level, while the center of Calistoga sits at an elevation of 365 feet. The Napa Valley and the Napa River thus drop 365 feet in a little more than forty miles. Although this might not sound like much (an average of less than 10 feet per mile), consider the Hudson River, which drops less than 1 foot per mile in its lower course—only 50 feet in its ninety-mile trip from Albany to New York Harbor. In the world of rivers, the Napa River is steep; in a wetter climate, it would be eroding its banks and reworking the valley fill with considerable energy. As it is, during the rainy season it flows strongly, carrying a large load of sediment eroded from the surrounding lands. One of the critical components in vineyard engineering is to ensure that runoff and erosion do not clog the river with sediment from the hills, exacerbating its tendency to flood.

Napa's rough topography—deep canyons, steep slopes, and jagged peaks—is a fundamental aspect of the regional terroir. A slope aspect map (Figure 63) vividly depicts the faceted character of Napa's mountainsides. Slope aspect—the direction a slope faces—determines sun exposure; each change in direction alters the amount of time, and the time of day, during which grapes are bathed by the sun's rays and thus potentially alters growing conditions. With geologic age, erosion smooths things over, removing the edges, rounding the hills, generally subduing the form. The older slopes of Bordeaux and Burgundy, predominantly east-facing, are less faceted and more uniform. While they are surely easier to develop and farm, they do not provide the diverse growing conditions that characterize the Napa region.

It's easy to gloss over the details of slope orientation and simply assume that the valley runs basically north-south, with mountains trending in the same direction. Vine rows in the Napa Valley are commonly oriented parallel or perpendicular to Highway 29 or the Silverado Trail, both of which run along the valley generally northwest-southeast. Winegrowers often talk about these row orientations as north-south or east-west, when they are more nearly northwest-southeast and southwest-northeast, respectively. Is this a minor point? Perhaps not, especially for those winegrowers who are aware of, and work with, the true orientation of the rows.

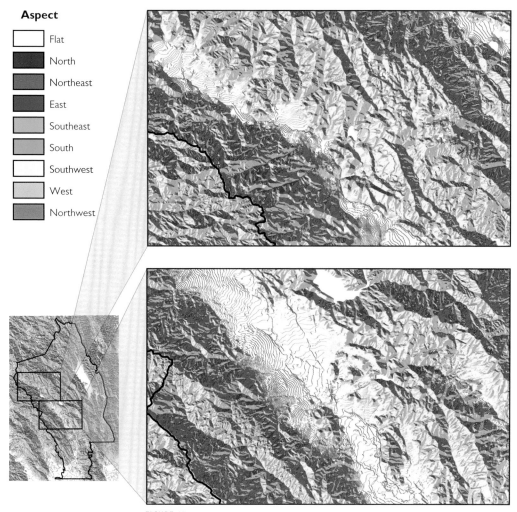

Aspect

☐ Flat
■ North
▨ Northeast
■ East
☐ Southeast
▨ South
☐ Southwest
☐ West
▨ Northwest

FIGURE 63. Slope aspect maps reveal the faceted and diverse character of the hills surrounding the Napa Valley.

MATTERS OF TEMPERATURE

Buffered as it is from the climatic extremes of the cool, foggy coast on the west and the fiery Central Valley on the east, Napa's consistency of climate is a major element of its terroir. Mention Bordeaux to most Napa winemakers, and they're likely to snicker a bit and quickly point out with competitive and sometimes vengeful glee that the great years in France are the warm ones, historically the single year in three or four during which the grapes can truly ripen. Napa has such years one after the other, almost without interruption. The implication is that the lesser years in France are not worthy of consideration, a narrow and limiting view. The French, not to be outdone, tend to criticize Napa wines as overripe, too intense, a result of excessive heat. In truth, even a few Napa winegrowers are wondering whether parts of the valley are too warm for anything other than the sometimes overwrought wines in which power and intensity dominate. Among those who argue that Napa's best years are cooler than normal, some adventurous winegrowers are developing Cabernet vineyards in the southern reaches of the valley, which have been traditionally considered climatically marginal for that grape.

If you've visited or read much about Napa, you've likely come across the notion that the valley has a regular south-to-north temperature gradient, with the coolest temperatures in Carneros, just north of San Pablo Bay, and the hottest in Calistoga, thirty miles north. The assumption is that breezes moving north out of the bay cool the valley and that their cooling effect decreases regularly toward the north, with Calistoga being the hottest spot. Bo Barrett, however, whose family owns Chateau Montelena, off Tubbs Lane in the northern tip of the valley, has a different take on temperature.

At first glance, Barrett does not appear to be someone who will provide a lot of insight into winegrowing. A deceptively laid-back ex-surfer, he has a casual, disinterested drawl, which we first heard on his answering machine: "Hi, this is Bo. I'm out of the office, off makin' trouble somewhere else. Leave me a message." But Barrett has been working at Montelena for thirty years, and he has been quietly innovative most of that time. In 1986, well ahead of the curve, he was talking about soils and wine on marketing tours and had begun making a few barrels of wine from each of several distinct terroirs, finding consistent differences in Cabernet wines grown on different parts of the estate. He knows every nook and cranny of his vineyards, every change in sediment and soil. And he makes wine that has been at the top of the list in Napa for three decades. So when he mentioned that the conventional wisdom about temperature in Napa was a bit inaccurate, we paid attention.

Barrett objects to Calistoga being called the hottest part of the region, a statement that does not jibe with his experience: "When I'm sweatin' here in hundred-degree heat, it's always ten degrees or so hotter down there near Dutch Henry Canyon," seven or eight miles down the valley. When you look at a map, this makes sense—Dutch Henry Canyon is slightly south of the most restricted part of the valley, the hill topped by the Sterling winery. Heat rising up the sloped valley floor seems to pool at this restriction.

Data from DAYMET, a not-for-profit Web site (www.daymet.org) that provides

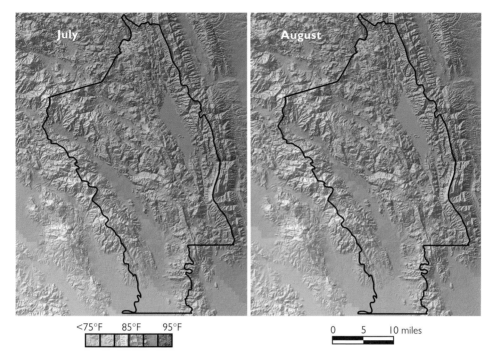

FIGURE 64. Average maximum temperatures in July and August. Note that the area with the hottest temperatures lies at the base of the Vaca Mountains. (Source: www.daymet.org.)

climate data for the entire country, support Barrett's observations. Using an algorithm that relates temperature and pressure to elevation, DAYMET extrapolates data from scattered weather stations into areas of highly irregular topography, such as the Napa Valley. DAYMET data for maximum summer temperatures, averaged over the period 1980–1997, show that the hottest segment of the valley in the summer is surprisingly large (Figure 64). The area of highest temperatures in July stretches from south of the Stags Leap District through Calistoga. But the area of highest temperatures in August lies along a smaller strip at the base of the Vaca Mountains, extending from north of Rector Canyon to Dutch Henry Canyon. The high temperatures seep up side canyons as well, accounting for the "banana belt" in the hills south of the Hennessey Reservoir.

These maps based on DAYMET data demonstrate the relationship between topography and temperature, particularly in the hills, where average temperatures decrease with elevation. They also suggest that the notion of a regular increase in temperature northward through the valley is difficult to support. Although these maps are generalizations extrapolated from two or three weather stations, they do indicate the degree of local temperature variation that results from Napa's rough and

CLIMATES: MICRO-, MESO-, AND MACRO-

Over the past couple of decades, Australian viticulturalist Richard Smart has exerted a strong and positive influence on the evolution of trellising systems for vineyards. His illuminating book *Sunlight into Wine,* co-authored with Mike Robinson (Adelaide: WineTitles, 1991), summarizes this work. Smart defines a microclimate as the conditions that exist within the grape cluster as it hangs on the vine, a mesoclimate as the climate of a vineyard, and a macroclimate as the regional condition in which the first two exist.

In California, the terms "microclimate" and "microenvironment" usually refer to local conditions that differ from those of nearby areas. The size of the microclimate or microenvironment is left undefined, though the terms can often imply a single vineyard or part of a vineyard. In this book, we follow local usage, finding the looser, regionally accepted terms less confusing than an attempt to introduce new descriptions. When we discuss a microclimate or a microenvironment, then, we are referring to local climatic or environmental conditions in an area of unspecified size that generally does not encompass more than a single vineyard.

Information about how many microclimates or microenvironments exist in Napa will always be elusive, dependent both on definition and on detailed measurement of local conditions. How different, for example, must two portions of a vineyard be to qualify as separate microclimates or microenvironments?

Such distinctions are an integral part of the winemaker's dance and are influenced by individual perception and vision. Al Brounstein chose to keep his three original vineyards at tiny Diamond Creek as separate entities, whereas the Mondavis choose to maintain the more than six

(continued)

dissected topography. Each small stream appears to have a different temperature regime from the ridge that separates it from the adjacent drainage. Combine this with angle of exposure to the sun, and significantly varied microclimates result.

ON RIPENING GRAPES

One of the primary measures used to characterize regional climate is the growing degree day, a measure of heat summation for the growing season developed by A. J. Winkler and his colleagues as a classification of winegrowing areas. In the groundbreaking book *General Viticulture* (Berkeley: University of California Press, 1962), Winkler and his coauthors calculated growing degree days by adding up the total number of hours above 50 degrees Fahrenheit from April to October—the growing season for grapes. They then divided the winegrowing areas of California into five categories based on these degree days. They determined that most of Napa belonged to region II, with 2,501 to 3,000 degree days. Carneros, with fewer than 2,500 degree days, fell in region I. In Winkler's 1962 data, Oakville, with 2,300 degree days, was placed in region I; St. Helena, with 2,900 degree days, was assigned to region II; and Calistoga, with 3,360 degree days, was part of region III. These designations have been accepted, and quoted, ever since.

More recent calculations of growing degree days in Napa, however, summarized by our colleague David Jones, suggest that Winkler's data are either inaccurate or not applicable to current conditions. Jones observes that the original Winkler data have had "a profound influence on perceptions of wine quality produced in the various climatic regions. Modern data . . . do not agree with Winkler's original climatic assignments. For example, Oakville, assigned by Winkler to region I, is a solid region III. St. Helena is not a cool region II, but a hot region IV. These differences are so profound that old references to climatic regions should not be used unless verified by modern

(continued)

hundred acres of To Kalon as a single vineyard from which they blend a variety of wines, including the new To Kalon Reserve. Brounstein sometimes subdivides his vineyards into still smaller microclimates. Similar, though perhaps not quite so local, distinctions could be made in To Kalon, but the dance there is to a different tune.

data" (see www.esri.com/news/arcnews/winter0102articles/the-wine-country .html). Using data from the University of California at Davis, Jones reports 3,289 degree days for Oakville and 3,767 for St. Helena. Degree day data from DAYMET (Figure 65) indicate that much of the central-eastern part of the Napa Valley lies in region IV, with Carneros, Calistoga, and much of the mountain slope in region III, an assessment that supports Jones's view. Only the upper slopes of the mountains are in regions I and II.

Although we may have opened the proverbial can of worms in raising this issue, it is important to note that people have made significant decisions on the basis of growing degree day designations. John Caldwell, for example, planted his Coombsville vineyard to Chardonnay when the county farm adviser told him that the vineyard was part of region I and suitable only for Chardonnay and Pinot Noir. After Caldwell began to measure temperature and moisture, he found that the vineyard was actually a high region II, and he replanted it to Napa's premier grape, Cabernet Sauvignon. According to the DAYMET map, Coombsville is mostly in region III, though Caldwell is located in the eastern part of Coombsville, on the lower slopes of the hills, right on the edge of regions III and IV.

Jones's calculations and Caldwell's data suggest that the DAYMET growing degree day maps are reasonable representations of existing conditions. Yet other data indicate that the situation may be more complex. Degree day data from Oakville and Carneros provided by Robert Mondavi Winery (Table 1) place Oakville on the cusp of regions II and III, though the DAYMET map shows Oakville nearer to regions III and IV. As Jones points out, in order to compare these sets of data, you must ensure that they have been collected using the same standards—placing the instruments closer to or farther from the ground, for example, can skew the numbers significantly. Jones has shown that degree days based on detailed local data can be

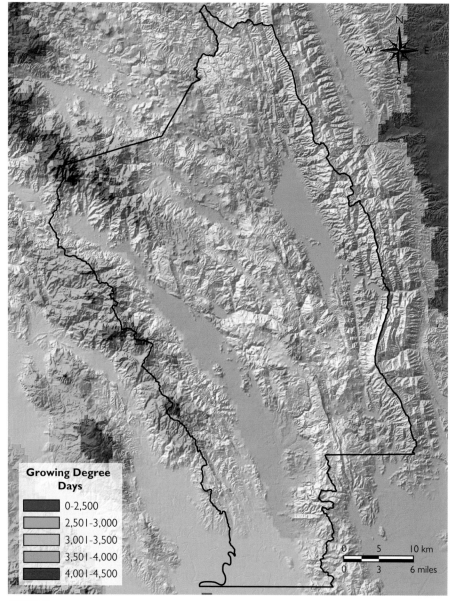

FIGURE 65. Average annual growing degree days, 1980–1997, measured as the total number of hours above 50 degrees Fahrenheit during the growing season, April 1 to October 1. (Source: www.daymet.org.)

immensely useful in designing and laying out vineyards, although he cautions that for general purposes they can be misleading.

Using GPS (Global Positioning System) and GIS (Geographic Information System) technology, Jones mapped the distribution of soils in his Eldorado County vineyard, focusing on the residual materials that he believes are most important in influenc-

TABLE 1

Growing Degree Days Comparison, Oakville and Carneros

	OAKVILLE	CARNEROS
DAYMET data (18-year average)	3,500	3,100
Robert Mondavi Winery data (17-year average)	2,975.7 (2,603–3,348)	2,459 (2,169–2,784)

SOURCES: www.daymet.org; Daniel Bosch, Robert Mondavi Winery.

ing the character of grapes. Then, by using data from nine weather stations on his 130-acre vineyard, he found that degree day variation closely matched the topography, reflecting elevation and exposure to the sun. He planned the Lava Cap vineyards based on this work and an analysis of wind patterns. He planted Chardonnay and Sauvignon Blanc, which need cooler conditions and protection from frost, high on north-facing slopes, away from direct sun exposure and above the coldest parts of the vineyard. Zinfandel gets maximum sun exposure on west- and southwest-facing slopes. Cabernet Sauvignon and Merlot occupy the cooler, north-facing slopes, protected from frost by natural air circulation.

Without sufficient direct exposure to the sun's rays, grapes will not mature fully; with too much, they get sunburned, adding a cooked flavor to the wine. In Napa, maps of maximum average temperature for July and August clearly show that the eastern hills, the Vaca Mountains, are hotter than the Mayacamas. Exposed to the hot western sun, these ridges bake in the afternoon, at a time when air temperatures are already high. The Mayacamas bask in the gentler early morning sun, the cool of the night slowly lifting from the vines as the sun climbs the eastern sky. During the hot late afternoon, the shadow of the mountains protects vineyards on the lower slopes and along the western edge of the valley from direct sun.

Sun and heat are essential for ripeness and maturity, but greater heat concentrates certain elements in the grape while driving off the more volatile ones, those that vaporize most readily, including many of the aromatic and some of the fruitier components. The general take in the valley is that wines from the western side—the Oakville and Rutherford alluvial fans, in particular—are fruitier, more supple, less tannic than their counterparts from the eastern side of the valley, which tend to be richer and more concentrated, with a somewhat hard-edged tannin profile. The exception on the eastern side is the Stags Leap District, where afternoon breezes seem to cool the grapes, helping them retain the more volatile components and develop more supple tannins. These variations are part of Napa's strength in diversity.

THE TANNIN EFFECT

The process of tanning leather—stabilizing animal skins so that they will not continue to decay—got its name from the substances used in the process, tannic acids derived from the bark of trees. Molecules of tannic acid attach themselves to proteins in the skins and prevent them from disintegrating under the onslaught of bacteria and other organic and inorganic substances that promote decay. Tannins in wine—from skins, seeds, stems, and oak barrels (or oak chips)—similarly try to attach themselves to proteins in the mouth, tugging at them, creating the "bite" of astringency or dryness. As tannins mature, either in the grape on the vine or in the wine in barrel and bottle, they polymerize, attaching to one another to build longer molecules. We experience these longer, more mature tannins as smoother, less biting, with lower astringency. The French explain this by saying that the shorter tannin molecules find their way into tiny crevices in the lining of the mouth, while the longer molecules slide over. As David Ramey of Ramey Wines notes, however, "This is still a theoretical idea—the French don't mind printing ideas with no backup."

Although modern trends in wine style have moved toward the smooth mouth feel of mature tannins, many wine drinkers still enjoy the bite—or "grip," as the Brits call it—of more youthful tannins, particularly with food. Imagine eating a meal of rich goose, or a great prime rib or porterhouse steak. Much of the flavor of these dishes comes from fat, which tends to coat the mouth with a thin film. Nothing cuts through that film, refreshing the mouth for the next incursion of richness, like a fine red wine with a bit of tannic bite. Wines with smoother mouth feel, delicious in the tasting room, are not as effective with such food.

(continued)

For all the current popularity of the International style, with its intense, fruit-forward power, many wine drinkers still prefer subtlety and nuance.

RAINFALL

Yearly rainfall patterns are not quite the concern they once were in Napa, before drip irrigation became available. When Warren Winiarski planted his first vineyard in the Stags Leap District, he and his family irrigated it by hand, carrying water to the vines in buckets, a technology more primitive than that of the Chinese or the Egyptians of several thousand years ago. Now most winegrowers use drip irrigation controlled by timers. As long as the winter rains fill Napa's reservoirs and replenish the underground aquifers that feed its wells, everything is fine, at least until the harvest.

While most rain falls in the winter months, rains at harvest can cause near panic. You can imagine the drama—as a winegrower, you've worked all season to produce small berries with concentrated flavor, and suddenly you're faced with the possibility that the grapes will suck up moisture like some desert wanderer handed a case of cold beer. The berries can plump up with water, diluting the juice, negating your careful husbanding of quality over the past seven months. It can be devastating. With the reds, you hope that the rain ends quickly and is followed by sun and warm weather that can drive off the added water, shrinking the berries and restoring at least some of the concentrated flavor that was so quickly lost. But letting the fruit hang is always a gamble—the

TABLE 2

Total Annual Precipitation (inches), Robert Mondavi Winery

	OAKVILLE	CARNEROS
1994	23.3	21.4
1995	64.6	36.8
1996	40.2	27.4
1997	39.8	36.4
1998	60.5	39.6
1999	33.3	19.5
2000	37.9	20.1
2001	25.6	14.8

SOURCE: Daniel Bosch, Robert Mondavi Winery.

(continued)

Like so many of the gustatory pleasures in life, wines with a bit of tannic bite may be an acquired taste, but they are worth the effort. For those of us who began drinking wine when most of the affordable bottles were at least a little on the rough side, a bit of "grip" in a wine these days is a welcome surprise.

weather might stay cool and moist. With Chardonnay and Sauvignon Blanc, Napa's primary white varietals, you have fewer choices. The Chardonnay grapes soon rot when ripe and wet, and they must be snapped off the vine as quickly as possible. You take the best you can find and sell the rest for the jug market.

Regardless of the season, rainfall increases up the mountain slopes, and also up the valley. The city of Napa averages around 20 inches a year, Calistoga more than 30, and Mount St. Helena more than 55. But the year-to-year variation is marked and uneven. From 1994 to 2001, precipitation at a Robert Mondavi Winery station in Oakville ranged from 23.3 inches to 64.6 inches, while in Carneros it varied from 21.4 inches to 39.6 inches (Table 2). Regional precipitation patterns show similar irregular variation; for instance, in 1995 and 1996, rainfall was heavier in the Vaca Mountains than in the Mayacamas (Figure 66).

You are likely to hear from most valley residents that total rainfall in the Mayacamas Mountains exceeds that in the Vacas during most years, and you might assume that the sparse vegetation in the Vacas supports this view. DAYMET data, however, reveal that rainfall amounts in these two ranges are about equal (Figure 67). Other data, from Steve Lagier of Lagier-Meredith for the Mayacamas and from the Napa Water Resources District for the Vacas, as well as from a weather station above St. Helena, indicate that rainfall in the Vacas is usually within 10 percent of that in the Mayacamas (Table 3). If this is so, what controls the difference in vegetation?

The vegetation does indeed reflect the available moisture, but for reasons other than the amount of rainfall. The hot afternoon sun bakes the vegetation and the ground on the eastern hills, forcing moisture from both. And on the west, fog drifting over the hilltops in the summer adds to the humidity of the Mayacamas Mountains.

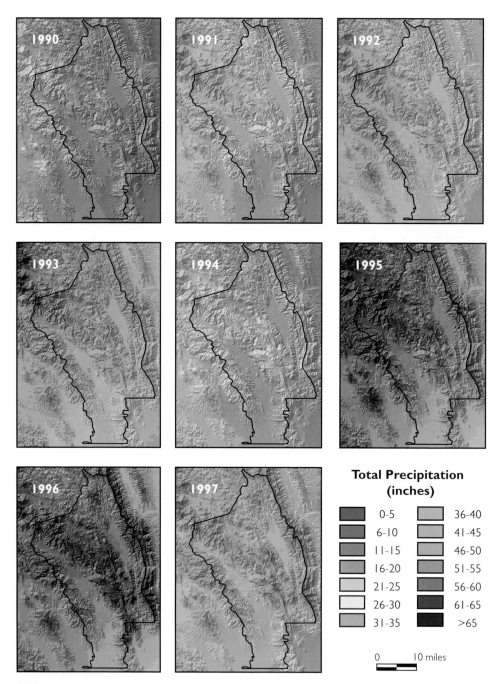

FIGURE 66. Average rainfall for the years 1990–1997. (In 1995 and 1996, more rain fell on the Vaca Mountains than on the Mayacamas.) (Source: www.daymet.org.)

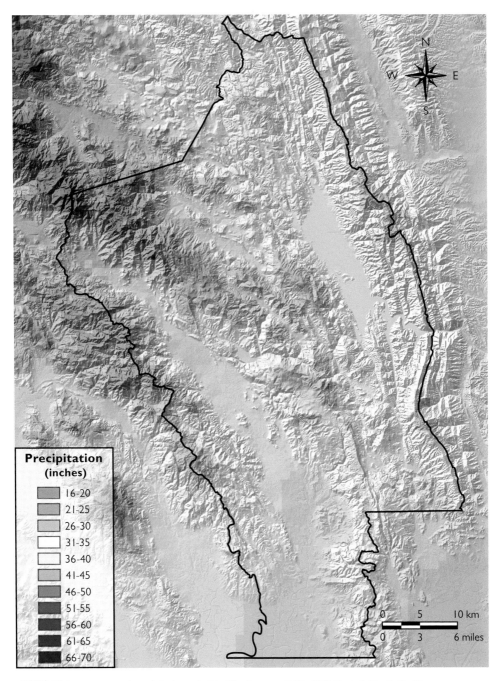

Precipitation (inches)

	16-20
	21-25
	26-30
	31-35
	36-40
	41-45
	46-50
	51-55
	56-60
	61-65
	66-70

FIGURE 67. Average annual precipitation calculated for the years 1980–1997. Precipitation in the Mayacamas Mountains and the Vaca Mountains is approximately the same. (Source: www.daymet.org.)

TABLE 3
Rainfall in Inches, Vaca and Mayacamas Mountains

	VACA MOUNTAINS, ATLAS PEAK (1,660 FEET)	MAYACAMAS MOUNTAINS, ABOVE ST. HELENA (1,780 FEET)	MOUNT VEEDER, LAGIER-MEREDITH VINEYARD (1,300 FEET)
Jan. 1–Dec. 31, 1997	32.52*	37.28	35.40
Jan. 1–Dec. 31, 1998	60.64	66.20	66.80
Jan. 13, 1995	2.80	3.70	——
Jan. 1, 1997	4.92	4.64	——
Jan. 22, 1997	5.20	3.48	——
Nov. 26, 1997	1.32	1.56	——
Jan. 11, 1998	1.92	2.96	——
Feb. 2, 1998	3.68	3.64	——
Apr. 23, 1998	0.88	3.72	——
Nov. 23, 1998	2.60	2.72	——

*No data from Oct. 4 to Nov. 5. During this time, 2.2 inches fell in St. Helena station.

Writing about the effect of fog in central California in her book *An Island Called California* (2nd rev. ed.; Berkeley: University of California Press, 1984), Elna Bakker points out that "parts of the Berkeley Hills receive moisture equivalent to 10 inches (25 cm) of rainfall each year from fog drip alone. Fog not only lowers air temperature and raises humidity, it eases the effect of summer drought by forming drops that build up behind veins and other tiny dams on leaf surfaces. When heavy enough, they fall in sparse but noticeable showers" (p. 76). When the fog rolls over the top of the Mayacamas Mountains, as it does regularly on late summer afternoons, you can see similar effects.

"The afternoon fog just creeps down the drainage, down Diamond Mountain Creek, in the late afternoon and cools the vineyards from the afternoon heat. It's just a blessed spot for Cabernet." So said Al Brounstein, standing on the island in the tiny lake he created, which separates the three vineyards that he scratched out of near wilderness thirty-five years ago. Fog plays many roles in Napa, stealthily moving in from the south and from the west, up the valley and over the Mayacamas ridge, across the low spot northwest of Calistoga, at times lying low, at others shrouding the tops of the ridges. In the summer, northwesterly winds drive surface water away from the coast, allowing deeper, colder waters to well up. Winds from the Pacific flow onto the coast and are cooled by this water, their moisture condensing to form thick banks of fog that envelop coastal towns, valleys, and ridges. The offshore fog bank slides back and forth, drawn in to land as hot air rises from the valleys during the day, nudged back out at night when the inland air cools.

In Napa, the fog often lingers until late morning, protecting grapes in the valley from the intense summer sun but increasing the daily temperature variation. From the top of Howell Mountain or Spring Mountain, you can look down on the fog bank, its brilliant white top glaring in the sun. The fog usually tops out at fourteen hundred feet, an elevation that marks the boundary of the Howell Mountain appellation. Vines above that contour are warmed from early in the day, making up, at least in part, for the otherwise cooler aspect of the highlands. The Mayacamas Mountains, however, are also influenced by the cool winds that come across the ridge with the fog in the late afternoon, eventually sliding down the slopes and draws, cooling off the hotter niches such as Diamond Creek.

Air movement, from almost imperceptible breeze to blustery wind, is another key factor of Napa terroir. Air is moved by temperature differences, hot air rising and cool air falling. The cooler daytime temperatures of higher elevations are ameliorated at night by warmer air rising from the valley floor. Cooler, denser air from the hills moves downslope, providing a bit of local cooling to the hotter valley. Araujo Estate's Eisele Vineyard, for example, lies on a small alluvial fan tucked into the head of a draw near the end of Pickett Road in the northern end of the Napa Valley. You might assume that it heats up in the late afternoon, but Bart Araujo talks of the breezes that flow down Simmons Canyon from the Palisades above, cooling the vineyard and helping preserve acidity, which can be driven off when there's too much heat at night.

Warren Winiarski speaks of the winds that blow through the Stags Leap District during the late summer afternoons. The vale created by the Pine Ridge knoll on the west and the Vaca Mountains on the east (Figure 68) funnels this breeze, cooling the grapes late in the day. The winds increase in velocity as they are funneled through the Stags Leap vale; how much this affects vineyards south of Pine Ridge and Stag's Leap Wine Cellars is unclear. A blind tasting of wines from these vineyards—from Clos du Val on the south to Shafer on the north, from S. Anderson in the northwest to Mondavi on the southwest—might be revealing.

A cooling breeze, of course, may become a drying wind that can extract moisture from a leaf or grape as quickly as a piece of bread sops gravy from a plate. If moisture is not replaced by uptake through the roots, its loss from wind increases stress on the plant, especially at key times such as near harvest. Although documentation of wind patterns and velocities in Napa is unavailable and their overall effect on vine

FIGURE 68. In the Stags Leap District, afternoon winds blow through the vale formed by the Vaca Mountains on the east and small hills that lie to the west, cooling the grapes at the hottest time of day. Aerial photography © 2003, AirPhotoUSA, LLC.

productivity or grape quality is essentially unknown, winegrowers are beginning to consider these issues.

Some climatic observations made by John Gladstones suggest the positive effects of cooling winds and breezes (as opposed to the hot Santa Ana winds, which tend to dehydrate grapes). Gladstones concludes that short-term temperature variation—day-to-night, day-to-day, and week-to-week—strongly influences grape and wine quality. He maintains that "relatively constant, intermediate temperatures during ripening" lead to the most complete development of color, flavor, and aroma in grapes (*Viticulture and Environment*, p. 19). Extremes of temperature, whether high or low, inhibit the enzyme activity that is essential to the full maturation of these qualities. High temperatures also drive off the volatile compounds in the berry, the elements that provide aromatic and flavor overtones. Gladstones's bottom line: the highest-quality grapes come from places where they ripen fully in the most equitable temperature regime.

The implications for Napa are unclear, particularly because the temperature data needed to define such zones are proprietary and unavailable. But perhaps the notion of temperature equitability added to the mix of terroir will provide another layer of definition in the already diverse array of microenvironmental conditions in Napa. Do the sites in each AVA that have the most equitable temperature also have the best potential for great wines? Did Bill Harlan's research, which led to identifying the area between 325 and 500 feet in elevation as the most highly regarded zone for viticulture around the world, tap into a zone of temperature equitability? Given the topographic variation typical of many Napa properties, do vineyards contain particular sites with more even temperatures and better fruit? The notion of defining local terroir becomes more complex at every turn.

five

CIVILIZING THE VINE

AFTER THE PARIS TASTING of 1976, in which his Stag's Leap Wine Cellars Cabernet Sauvignon was deemed the best, Warren Winiarski and others in Napa realized that they did in fact have land that could produce "wines of global interest." Winiarski believes that the Paris event provided the motivating force that led Napa winegrowers to search for ways of improving the fruit.

By the late 1970s, winemakers had largely overcome the problems posed by the absence of experienced mentors by approaching winemaking with courage and audacity—they knew they could produce great wine, and they plunged into the task with little concern for their ignorance or limitations. In doing so, they slowly achieved an understanding of winemaking that allowed them to work with clarity and purpose, avoiding some of the uncertainties that had plagued the early years of the Napa renaissance. They did, of course, make misjudgments along the way, the kind of missteps that led, for example, to the highly tannic, over-oaked Cabernets of the 1970s and early 1980s. But as winemakers became more confident, the focus began to shift, however slowly, from winery to vineyard.

This change, initiated in the late 1970s and clearly in progress by the mid-1980s, would take an additional decade to realize, an agonizing time during which the scourge of phylloxera forced winegrowers to tear out and replant nearly every vine in the valley. Opportunity, however, is often the companion of disaster—the necessity of replanting allowed winegrowers to reconsider every aspect of winegrowing, from choice of rootstock and clone to spacing, trellising, and pruning.

For Winiarski, the focus on better fruit arose in the 1970s, but the motivation for action came from his recognition, in the early 1980s, that something was wrong in the vineyard. He also realized that the problems affecting his fifteen-year-old vineyard, whatever they might be, called into question the well-accepted idea that older vines make better wine. And then two events came along almost simultaneously: an opportunity to buy Nathan Fay's vineyard next door, and a chance meeting in Australia with Danny Schuster.

Winiarski had earlier bought a piece of land next to Fay's, after tasting the wine Fay had made from selected pickings of his own grapes. Winiarski by then had tasted as much unblended Cabernet as possible, exploring the expression of that grape throughout Napa. At that time, there were only some four or five hundred acres of Cabernet in the valley; Nathan Fay's vineyards contained the only Cabernet plantings south of Rutherford. Winiarski had "developed a kind of sense of the Cabernet 'geography' of the valley" and thought that he knew roughly what to expect from Fay's efforts in Stags Leap.

Nevertheless, he recalled, "I was unprepared for the experience when I first tasted Nathan's wine—and even before that, when the perfume of it spread through the small room where we stood together. That wine was, to my senses and mind, the best expression of the varietal of all the alternatives I had experienced before. That moment became, for me, an epiphany of perfection. I recognized immediately that this was the kind of wine I wanted to make." Winiarski proceeded to buy the parcel of land next to Fay's, which became his SLV vineyard, the one that produced the wine judged best at the Paris tasting.

Right from the beginning, in 1951, when Nathan Fay bought his 205 acres in what would become the Stags Leap District, Fay had set out with calm determination to grow the best grapes possible. He decided on Cabernet Sauvignon because it was the heart and soul of so many of the great red wines of Bordeaux, and he stuck to this decision even when most of his friends in the wine business predicted that he would go broke. Stags Leap was too far south, they warned, too cool, with those winds that funnel through the area in the summer. Conventional wisdom held that the only place to grow Cabernet in Napa was the hotter territory of Rutherford and Oakville, where the late-ripening grape could develop sufficient sugar—certainly not farther south.

But after much study and consultation, Fay planted fifteen acres to Cabernet in 1961. He kept planting over the years, reaching toward the slopes of the Vaca Mountains, with the Stags Leap palisade looming overhead, eventually filling ninety acres with mostly Cabernet Sauvignon vines. It was a gamble. He could have planted the "rent payers"—the heavy-yielding Zinfandel and Petite Syrah rather than the shy-bearing Cabernet. But Cabernet is what he wanted, and great Cabernet is what he grew. He always kept a few tons—the handpicked best—for himself, to make his own wine, which he shared with his friends and colleagues. In an online *Wine Spec-*

tator article, "The Man Who Made Stags Leap," published November 9, 2000, shortly before Fay's death, Daniel Sogg quotes John Kongsgaard: "That's the charming thing about it. Nate was just an innocent, friendly 'aw, shucks' kind of guy humbly pouring his wine for his social buddies, and he started a revolution."

Fay appears to have been a natural winegrower, a man who danced the dance without effort, the Gene Kelly of his time, place, and chosen vocation. Again John Kongsgaard: "I remember being at a Napa Symphony fundraiser at Robert Mondavi . . . and it occurred to Nate that he should sulfur [his vines, to protect against powdery mildew], so he slipped out. He always had his ear to the ground like that, not because he was trained, but just really a sensitive guy. He wasn't a crazy perfectionist, just good and steady and always on it. He never got excited, never lost his cool."

Fay sold most of his fruit—to Krug, to Robert Mondavi, to Francis Mahoney at Carneros Creek, to Joe Heitz, and to a few others. Winiarski remembers that "Nathan's fruit was regularly outstanding during the late sixties. His 1968 Cabernet influenced a lot of people—Francis Mahoney; John Kongsgaard, who decided to become a winemaker when he tasted that wine; lots of others as well. In the mid-seventies, Nathan's fruit made some fabulous wines at Krug." But in the 1980s, something began to happen to Fay's fruit; some sensed that its quality had begun to suffer. As the vines got older, the quality unexpectedly diminished. And then, in 1986, Winiarski had the opportunity to buy Fay's vineyard.

On the surface, this was a simple choice. The original Fay property had, after all, changed Winiarski's life. Wine from this vineyard had convinced him to buy his own Stags Leap land, which had produced the wine that made him famous. Yet he also knew that something was going on in Fay's vineyard that he didn't understand, something that might compromise its future. Nevertheless, being perhaps as much of a gambler as Nate Fay, Winiarski plunked his money down and then worried about the mistake he might have made. Had the soil been changed through cultivation? Had the Bay Area climate changed in a way that affected Stags Leap? Did the problem lie in the way the vines were pruned, in a complicated and unsystematic manner? He knew that the quality was declining, he didn't know why, and he wondered whether he would lose his shirt, or more, on the deal.

Then, while serving as a judge at the Sydney Wine Show in 1986, he met Danny Schuster. After ten minutes with Schuster, Winiarski identified the problem in the Fay vineyard and assured himself that buying the property was a safe bet. He became convinced that the reason for the decline of the fruit was neither the ground nor the climate (though that might have had an effect), but was, rather, the way the grapes were grown.

Schuster had grown up in Germany, where he had steeped himself in vine physiology. Although he worked in the vineyards of France as a young man, he was drawn to Australia by the beaches and the bikinis, wine being secondary at best. Eventually, he bought property in New Zealand, becoming the first winemaker on the South Island, in 1971. At the 1986 Sydney Wine Show, he connected with Winiarski, chauffeuring him around town in wine writer James Halliday's car. As he drove, Schuster began to talk about vine physiology and its importance in growing great grapes.

Winiarski quickly saw the significance of Schuster's insights, recognizing that he and his colleagues in California had been going about the business of growing grapes all wrong. They had developed an agronomist's view, seeing viticulture purely as farming, not as a specialized occupation that needed particular sensitivities. Winiarski now likens viticulture to horticulture, describing it as a business in which you care for plants, not crops, for individual vines rather than vineyards. And despite Maynard Amerine's emphasis on science—on plant physiology and wine chemistry—no one in Napa in the mid-1980s seemed to be looking at the real needs and potential of the vines.

At that time, the process of laying out a vineyard was dominated by mechanical concerns, sizing up the inputs and outputs. Minimize the tractor runs, make them as long as possible, design for the smallest number of turns to reduce wear and tear on the machinery. Decrease the number of point rows that intersect field boundaries at an angle—they spell trouble for the tractor and take up too much space. Planting a vineyard this way made it vastly more difficult and expensive to respond to changes of sediment and soil, but this had never been an issue. The central question of whether this approach made beautiful fruit never entered the equation.

Winiarski had already been moving toward a new objective: to produce the best fruit not just from the vineyard but from each separate block within it. The way the blocks were laid out, with little awareness of how the substrate within them might differ, meant that he now needed to look closely at every inch of the vineyard, every vine, every foot of sediment and soil, to understand the interplay of vine and Earth that was reflected in the fruit. He needed to become a horticulturalist rather than a grape farmer.

A naturally growing grapevine does not look like the vines you see in Napa. Left to its own devices, the vine's strongest shoots will extend themselves to the detriment of others—the plant will become a true vine, climbing and clinging to the surrounding growth, reaching farther each year. It will bear hundreds of clusters every year, each with a small number of berries. And it will allocate just enough energy to ripen those berries to a degree of sweetness that will attract the birds and animals who spread seed as widely as possible. That degree of sweetness, however, is not the sweetness we humans seek. For that degree of ripeness, for full maturity, the grower must direct more of the plant's energy to the berries. Winiarski calls this "regulating" the plant—and it is this regulation that domesticates and civilizes the vine. This is the work that, in Winiarski's words, "lets the terroir speak."

It was to this work of regulating the plant that Danny Schuster's comments were particularly directed. As they talked, Winiarski quickly realized that the Fay vineyard had become the victim of old vine syndrome, a spiral of descending quality that reflected a lack of awareness of the life cycle of the vine and its effect, both short- and long-term, on the fruit.

In the Napa of that day, less than twenty years ago, the vines were generally left to grow into the California sprawl, a form in which shoots thrust out in all directions with few limits to growth. The result is an endless number of leaves that support only two clusters of fruit per shoot. The vines accumulate more solar energy than they need for supporting themselves, growing the fruit, and saving a little nourishment for the next year. Each vine sends the extra energy, the food left on the plate, into the roots and old wood, increasing the plant's capacity to grow the following year, when the vine will produce more leaves, more shade, and even less fruit. The less fruitful the plant becomes, the more leaves it grows, the more energy it stores, and so on, each year producing lesser amounts of lower-quality fruit on bigger vines.

Once Winiarski recognized that the major problem in Fay's vineyard was this excessive plant vigor, which had triggered the cycle leading to old vine syndrome, he set Stag's Leap Wine Cellars on a new path. He began by controlling water, putting in deep drainage where it was needed. He followed this by replanting with another, less vigorous rootstock and introduced a different canopy structure, one that let him easily eliminate leaves, a task that the California sprawl had made virtually impossible. Controlling the number of leaves allowed him to balance carbohydrate, produced by photosynthesis, with the fruit that fed on it. It encouraged the plant to transfer energy as rapidly as possible to the reproductive part of the vine—fruit and seed—rather than to the vegetative side.

He could see that the difference between mountain sites and vineyards at lower elevations stemmed not from the facts of geography and topography but from their implications for plant growth. Because mountain sites are better drained, excess water is not a problem, and the soils are likely to be thinner and less agriculturally vigorous. Mountain vines, then, tend to grow in balance, with fewer leaves to feed more fruit, at least in comparison to their peers growing on thicker and more vigorous substrate.

His chance meeting with Danny Schuster set Winiarski on an exploratory path that he still treads, always attempting to allow the fruit to express more fully the power and potential of the land. Michael Silacci, winemaker at Stag's Leap Wine Cellars before moving to Opus One, remembers a particular harvest: "Warren came into the vineyard. All the indications were to pick now. He took a cluster in hand, waved it gently at me, and said, 'Mike—these are like jewels. I understand why you want to pick now, and you can do that, but perhaps if you wait just a couple more days, you can eke out a bit more perfection.'" Winiarski once put it this way: "We're always striving for uniform expression, to have it all ripen evenly so we can pick it all at once. But the less uniformly you treat it, the more you can grasp the window of perfection. If you neglect the differences, you lose the opportunity."

PHYLLOXERA AND TODAY'S GRAPEVINE

Winiarski was not the only winegrower to change course during these years. The revolution that Nathan Fay began by planting Cabernet Sauvignon in Stags Leap dirt in 1961 was only one manifestation of an energy that was building in Napa, leading to the renaissance of the 1970s and 1980s. But the Napa of today was also shaped by the threat of phylloxera, which began to kill off vines throughout the valley in the mid-1980s. The need to tear out and replant virtually the entire valley in order to prevent disaster provided an unprecedented opportunity to reevaluate longstanding vineyard practice. At the same time, scientists and viticulturalists around the world were bringing new insights and new techniques into the vineyard, and new rootstocks and clones were becoming available in Napa. Although the task of replanting brought significant economic hardship—replanting an acre of vines today can cost more than sixty thousand dollars—the pain was more than offset by the advances in quality and the ability to explore character and diversity.

The vines that produce most of today's wine are the result of considerable thought and research dating back to the mid-1800s, when phylloxera, a noxious louse that feeds on vine roots, destroyed the vineyards of France. This microscopic bug has a multichannel proboscis that sucks and injects at the same time, pulling fluid from the root and inserting a compound that slowly destroys the root structure. Introduced to the Mediterranean basin on plants brought from America in the 1800s, phylloxera first made itself known during the mysterious dying-off of vines in the southern Rhone and Bordeaux regions in the late 1860s. It spread rapidly to other districts, with disastrous effects. The vines of France slowly deteriorated and died, devastating the industry and setting horticultural scientists scurrying for a cure.

They found it, perhaps to their chagrin, in North America, where native grapevines in the eastern part of the continent had developed an evolutionary mechanism that allowed them to coexist with phylloxera. American vines attacked by phylloxera adapt to the situation with a simple solution: when bitten by the bug, the plant forms a kind of pocket, in effect sealing off the bite from the rest of the plant. This defense limits the damage to a local area, preventing the pathological results experienced by the wine grape stock of Europe.

The solution, then, was to import American phylloxera-resistant rootstock into Europe and graft onto it the buds of European vines, the *Vitis vinifera* grapes that had proved themselves over centuries to be the best for making wine. The first rootstocks taken to France were varieties of *V. riparia* and *V. rupestris* from the eastern United States. While these stocks were resistant to phylloxera, they did not adapt well to the soils of Bordeaux and other French wine regions, many of which are developed on a substrate rich in calcium carbonate.

In 1887, a French delegation traveled to the United States to find a phylloxera-resistant vine that would adapt well to the calcium-rich soils in France. They found such a plant—the species *V. berlandieri*—in the hills and limey soils around Austin, Texas. But the French winegrowers discovered that *V. berlandieri* neither roots nor grafts particularly well, so they hybridized this species with *V. rupestris* and *V. riparia*, both of which have characteristics important to winegrowing. *V. riparia*, found along watercourses and in wetlands, is a vigorous rootstock adapted to moist conditions; *V. rupestris* is tolerant of drought. When phylloxera came to the Napa Valley in later years, forcing winegrowers to replant nearly every acre, both of these characteristics would stand the industry in good stead.

The first replanting in Napa occurred in the late 1800s. Although phylloxera is native to the Mississippi Valley, it probably came to California by way of France, on *V. vinifera* plants imported in the early days of the industry. Napa winegrowers began to recognize the effects of phylloxera in the early 1870s, but little was done in response until the early 1880s. At that time, most growers considered the species *V. californica* to be the most resistant rootstock, though one lonely and unheeded voice, that of Morris Estee, suspected this assessment. By the end of the decade, the susceptibility of this species to phylloxera had become apparent to even the most stubborn winegrowers, who were forced to accept that virtually all the vineyard acreage in the valley required replanting.

Those who recognized the problem with *V. californica* supported *V. rupestris* and *V. riparia* as the most resistant stocks. Each had many varieties, however, and no one yet knew which variety would be most effective for specific growing environments. By the mid-1890s, French viticulturalists had been systematically investigating this question for two decades. Based on their work, Professor Arthur Haynes decided that the *V. rupestris* variety that the French called St. George was the all-around best chance for renewing the California vineyards. A variety called AXR-1 also arrived in California at about this same time; it too came from France. St. George rapidly took hold and became the favorite rootstock of California winegrowers during the last two decades of the nineteenth century.

Nearly one hundred years later, when the winemakers of Napa planted their vineyards in the three decades after 1950, the selection of rootstocks was severely limited—St. George and AXR-1 still held sway. St. George, a deep-rooting variety, tolerated drought; and AXR-1 was a fine general-purpose rootstock, suitable for a variety of grapes and adaptable to diverse soils and climates. Both were believed to be resistant to the depredations of phylloxera. Thousands of acres of vineyards were planted during this period with these two varieties, predominantly AXR-1.

Little did the growers know that AXR-1, like *V. californica* before it, had a fatal flaw, a hidden susceptibility to phylloxera that would not show up for twenty years. Like Morris Estee a century before, A. J. Winkler had maintained for years that AXR-1 might not have enough resistance to phylloxera, but no one had heeded his warning. Apparently, somewhere in its ancestry AXR-1 had been crossed with *V. vinifera* stock and had picked up some *vinifera* genes—the right ones, it seems, to undercut the evolutionary resistance of its American heritage. The implications of this genetic history surfaced in the mid-1980s, as vines planted between the 1950s and the 1970s began to fail. Slowly, the winegrowers of Napa came to grips with the necessity of replacing every AXR-1 vine in the region.

Most of the stock currently in use was developed for the high-calcium soils of France, not the less calcium-rich soils of California. In Napa, winegrowers commonly add calcium, in the form of ground limestone or dolomite (a carbonate with calcium and magnesium), to compensate for its absence. Rootstocks intended for the general conditions of California are now being developed, but it remains to be seen how well they will adapt specifically to the broad range of conditions in Napa. Despite nearly two decades of planting and experimentation, no consensus has been reached in Napa, or anywhere else in California, concerning the best rootstock to use for each variety in specific circumstances. The effort is ongoing, now focused on the interaction of Earth and vine, where winegrowers are finding that they still have much to learn.

THE QUEST FOR A BALANCED VINE

In decades past, anyone who aspired to own a Napa Valley vineyard—and who had the entrepreneurial drive and financial resources—could decide on a general location, look for a piece of land, and establish a vineyard. In the early years of the Napa renaissance, Winiarski was joined by individuals such as Al Brounstein, who knew with absolute certainty that he wasn't interested in "one of those simple wines from down in the valley" and therefore bought more expensive mountain property. In the early 1970s, Bernard Portet arrived in the valley intending to stay for a couple of weeks—and he has now been at Clos du Val for thirty years. At about the same time, Tony Truchard's brother was drilling for oil in their home state of Texas. Tony was looking for land in Napa, and he had visions of oil supporting the purchase of a vineyard in St. Helena. "Carneros was not prosperous then," he recalled. "It was sort of low end, and we thought if the well came in, we'd buy something a bit nicer." But the well was dry as dust, and the Truchards began their operation with a spread of 21 acres in Carneros, now grown to 270 acres.

Even in the late 1980s and early 1990s, it was possible to luck out. Having studied the character of superior Bordeaux vineyards, Paul Frank knew that he wanted a particular kind of land, with the potential to produce great wine. After searching for several years, he found it, in an area of thin alluvial soils south of Rector Canyon, just down the road from Screaming Eagle. He then sank a good part of his life savings into creating Gemstone Vineyard. A few years later, when property was even tighter, Jan Krupp was able to buy the hundreds of acres that make up Stagecoach Vineyards because the rocky and cool nature of the site scared others away. When we asked Leslie Rudd about the research that had gone into picking his property, he told us that in the end he'd sent letters to fifty winegrowers to see whether any of them were interested in selling. He received only one reply, from Steve Girard, whose father was then eighty-two and ready to quit. Rudd got a fine piece of land—as he says, "We didn't know how good 'good' was."

If you're serious, not simply driven by fantasies of celebrity and glamour, you're likely to have a vision of the varieties of grapes you want to grow and the quality of the wine you want to make. Today, we know much more about where to plant specific varieties than growers knew in the 1960s: late-ripening Cabernet in well-drained soils in warmer spots, early-ripening Merlot in cooler regions and on clay soils, Chardonnay and Pinot Noir in the coolest locations. But the details are often subtle, and our understanding of how to match variety to place is still incomplete.

Once the grapes are planted, the modern winegrower's focus is on the ideal balanced vine, one with fourteen or fifteen leaves per shoot that feed energy to two clusters of grapes at the base. The shoots will stop growing at veraison, the time at which the grapes change color, soften, and begin to develop complicated chemical compounds. When growth stops, hormonal action redirects the sugars created by photosynthesis from the growing tips of the shoots to the grapes. There, the sugars drive processes that develop thousands of phenolic compounds, which provide the grape characteristics we prize so highly—the color, the complex flavors and aromas, and the tannins that, together, make great wine.

"A great site, the ideal case, is where the nature of the soil limits the vine's capacity to grow naturally. If you never had to take a knife to the vine, never had to prune it, it would be a better plant." So says John Kongsgaard, who gets the grapes for his Arietta Merlot from just such a site, a block in Lee Hudson's vineyard in Carneros that neither of them believed would ever produce fine wine. Hudson notes, "I'm not that successful with Merlot, as a rule. We try to manage it all to get the same quality, but in other blocks, the berry size is too small or too large or there's not enough fruit. In this block, we just don't need to work to get some of the finest fruit that comes from this property. . . . It's crappy-looking soil, but with the right rootstock, the right scion, it all works."

Most winegrowers recognize that the best wine comes from such naturally balanced vines and that intervention, in the vineyard or later in the winery, never quite makes up for the lack of this quality. Thus, as a winegrower, you do everything you can to pick a site that will grow balanced vines. If you miss, or if such property is beyond your reach, you work with the land you get and, from the beginning, make choices that will best promote natural balance—variety, rootstock, and clone, all fitted to variation in the vineyard.

Charles Taylor and Terry Mathison of Rudd Wines look for clay horizons or rock layers only a few feet from the surface—conditions that will limit downward growth of roots. "We don't want a full soil profile that will fill with water in the spring— it leads to too much early vigor. Even with good drainage, the roots just keep going down; and as they do, the shoots keep growing out. The hormonal steps that stop shoot growth aren't triggered at the right time. So, for us, naturally limited root growth is the key to producing the quality of fruit we're looking for." Taylor adds, "Mind you, we're not saying that you can't grow fine Cabernet here in this well-drained material. [We're just saying] that we think it won't grow the kind of grapes we're looking for."

This conversation with Taylor and Mathison took place above a backhoe pit, one of several dug to examine the substrate in a new vineyard Rudd Wines was developing on Mount Veeder. The hole revealed about seven feet of gravel, sand, silt, and clay in dark, purplish-brown, irregular layers. Mathison judged that the sediment simply had too much space for water; if there had been more rock and gravel, there would have been less room for water, and they might have chosen to plant Cabernet. Another grower, one with greater need for Cabernet grapes or a different view on how to produce fine fruit, might choose to put in a shallow-rooted, less vigorous stock; pick a Cabernet clone adapted to vigorous growing conditions; design and install an effective drainage system; and further control excess plant growth through trellis design. Either choice—that of Taylor and Mathison or that of our hypothetical grower—would be made in response to the eternal quest for a naturally balanced vine.

Only a few years ago, rootstock choices were limited to St. George and AXR-1, but now the possibilities are considerably broader. Matching rootstock to location—to sun exposure, to sediment and soil, to availability of moisture—is no simple task. Vineyard consultants dig soil pits; analyze sediment and soil for chemistry, organic content, and moisture potential; map out the results in terms of soil vigor; and advise growers about which variety to plant and which rootstock to choose. They use proprietary software to process the data and spit out the results. When pressed for details, these consultants are reluctant to reveal the basis for their suggestions. For some winegrowers, this process is a bit too mysterious, too far from the realities of the land—it goes against their need to understand, as best they can, what they're doing and why they're doing it.

We asked Jan Krupp of Stagecoach Vineyards how he decided on rootstocks. "Well, I took courses at [the University of California at] Davis. I talked to everyone I could. I read, I tasted a lot of wine. I also learned from our home vineyard that I planted in '91. I was trying to understand what might appeal most to winemakers, so I also talked with my neighbors at Atlas Peak and with [John] Caldwell and [Joe] Cafaro. I talked to three different consultants, all bright guys. Each of them told me something different: use this clone or that, run the rows this way or that, this is good Merlot, this is really great, some say this other one makes the greatest Merlot in the world. Everyone seems to know what they're talking about, but how do you figure out who really has a bead on what I'm trying to do here?"

Eventually, Krupp combined all this information with what he had learned while preparing his 650 acres and came up with a plan for a hundred separate blocks, determined by visual differences in soil, sediment, and bedrock, each with a combination of variety, rootstock, and clone chosen for that specific place. Krupp's experience is not unusual. Chris Howell at Cain Vineyards uses consultants, backhoe pits, and soil analysis but admits that he's "never very happy with what I hear. It turns out I know more from experience than anything else."

Choosing a clone requires a different process. The various clones are less well defined, their influence on quality and character less well documented, their ability to reflect terroir not yet clear. John Caldwell, perhaps the clone king of Napa, says,

"In France, there's no 'best' clone. They focus on mixing clones to develop complexity. They say the blend is always better than what seems to be the best of the available clones." Caldwell believes that in the long run Napa will benefit more from clonal diversity than France: "Clones can't influence the wine much at 21 or 22 Brix, which is often what the French are dealing with in their cooler climate. Clones shine when the grapes are fully ripe, [which happens] only every three or four years in France, but here pretty much every year."

Caldwell should know—he's been growing and importing clones from France for twenty years. He started out as a "shoe salesman" who owned five stores in Napa. But one day in 1982, he jumped onto a D6 Caterpillar tractor in his fancy calfskin boots and started shoving dirt around the vineyard he was developing. When he stepped on the gas and saw "the black stuff boiling up behind the Cat, I got all emotional and never turned back." Caldwell is a small guy, with a bald pate, bright and lively eyes, a mischievous outlook, and an entrepreneurial spirit. He's also a smuggler.

Caldwell is in the wine business because he was unable to subdivide his land. He originally had fifty-four acres, bought from a family who had owned the property since the 1880s. He put a blacktop road through it, intending to subdivide it into five ten-acre plots. But the county changed its game plan, limiting development in the area, so he had a fancy road going nowhere. His friends suggested that he plant grapes as a cash crop, an idea that began to sound pretty good. After starting with Pinot Noir and Chardonnay, he replanted to the real moneymaker, Cabernet Sauvignon.

Since the French had been making the best Cabernet wines in the world for a long time, Caldwell figured that he'd better get over there and see what he could learn. Visiting Château Haut Brion, he quickly picked up on the clonal research these winemakers had been doing since the 1970s, which had improved their wines, and their profits, significantly. At the time, Caldwell had no idea what a clone was, but when he saw that the American-owned Haut Brion was sinking real money into the research, he decided that, yes, indeed, he wanted some of these clones from France.

Later, when Caldwell heard that a friend at the University of Toronto had some extra budwood from France, he took the next plane to Buffalo and set about getting it into the States. That his approach (smuggling) was illegal might have given the somewhat roguish Caldwell momentary pause. But he had heard rumors in California that others had taken this path, so he considered it a challenge rather than a criminal act. What developed into a colorful adventure carried with it a significant amount of anxiety (especially when he was caught and barely avoided serious confrontation with the law), but it did result in Caldwell attaining enough French budwood to plant a couple of acres, a block that he kept separate from the rest. This block yielded its first vintage in 1986, and winemakers liked it from the start. Randy Dunn bought some of the grapes, and when the Dunn 1986 Napa hit the market and earned a 90–92 rating from Robert Parker, Caldwell's vineyard was made.

Anticipating a future in the clone business, Caldwell started a vineyard nursery in 1985 using French rootstocks, this time brought in legally. Although the plants had been adapted for the high-calcium conditions of France, he considered them the best available, the foundation of the finest red wines in the world. He also began selling budwood from his vineyard, cuttings collected from pruning. By 1990, this business had taken off, with not a single cutting left to be burned. But Caldwell was still focused on those French clones. Although the field selection he was selling came from French budwood, he'd brought it in illegally and couldn't publicize its origin; and he was not able to mine the rich reserves of clonal research that had been underway in France for decades. Finally, he was licensed by ENTAV (Etablissement National Technique pour l'Amélioration de la Viticulture), the agency for viticultural improvement located in the south of France; and he now uses UPS to import the same clones that once arrived hidden in suitcases, packed in innocent packages, and stashed on private planes.

CLONES

A clone of a grapevine is much like the clone of a sheep or a cow or a fruit fly: it's an exact genetic copy of the parent (or as close as you can get to that ideal). The French, good regulators that they are, have established a precise protocol for cloning grapevines. It begins in the vineyard, where you identify a plant that stands out in some way, perhaps by bearing more and better fruit than its neighbors, showing greater tolerance to drought, or producing fruit with special character. After observing the plant for a couple of years, you take budwood to create ten "mother" plants. You carefully follow these plants, recording their viticultural characteristics.

Each year, you make wine from each mother plant, comparing it with all the others. If one of the plants continues to demonstrate its valued attributes, shows no problems, makes good wine, and (for France) ripens early, in its twelfth year you might submit it to the institute that recognizes and registers viticultural clones. The wine tasters at the institute analyze your entry, and if they approve the clone, it becomes part of the institute's library of clones.

Each mother vine will produce perhaps three hundred buds per year. You can establish a clone block with budwood from the mother plants. That way, if you need to increase the block, you can always "go back to mama," as John Caldwell puts it, referring to the ten original mother plants.

If you spend much time in Napa talking with winegrowers, you will surely hear talk of clones. In addition to numbers such as 191, 337, and 343, you are likely to run across names—the Grace Family clone, for example, or Bulmaro, or even P. These names don't refer to true clones that have gone through the rigorous selection process that is standard in France. Rather, they are names of pseudo-clones, which are field selections, cuttings taken during pruning from a favored vineyard, as Caldwell's cuttings had been. The Grace Family "clone," for example, comes from cuttings from the Grace Family Vineyard, one of the early and extraordinarily successful small vineyard operations of the late 1970s and early 1980s. Dick Grace calls his source the "Bosche clone," but the cuttings were actually field selections from the Bosche Vineyard in Rutherford.

A true clone and a field selection are quite distinct. All individuals of a true clone can be traced back to a single plant, whereas field selections come from many plants that may have a poorly established lineage. You should not be thinking, however, of the family purebred poodle who sneaks out for a fling with the neighbor's Rottweiler, the result being a mix of two varieties. While field selections may not be as genetically distinct as clones, they are nonetheless a specific variety such as Cabernet Sauvignon or Merlot, not the grape equivalent of what might be called Roodles or Pooweilers.

Clones, or field selections, and rootstocks come together in the nursery or in the vineyard. Bench grafts are performed in the nursery, with the scion—the bud to be grafted—attached to a piece of vine wood, which has been planted in a pot to grow roots before being sent to the buyer and transferred to the field. For vineyard grafts, the rootstock is planted in the spring and the bud grafted the following September. Some prefer field budding because the root is already working and begins feeding water to the graft immediately. Bench grafts need more water, as the plant must support both new root growth and establishment of the bud.

This insight came from Manuel Montes one day in Backus Vineyard, where we were meeting with a group of vineyard workers from Joseph Phelps. Montes showed us how to make a field graft. He pulled out a knife—a large and seemingly unwieldy pocketknife, with a black handle and a hefty, very sharp blade—which he used to cut a cane from one of the young vines. With his tough-skinned, blunt-fingered hands, he gently held the cane and cut from it with surprising delicacy a wedge-shaped sliver that included the bud at the top. The sliver was perhaps a third of an inch wide and a quarter of an inch thick at the top, tapering to a flat edge at the lower end, about an inch long. He held this fragile piece of vine in one hand while he grasped the stem of an attached cane and made an angled slash in its side, cutting about a third of an inch into the meat of the cane at its deepest end. Carefully bending the cane, he opened the slash and slipped in the graft. When he released the cane, the fit was so clean that we could not see the join. Had this been a real graft, he would have proceeded to wrap it with twine to keep it tight. The whole process took about two minutes.

This graft was an act of dedicated art and skill, its precision driven by a hidden biological necessity. Like all woody plants, the vine has an outer layer of bark and a thin layer of cambium underneath it that transmits nutrients from the roots to the growing tip of the plant. If the cambium is interrupted, the flow of nutrients is blocked, and the plant (or bud) dies. In a vine graft, the cambium of the vine stem and the bud sliver must match precisely, or the grafted bud will shrivel and die from lack of sustenance. The precise fit we saw Montes create is essential to the survival of the bud.

A skilled and experienced vineyard worker is also a knowledgeable horticulturalist who understands plants and cares deeply for them. Montes's simple demonstration of an act that these workers perform thousands of times a year (some make more than three hundred grafts a day) exhibited a grace and skill that gave it special power and emphasized the intimate connection these vineyard workers have with the world in which they work.

The vines in upper Backus that day were approaching three years in age and were ready for cutting back to a single cane. They had the awkward look of youth, with small canes shooting off in all directions. This year, they would be pruned back to one or two canes, from which the next year's growth would sprout. One of the Backus Vineyard crew knelt before a plant and eyed it for a few moments. Then he took his shears and lopped off the entire top of the plant, cutting through the widest part of the vine with one definitive snip of the blades, as if to behead the plant quickly and cleanly. Shocked as surely as if we'd touched a live wire, we jumped back, physically affected by the cut. The young healthy plant had suddenly been whacked to one-third its size, left with a single sprout, a lone, bare arm.

THE PEOPLE BEHIND GREAT WINE

Vineyard workers, the people who actually manage and care for the vines, are key to the production of great wine. Many of these workers love the plants they tend, talking to them, getting to know them as individuals, nurturing them with care and commitment. They know that the quality of the wine made from the grapes these plants bear is in their hands, and they are proud of the responsibility and honored to be a part of the action. Yet, outside the industry, they are unknown and get little of the credit.

Some have moved on to successful careers in the industry. Bulmaro Montes has been with Joseph Phelps for twenty-seven years, since he was sixteen. His father and brother came to California from Mexico before Bulmaro was old enough to work. Perhaps his role as vice president for viticulture at Phelps has helped to forge the bond that the Phelps organization has established with its vineyard workforce. While many winegrowers depend on migrant workers for harvest, Phelps prefers to hire for the period of January through October, depending on fewer temporary workers during the harvest. The Phelps crews are responsible for specific areas, which allows the workers to learn and understand the idiosyncrasies of a particular place. The vineyard supervisor seeks their counsel and passes the information up to the vineyard manager. The vineyard workers offer input concerning the development and maintenance of the vineyard, from choice of rootstock to vine spacing and trellising. These are the individuals who look at the vines and grapes every day and monitor progress during the season. They carry with them a mental picture of the ideal vine and work to help each vine reach its potential.

Napa, and the California wine industry in general, depends on these workers. Many receive

(continued)

(continued)

a low wage, however, and the work is long and difficult. Their children, many of whom have been brought up in the United States, often do not want to follow in their footsteps. The next generation of vineyard workers is likely to be similar, men and women coming mainly from Mexico to make a living in the United States.

The economies of this labor force allow winegrowers in Napa the luxury of handpicking grapes, an approach often touted as a primary component of producing fine wine. In years during which ripening is uneven, for example, workers make several passes through the vineyard, each time handpicking only the most mature fruit. Changes in global economics or immigration policy that would either increase the cost of these workers or reduce their availability would affect the production of fine Napa wine in a variety of ways, from increasing costs to encouraging further mechanization.

For now, however ironically, the quality of much of the wine in Napa is in significant part a reflection of the care given to vine and grape by knowledgeable, and professional, vineyard personnel, many of whom make only a bare living. When you raise your glass, remember them as well.

It was a powerful act, filled with confidence and the knowledge that this drastic move was necessary for the future of the vine and the vineyard—without it, the fruit would never attain the character that this piece of land could produce. To the two observers standing nearby, it was like a shot to the heart.

SHAPING THE VINEYARD

If you had driven into the valley two or three decades ago, you might have been impressed by the vigorous and healthy look of the vines, shoots waving in the wind in all directions like the arms of octopi searching for prey. In those days, growers generally took a laissez-faire approach to growing grapes, exerting little control over the vines while keeping an eye on degrees Brix, waiting for the number that triggered picking. The winemakers' view was simply, "Give us grapes at 22.5 or 23 Brix—or, if we're lucky, 24—and we'll work our magic." Grapes were just raw material; quality was a result of what happened in the fermentation tanks and the barrels, where the winemaker would use skill, intuition, and art to craft great wine.

Gradually, however, it dawned on winemakers that grapes are the key; that great wine comes from great grapes, not necessarily from great winemakers; and that they needed to pay more attention to what was happening in the fields. Driving through Napa today, you still see a few vineyards with the old California sprawl, but more are vertically trained, closely hedged, tightly arranged, and neat. It's as if the vineyards reflect the hairstyles of the times, from the long, loose, and often dreadlocked styles of the 1960s and 1970s to the close-cropped, tidy look of the 1990s.

Reason, of course, rather than fashion motivated this new look, which vineyards the world over have adopted. The change most directly reflects the work of Australian viticulturalist Richard Smart, but it can also be traced back to research by Nelson Shaulis at Cornell University, who began in the 1950s to investigate ways to increase the quality and yield of Concord grapes. Few winegrowers paid heed to this work on the lowly Concord, but in the 1970s Smart in Australia and Alain Carbonneau in France began to adapt Shaulis's conclusions to *vinifera* grapes.

Shaulis's fundamental discovery was that grape quality and yields increased if you exposed the fruit to the sun, which required manipulating the vines. This notion led to radical rethinking of a winegrowing belief that had held sway for decades, namely, that the wines of highest quality tend to come from vineyards of low vigor and low yields. In California, this idea had caused growers to conclude that hillside and mountain vineyards were the most likely to yield the quality fruit required to make great wine.

Smart questioned these assumptions about vigor and yield, mountain versus valley, by stating, "We do not believe that low vigour and low yield are the *cause* but rather [are] *associated* with high quality" (*Sunlight into Wine,* with Mike Robinson [Adelaide: WineTitles, 1991], p. 12). He noted that in such vineyards, the canopy is open, exposing the leaves and fruit to the sun. He concluded that the grape quality does not result from low vigor and low yield per se but rather is determined by the growing conditions that promote an open canopy and influence the climate within that canopy.

According to Smart, experiments from other winegrowing regions indicated that shading the grapes and/or leaves tended to lower fruit quality by decreasing sugar content, acid, and the phenolic compounds that produce the best colors, flavors, and aromas. Such shading also accentuated less desirable aspects, particularly the herbaceous and grassy elements. The answer seemed evident: open the canopy, expose the fruit, and increase both quality and yield.

In Napa, winegrowers began to combine Smart's work on exposing leaves and fruit to the sun with a growing appreciation for grapevine physiology, bringing a revolution to the vineyards in the late 1980s. The timing was perfect: Napa winegrowers could implement these new and radical approaches at little or no extra expense while tearing out the vineyards and replanting them with phylloxera-resistant rootstock.

Napa's diversity of physical terroir has sometimes made it difficult to apply these new understandings and the resulting solutions, however. In the hills, where sediment and soil commonly form only a thin veneer over bedrock, roots do not extend very far, plants are naturally limited, and vines achieve balance with little manipulation. Mia Klein says of the Dalla Valle vineyards, a few hundred feet up the slopes of the Vaca Mountains: "In places like this, you don't need to work hard.

There's a natural limit to the vegetative cycle that's good for the fruit. The plants don't grow too large; the canes barely fill the areas between the vines, which is a good sign. Cabernet Franc always wants to grow more vegetation and set more crop, but up here, it can't do it, so we get concentrated fruit, perhaps the best of its kind in California. We don't need fancy trellising to support a lot of growth, and the fruit is exposed throughout the season. We irrigate a couple of times before veraison and then use deficit irrigation, watering for short intervals every ten days. But the drainage is extreme here, and the water doesn't hang around for long—we just try to keep the vines going until the fruit ripens and matures."

Where sediment and soil are thicker—four, six, eight feet—and more vigorous as a result of water-holding capacity, nutrient content, or both, growers are forced to think and plan a bit more. Philippe Melka describes the process: "First the soil, then the rootstock, then you build up from there. You choose variety, and clone, then the vine spacing and the trellis system. You either work with the soil or against. With vigor, using large spacing and strong vines; or against, with close spacing, more competition to devigorize the vines. I think it's better to work with the elements. With deep, vigorous soil, space ten feet by four, open trellis, more sun to give quality and good tonnage. With poor soil, maybe five by three or six by four, close spacing, little growth, smaller roots. The vines feel like they're in their element. People seem to get a notion of what is best and then apply the same spacing everywhere. This is no good on variable soil. People think close spacing will give them good quality and more fruit yield, but probably the yield comes out about the same, 3.5 to 4.5 tons per acre at most sites for Cabernet Sauvignon."

Vines in most of Napa's vineyards are now trained vertically, with wires that hold the shoots upright. Fruit clusters form at the base of the shoots, hanging below the canes, exposed to the sun. You might notice as you gaze down rows of vines that some have a more orderly look, with a rigid lower boundary parallel to the ground. Rising from these horizontal limbs are dark stubs with canes growing up through the containing wires, forming a linear, vertical wall of green. These are cordon-pruned vines (Figure 69), with permanent canes attached to the lower wires, some trained bilaterally, with cordons in both directions from the vine stem, others with a single cordon. The dark stubs are the "spurs" from which each year's shoots grow; in the winter, the shoots are pruned back to near the top of the spur, leaving two buds for the succeeding year's growth.

Cane-pruned vines (Figure 70) are less orderly, with no permanent growth other than the main stem. Each year, the shoots are pruned back to one or two canes that are attached to the lower wire. The next year's growth rises from buds on these canes

FIGURE 69. Cordon-pruned vines have canes attached permanently to the trellis wire early in their history. Fruit-bearing canes grow vertically from spurs that are cut back each year to two buds at the base.

and is held vertically by the two-wire trellis. Cane-pruned vines require more attention than cordons—you must carefully choose the strongest and healthiest canes, the ones that will support the best fruit the following year. Spur pruning on cordon-trained vines, in which you simply cut the shoots back, leaving a couple of buds on each spur, takes less thought and focus. Winemaker/consultant David de Sante compares cane pruning and cordons to chess and checkers: "In cane pruning, you look closely at every vine, see how it has done through the growing season, and think about what it might become the next year. The advantage of cordoned vines is simplicity. You don't have to think much about pruning, and you can train crews easily, as everyone does it the same way."

Ideally, on a balanced vine, the shoots grow three to four feet during the season of grand growth, from March to July, and then stop when the grapes turn color and soften at veraison. On more vigorous sites, the shoots might grow out five or six feet from the canes. As you drive through the valley in June and July, you'll see these shoots stretching past the trellis wires, waving in the wind. By early August, however, the vines are trimmed and hedged, cut back with the precision of a Marine Corps drill parade. This act tends to convince the vine that it's time to ripen the fruit.

Some growers still prefer the California sprawl (Figure 71). Daniel Bosch, at the Robert Mondavi Winery, argues that this growth habit "gives more uniform light

FIGURE 70. In cane pruning, fruit-bearing canes grow vertically from canes that are attached to the horizontal trellis. Each year, these horizontal canes are cut back and replaced by others chosen for their strength and health.

on the clusters." John Williams, at Frog's Leap, prefers the style of wine that comes from the sprawl: "People want to get the grapes in the sun, get high phenolics, and make dark wine. They favor the huge differences that come from sun exposure, exotic yeasts, high maturation, oak perfume. To me, it's more like a woman with a red dress and lots of makeup—perhaps a bit too obvious. Here [at Frog's Leap], the fruit grows at a variety of levels in the plant, a variety of exposures, which gives a broad range of texture and flavor components. It's possible to have fruit character, but if you connect with the soil and minerals, [the grapes] will taste like where they came from." Joel Aiken, at BV, speaks of a block pruned in the California sprawl that "looks horrible but often gives the best wine."

Here and there, you'll see a U-shaped, or lyre, trellis system (Figure 72), in which shoots are trained in two near-vertical ranks on either side of the vine, allowing the plant to respond to the nutritional richness of the substrate by growing large while also opening the inside of the canopy to the sun, to avoid the shading of leaves and fruit that normally afflicts large vines. Growers are experimenting with this and other solutions to the problem of excess vigor. Some choose very close spacing, believing that competition for water and nutrients will control excessive growth. This belief, however, may not jibe with reality.

Vigorous sites generally have fine-grained and loose substrate through which you

FIGURE 71. Classic California sprawl, in which canes grow freely in all directions, their length determined by the vigor of plant and substrate. Each year, the canes are pruned back to the spurs from which they grow.

FIGURE 72. Lyre trellises are designed to split the canopy into two parallel parts, allowing the vine to support twice the number of fruit-bearing canes. This technique is used to control plant vigor where the substrate is rich in water and nutrients. The inset shows the metal framework from which the trellis gets its name.

can dig for six, eight, ten feet or more; vine roots can penetrate this material with ease. With little reason to stop, the roots mine downward for food and water, finding a rich source of nourishment that allows the plants to grow large. In addition, the steady supply of nutrition subverts the natural process of hormonal change that moves the plant from feeding the shoots to ripening the grapes. You can hedge—cut the shoots back to three or four feet—but David de Sante observes that "the pump doesn't stop working just because you cut the top of the vine back," suggesting that a hedged vine still tends to feed the shoots and leaves. Somehow, you must convince it to stop vegetative growth and start the process of ripening fruit and maturing seed. Withholding water after veraison aids this, creating stress that encourages the vine to shift its focus to the fruit.

In the early days of the Napa renaissance, many growers watered the vines by hand, carrying buckets into the fields. Now drip irrigation is everywhere. John Williams contends that this is not necessarily good: "The old-timers used to irrigate by hand, saturate the ground. It made for deeper roots. Then, when they replanted the vineyards, many put in *riparia*-type rootstocks, shallow-rooted stuff, the kind they use in France [where the ground is often saturated with water from summer rain]. 'No,' they said, 'you can't use St. George with its deep roots. That's the old style.' The people who sold me this vineyard had another one across the road. When they pulled out the vines, the root balls were tiny because they'd been drip irrigated and stayed shallow. Here, we dry farm. We cultivate the vineyard, compact the soil, form a dust mulch so that water wicks up from below and goes to the vines. The roots go deeper to meet the water."

In earlier years, the "secret" to high quality was to irrigate until veraison and then turn the water off and stress the grapes. Too often, however, the result was over-stressed vines and wines with harsh tannins. The new emphasis on balanced vines has turned this approach on its head. Now most growers use water sparingly early in the season to avoid excessive growth and then water just enough after veraison to keep the vines going, allowing a long "hang time" for full ripeness and maturity. The idea is to provide only enough stress so that, in Michael Silacci's words, "the vines have a sense of urgency, not anxiety."

If you look closely beneath the vines in August, you might see dried-up leaves and shriveled, reddish-brown clusters of grapes littering the ground, the remnants of leaf stripping and "dropping clusters," or thinning the grape crop. Vineyard crews pull leaves to expose grapes directly to the sun, thus avoiding the vegetative flavors and aromas that come from too much shade. Sometimes thinning is excessive, and the clusters hang naked beneath the canes, like rows of bulls' testicles swinging free in the breeze. Thinning to this degree risks sunburn and dehydration. Winegrowers drop clusters when the vine is carrying more fruit than it can ripen or when they want to ensure that the remaining fruit will have the desired concentration.

Christian Moueix, who has properties in California and France, was the first producer to thin a crop in Bordeaux, in 1973: "There was a huge crop at Petrus. I thought it would not ripen correctly, so I thinned half the grapes in five acres." At that time, this was winegrowing heresy, so Moueix did his work in secret, at night, to avoid being seen by his colleagues. When he was caught, the local clergy publicly chided him. "Now it's extensively done, and I can't conceive of making a great wine without thinning to control yields. But you know, not much is new. In the first century, the Latin agronomist Columella wrote about crop thinning in his *De re rustica*. People [in Napa] sometimes think they are discovering something new, but often this is not the case," Moueix asserts. He quotes Columella: "An experienced grower should judge if his vine bears more fruit than it can carry. This is why we should not only remove excessive leaves, which one should always do, but sometimes a portion of the fruit as well, to help the vine exhausted by its own fecundity."

The crop load—the amount of fruit carried by the vines and produced by the vineyard—affects both wine quality and financial health. "Prior to veraison, the growers are looking at the crop, trying to evaluate the quality of the bloom set and gauge [whether] they need to take fruit off. There's no technology for this. Crop estimating is the biggest area of human decision-making in the vineyard," says Ed Weber, an agricultural specialist with the University of California Extension Service in Napa. "It takes experience and vision, for the vineyard and the wine. If you want to produce eight- to ten-dollar wine, you load it up. If it's going to be fifty- to hundred-dollar wine, you pay more attention, take much better care. It's all related to the site and its vigor. . . . I think sometimes in the past many have undercropped, thinking they would get higher-quality fruit, but they would probably do better with more. You always run the risk of underbalancing the vine, letting it grow too much vegetation for the available fruit."

This assessment is echoed by Dave Ramey, winemaker at Dominus during the 1990s: "A lot of people seem to think there's an inverse linear relationship between quality and yield, that with lower yields you get higher-quality fruit. My experience tells me that this isn't the case. At Dominus . . . they came in thinking they'd make great wines with low yields—maybe two and a half, two and three-quarters tons per acre. They found the wines were unpleasantly tannic at these low yields. At higher yields, they got softer and more supple tannins. There's probably an optimal curve for yield and quality for each site, but you find it only through experience and paying attention. Certainly it seems to me that you get better balance in the wine from less concentrated fruit, better tannic balance. Too much concentration is like having too much chocolate in hot chocolate."

These comments reflect an interesting conflict. The Gods of Wine, Parker in particular, have stated forcefully that great wine—great red wine, at least—cannot come from vineyards with yields of more than two to three tons per acre. Not a few winegrowers in Napa say that they are not entirely open about their crop yields, out of fear that Parker will downgrade their wine scores based on what he considers to be an excessive yield, say, five tons per acre. Yet experience suggests that high quality comes not so much from low yields as from vines that are balanced to their growing conditions. As Ric Forman, one of Napa's most respected winemakers since his arrival in the late 1960s, points out, "They say in France the yields are about a ton and a half per acre, but when you look closely, you find that many of the vines are dead or diseased. Newer vineyards come closer to four or four and a half tons per acre, and they make fabulous wine." Economic considerations apply as well; some growers maintain that even at five thousand dollars per ton you can't make a living selling grapes at the lower yields demanded by the wine critics.

It's a significant quandary. Doug Fletcher of Chimney Rock maintains that if he needed to lower his yields for marketing purposes, "I'd pull out every other vine and keep working with the remaining plants, just as I am now. This would let me maintain crop loads that are balanced to the vines and stay within Parker's ideal." There's more than one way to please the critics, but the trade-off here is loss of crop in favor of potentially better scores. Growers hope to make up the difference with higher bottle prices, a reasonable strategy in a rising market, but a worrisome risk if the economy is weakening. In the long run, wine, even fine wine, is a commodity that is sensitive to market forces.

Fletcher is perhaps Napa's strongest advocate of Richard Smart's principles and practices. According to Fletcher, Smart's key observation is that great wine correlates less with the character of the soil than with the look of the vine. "The canes should grow to about three feet, with thickness never bigger than your little finger, stopping growth naturally with about twenty to twenty-five leaves," Fletcher states. "There are some other [factors to consider, too], but basically, if the vine doesn't look like this, you're not going to get the best fruit. Can you make it look like this? Yes—and if you do, it will make great wine."

In the late 1980s, Fletcher began to experiment, trying to improve the Chimney Rock fruit. He pulled leaves, hedged vines, dropped clusters. Still not satisfied, he eventually adopted the collection of techniques espoused by Smart. "Vine balance is the overriding factor that affects grape quality," Fletcher explains. "In the old days, if pruning weights [a measure of substrate vigor] were high, the growers would increase the number of buds for the next year, trying to grow more wood, more leaves, more fruit in the same space. You get more leaves, but the inner ones are shaded and use more sugar than they produce through photosynthesis. This approach doesn't solve the balance problem. Trying to hold the plant back through competition encouraged by close planting doesn't work either."

Fletcher noticed that the vines at the top of one of Chimney Rock's hillside vineyards produced fine fruit, whereas those at the bottom grew grapes with unpleasant vegetative flavors. At the top of the vineyard, the vines were nearly balanced naturally, but the bottom was a jungle—overgrown vines, shaded fruit, "lousy" wine. Fletcher knew that the soils differed, but he did not realize that the vines at the top were rooted in just two and a half feet of residual sediment over bedrock, while those at the bottom could forage through twelve feet, accounting for their excessive growth.

"The pruning weights at the bottom of the hill indicated the vines needed about two times the number of buds as the vines at the top. So I pulled every other vine in the bottom one-third [to let the remaining vines grow larger]. In a single year, they became balanced, started to stress, and stopped growing at the same time as those on the top of the hill. They produced the same weight of fruit per foot of cordon, and we couldn't tell the difference between fruit from the top and the bottom. If there's a contribution from the soil, I don't know what it is. I think the flavor profile is dependent on vine balance, not on the character of the soil."

Fletcher maintains that wine of the same quality can be grown on the hillsides, at the edges of the valley, and even out on the valley floor, a place that some winegrowers consider better suited to sweet corn than to grapes. Is he implying that if everyone applied the same techniques, everything would taste alike? He denies that this is the case and adds, "Rutherford is different from Stags Leap. If you grow balanced vines in both places, the wines would still taste different." He seems to suggest that terroir does in fact influence the character of wine, despite his assertion about the overriding influence of vine balance. One way to approach this apparent contradiction would be to experiment with two adjacent pieces of rich, vigorous land near the river. Fletcher could oversee the redesign and care of one plot, as well as the winemaking, for five years; on the other plot, grapes could be grown and vinified as they have been in the past. Perhaps such an experiment is simply the dream of a couple of scientists, but it might help to answer an important question about the effects of Smart's techniques on grape character.

Today, the accepted key to success in Napa appears to be ripeness, a more complex notion than it was three decades ago. Then, the focus was on Brix. Most believed that 22 degrees Brix was fine—after all, it is what they ordinarily get in France. Then, says David de Sante, the 1974 vintage changed everything.

"Before, anything over 23 Brix was a bonus. They were not worrying about seeds, or the feel of the grape skin on the cheek, or the taste of the seeds on the palate. [For most,] 22 Brix was fine, 23 better. Then '74 was a hot vintage. Things ripened quickly, there were more grapes than anyone anticipated, and they let things hang, finally picking through a range of 24 to 24.5. Grapes this ripe had never been available. The '74 vintage caused a big shift in people's goals and expectations. In the late seventies and early eighties, ripeness became more a focus. Winegrowers began to relate better vintages to more mature grapes. Winemakers such as Tony Soter and Heidi Peterson Barrett began to push the ripeness envelope, going to 25 Brix and higher. Helen Turley [went] even further, perhaps taking things to extremes."

In the 1990s, a new approach to ripeness developed, a concern for "physiological maturity" in addition to sugar content. Christian Moueix became aware of this notion in the mid-1990s: "For twenty-five out of my thirty years of experience as a winemaker, I had no idea about this physiological maturity. Sometime in the past five years, we began hearing our interns talk about physiological maturity, the concept that as the grapes ripen, the phenolic compounds mature as well, and the tannins change structure. We used to taste only the juice and skin. Now we taste the seeds as well. When they turn brittle and develop an almond taste, this is an indication that the grapes are physiologically mature."

Moueix got his formal enological training at UC Davis, where he graduated in 1968, along with Daniel Baron. When Moueix founded Dominus in 1981 (with John Daniel's daughters), Baron became the first winemaker. By then, he had worked at Petrus with Moueix and had a good understanding of how the French approach viticulture. Baron believes that in the 1960s and 1970s the approach supported by the academics at UC Davis was oversimplified. "The consensus was to pick on sugars only, make alcohol. What else do you need? All the other stuff—color, flavor, aroma—will follow along, [people said]. The French were more subtle. They worked with different types of ripeness. They'd taste the pulp for sugar and acid, chew the skins to get a measure of the anthocyanins that produce color and aroma. For the tannins, they'd look at the seeds. They would track these characteristics independently. If you take only one into account, especially in California, you're likely to end up out of balance."

Still, the ultimate test for most winegrowers is in the taste, in chewing the grapes day after day, waiting for the precise time to pick. Michael Silacci describes his experience poignantly: "You can get a measure of ripeness from the numbers—they can be perfect for sugars and acids, for example—yet the grapes can still taste off. The sweetness is there, the acids are still bright, but somehow it all tastes disjointed. When the grapes are really ripe, it all wraps up in a sphere."

Harvesting decisions are complex, and the bigger the operation, the more complex they become. At Pride Mountain, they pick as soon as the seeds become brittle when crushed between the teeth, the measure of maturity that works for them. At Spottswoode, the forty acres of vines are across the street from the winery, and you can get from the vines to the crusher in minutes, allowing a great deal of control. The growers measure pH and acid in August, but Spottswoode winemaker Rosemary Cakebread says, "This is all sort of the school of numbers, but we don't really use them; we just want to know where we are. Then we walk the vineyard daily, checking color, the seeds, tasting the grapes. We can tell when the tannins are about right. With the winery close, we can work on our own schedule."

At Robert Mondavi, with 550 acres of vines in To Kalon Vineyard alone and other properties throughout the Napa Valley and farther afield, the decision-making process is far more daunting. According to Daniel Bosch, "We measure Brix, pH, tannins, color—get all the data. We look at the vines and grapes, chew the skin, check the seed color to see if [the seeds] have turned from green to brown. Then you try to make a prediction. Is it hot? Is it cold? Do I have time to wait? How much crop do I have to pick, how big is my picking crew, how long will it take to get the whole crop in? There's so much variability that we can never make it all uniform, but the land is more valuable if we make better-quality grapes. We can make up some of the differences [in grape ripeness throughout a block or a vineyard] by waiting to pick, but that has its own dangers, and variability also provides blending potential."

If anything is true of human beings, however, it's that today's great new idea will become tomorrow's dogma. And so it is with winegrowers and physiological maturity. Ric Forman describes a fundamental difference between California and France that needs to be considered in this new quest for ripeness: "You have to get certain flavors that come from mature grapes. In Europe, you can let the grapes sit on the vine for a long time, let them develop mature flavors, and they become ripe at 21 Brix. You're looking for seeds turning from green to brown; the pulp falling away from the skin, yellow pulp rather than green; a jammy, ripe flavor from the skins. In France, you can get all this at relatively low sugars. A warm vintage in France is a cool one in California. Here, getting mature flavors can mean high sugars, ultraripe grapes with pH greater than 4 [which can lead to instability], and huge alcohol, so high you have to add water to the fruit."

Daniel Baron expands on this view, pointing out the limitations of unthinking adherence to a notion. "In France," he says, "you can add sugar to ensure you get enough alcohol. So if you have mature flavors and pick at 21 Brix, it's not a problem. [In Napa,] we get sugar quickly, but not mature flavors, so often these days people are letting the grapes hang and picking at 27 Brix. The problem is that they keep referring back to Brix, so these high sugars become the new standard. Last year, we had grapes at 22.5 Brix, with mature seeds and tannins. They tasted great, but people weren't picking because they said the grapes weren't physiologically ripe. They said you need 26, 27 Brix. Now the buzz is about high sugars, but this is the way they were making wines here in the seventies."

Rosemary Cakebread defines the trend clearly: "We make our picking decisions on tasting. We know when the tannins are about right. The sugars turn out to be 26 or 27 Brix. Ten years ago, it was less. We're now pushing the envelope—you have to if you want to stand out. . . . The difference is in paying attention to getting high scores [from the critics]." Christian Moueix, well aware of the difficulty in Napa of achieving full maturity—brittle seeds—without also getting excessive sugar, observes: "In France, I've had maybe twenty vats of 26 Brix juice over thirty years. If I were to buy more land in Napa, I would move farther south [to cooler conditions]."

AN EXPERIMENT WITH TERROIR

Harvest is the transition from the vineyard to the winery—the process of making wine does, in fact, begin in the fields. Today, most vineyard managers and winemakers, if they are not one and the same, work together throughout the season. Chapter 6 will carry our exploration into the winery, but first we'll take a close look at one man's personal experiment in terroir, as he established a cutting-edge Napa Valley vineyard. This story exemplifies one of the major themes of this book: Napa's great microenvironmental diversity, which is still not fully realized.

When Paul Frank founded Gemstone Vineyard in the early to mid-1990s, he determinedly "set out to break all established conventions. I wanted to see what would happen if we did things that had not been done before in a small vineyard. Some told us we were designing a vineyard outside the parameters of economic reality, one that would be a logistical nightmare." Frank wanted to divide his small vineyard, some seventeen acres, into a number of microclimatic blocks. He set out to explore terroir directly by creating a vineyard specifically designed to reflect the character of the site.

Finding the right land took time. "I had been intrigued by locations in Bordeaux, where it's obvious that certain vineyards produce superior results while their neighbors are less successful. I put together a pretty good understanding of the character of the first-growth estates and then attempted to find similar property in Napa." The land he found, on the Silverado Trail just south of Rector Reservoir, is on a west-facing, sunny slope. It has cobbly, gravelly, alluvial soil over sandstone bedrock, avoiding the vigor of deep, rich soil.

Much of the early advice Frank heard insisted that only he would appreciate the effort needed to farm each block separately—no winery would be willing to pay the price required to make the project viable. To avoid viticultural suicide, so they said, he should grow and sell the lowest-cost product, planting a simple vineyard with one clone on a single rootstock. But Frank thought differently. He understood that with only seventeen acres his product could not be low cost. To be successful, he would have to create a niche by maintaining a unique quality and character. He wanted to grow grapes but think like a winemaker. And then a marketer suggested to Frank that if other winegrowers were getting the same kind of advice he was, perhaps he should do just the opposite, the winegrowing equivalent of "fishing in still waters."

At the time, most of the clonal material in Napa came from UC Davis and was predominantly heat-treated clone 7, one of the causes, Frank reasoned, for the similarity that so many people were tasting in Napa Cabernet. Many vineyards did not even know which clones they were planting. "One vineyardist told me, 'Paul, you're putting way too much emphasis on clones. You'll find that the clones are all site specific. They'll all wind up the same on your site.'"

The reality turned out to be quite different, as Frank describes: "Each clonal block has its own character, a certain consistency, but the performance year to year varies widely. I knew before I planted that some vineyards had a unique character, an identifiable quality. I believed then and still do that heat-treating [to eliminate disease] homogenizes budwood. With heat-treating, you can get healthy, vigorous wood producing quite remarkable wine, but [the wine is] very much the same. It may please many people, but it does not have distinctiveness and individuality." Frank ended up importing budwood from France, wanting to guard the unique character of his site

Early in the process, a wine broker told Frank that California was in the midst of a wine glut and if he didn't have customers now, he was unlikely to find any soon. Frank was "ready to call Dr. Kevorkian," having just put his life savings into the operation. But John Livingston of Livingston-Moffett Winery (and the valley's resident geologist) agreed with Frank that Gemstone appeared to be a superior site. Livingston guaranteed to bottle a vineyard-designated wine if Frank would sell him the fruit.

Frank began to think that perhaps the risk he had taken with his money and his sanity was worth it.

As he planted the vineyard, Frank continued trying to match certain places with the right material. "I found some Petit Verdot, an old clone from Sonoma that I was warned against. It's fickle, very difficult, doesn't want to ripen. So I put it in the most exposed part of the vineyard, in a particularly rocky site exposed on three sides with maximum solar interception and plenty of air so it would ripen properly. It has been remarkable, this intense structural element for the wine. It gives muscle, bones, and framework rather than fruit." Frank ended up with five clones of Cabernet Sauvignon, two of Cabernet Franc, two of Merlot, and one of Petit Verdot. His vision was to build a unique profile, not one designed to please everyone, but something that you could identify in a blind tasting of great Napa wines every time, marked by its distinctive character.

Shortly after his first vintage, Frank found himself pouring for a sommelier he knew in New York, an acknowledged francophile who stayed well away from Napa. Frank poured the Gemstone and held his breath while his friend sniffed, gurgled, snorted, and then said, "Thank God. I'm so tired of these overripe, clinging Napa wines. Finally some classic structure." And classic structure was just what Frank had been aiming for all along. He attributes this character in part to the physical aspects of the site that allow maturity at lower sugar concentration and to his determination to pick at the peak of physiological ripeness and full flavor, just before the acid drops. "If it's over 26 Brix, we've lost the battle. Sugar once was the object; now, for some, it's the alarm clock. Sugar is the nemesis of this valley."

Frank relishes his role as a small, niche producer. "I don't have to play to the broad market. I can set a style that I'm looking for and share this with some small cadre who share my taste." That group is growing. Robert Parker gave the 1999 Gemstone a 92 and a glowing review. It will be interesting to see whether Frank resists the temptation to grow with success. Volker Eisele puts it this way: "All these little labels, they start with five, ten, fifteen acres, and they become very successful. Then they begin to buy grapes because they can't meet the demand. They don't see what's happening, but quickly it becomes a brand, and the geographic identity is gone." Alternatively, if Frank stays small and demand continues to grow, Gemstone may end up becoming a "cult" wine available only to the collectors who can pay the price. That status seems at odds with the self-effacing character of Paul and Suzie Frank, though such success would surely validate the thoughtful way in which Frank approached his vision.

THE TOURS

part two

NORTH ON THE SILVERADO TRAIL

SHORTLY AFTER TURNING ONTO THE SILVERADO TRAIL FROM HIGHWAY 121, you'll see a rocky ridge ahead (Figure 73). The road here runs nearly due north—you are seeing the segment of the Vaca Mountains that rises up on the northeast side of the Stags Leap District. At Soda Canyon Road, the Silverado Trail bends left, to the northwest, and the view opens out. The ridge of the Vaca Mountains is on the right (Figure 74); on the left, in the distance, you can see the Mayacamas Mountains, which form the western boundary of the Napa Valley. The rounded hills on your right, in front of the

FIGURE 73. The view from the Silverado Trail, toward the Vaca Mountains. The high peak lies just east of Stag's Leap Wine Cellars.

FIGURE 74. The rounded hills in front of the main ridge of the Vaca Mountains are the result of movement on large displacement surfaces.

sharper ridge of the Vacas, as well as the hills directly ahead of you, formed as a result of slip on the displacement surface represented by the Stags Leap cliffs (a process described in chapter 2).

The top of this segment of the Vaca ridge rises in elevation toward the north, ending in the steep slopes and gray cliffs that hang over the Stags Leap District. The slopes are either green or brown, depending on the time of year. In contrast to the hills of the eastern United States, those in the West are a golden brown during the dry summer and a verdant green in the wet winter. The Vaca Mountains form the eastern boundary of the Napa Valley, although the border of the Napa Valley AVA is actually a few miles to the east, across a wide swath of highlands. Composed entirely of Napa volcanics, the Vacas run all the way up the east side of the valley, culminating in Mount St. Helena, the highest peak in the region.

On your right, toward the hills, you can look up the rows of vines (at Clos du Val, for example) and notice how they curve gently upward as they intersect the base of the hills (Figure 75). These slopes are alluvial fans, accumulations of coarse debris washed from the hills (as explained in chapter 3). Vineyards also climb the lower, steeper slopes of the hills themselves, although

FIGURE 75. Vineyard rows at Clos du Val and Chimney Rock climb the lower slopes of the hills.

FIGURE 76. Looking north up the Silverado Trail toward the Pine Ridge hill. Vineyards owned by Robert Mondavi Winery occupy the flat stretch of land; Hartwell Vineyards lies on the slopes above.

FIGURE 77. The vineyards of Stag's Leap Wine Cellars appear in the center of this image, behind a small hill. The Fay Vineyard consists of the two rows of vineyard blocks extending from the small hill to the mountains. SLV is the adjacent set of blocks to the right. Aerial photography © 2003, AirPhotoUSA, LLC.

the vines here are planted in material that is quite different from that found in the alluvial fans below. The vineyards on the upper slopes were developed before the enactment of stiff regulations that limit planting on hillsides with a slope greater than 5 percent. Now, out of concern for erosion and "visual pollution," environmental organizations are working to prevent further vineyard development in the hills, maintaining as well that the Napa Valley already has enough vineyards. The craggy cliffs that cap the ridge are made up of a variety of resistant volcanic rocks.

At the end of a long, straight stretch of road (Figure 76), just as you climb a small hill, you'll see Stag's Leap Wine Cellars on the right (Figure 77). This winery is home to SLV, the vineyard that pro-

FIGURE 78. A cliff made up of Great Valley sequence rocks, slightly north of the entrance to Pine Ridge Winery. These rocks were baked by heat from the volcanic plug that forms the hill at Stag's Leap Wine Cellars, just across the road. The outcrop is about twenty-five feet high.

FIGURE 79. An outcrop of Great Valley sequence on the east side of the Silverado Trail, north of Silverado Vineyards. Sandstones on the left grade into finer-grained sediments on the right.

duced the winning wine at the 1976 Paris tasting, a pivotal event for Napa wines, as the introduction recounts. The Fay Vineyard, directly north of SLV and also a part of Stag's Leap Wine Cellars, was the first Cabernet Sauvignon grown south of Rutherford when Nathan Fay planted it in 1961. Fay's wines influenced many Napa winemakers, including Warren Winiarski and John Kongsgaard. The caves at Stag's Leap Wine Cellars are dug into a volcanic plug, the remnants of one of the volcanic vents that fed the thick mass of Napa volcanics exposed in the hills to the east of the winery. Near the top of the hill, you can see volcanic rock in the banks on both sides of the road.

As the road descends gently on the other side of the hill, Pine Ridge Winery appears on the left. Here, the vines are planted mainly on sedimentary rocks of the Great Valley sequence. The high road cut just past the winery entrance (Figure 78) reveals the orange-red color of Great Valley sequence rocks that were baked by heat from the volcanic plug. Silverado Vineyards, owned by the Disney family, sits on the northern extension of the Pine Ridge knob. Where the road bends

FIGURE 80. One of the knobs that dot the valley in and north of the Stags Leap District. The knobs are toe deposits resulting from megaslides along displacement surfaces.

FIGURE 81. The Yountville Hills from the Silverado Trail. These hills are the toe deposits of the largest megaslide.

to the right, after the entrance to Silverado, a roadcut reveals layered sandstone and shale of the Great Valley sequence (Figure 79).

A short distance beyond this roadcut, the view opens up briefly on both sides. On the right, the vineyards of Shafer climb the steep hillsides at the northern end of the Stags Leap District. These slopes produce Shafer Hillside Select Cabernet Sauvignon, long considered one of Napa's finest wines. From here, up to Oakville Crossroad several miles ahead, the Silverado Trail winds through a series of hills and knobs (Figure 80). As chapter 2 explains, these unusual features are the toe deposits of a series of large displacements that formed after the Vaca Mountains were uplifted. In the distance to the west, on the left, arise the rugged and tree-covered Mayacamas Mountains, fronted by the long ridge of the Yountville Hills (Figure 81). These hills also formed as toe deposits of one of the large displacements. Highway 29 runs on the other side of the Yountville Hills.

Slightly south of Rector Reservoir, the road curves up a slight rise onto a straight, flat stretch. Here, you are driving along the upper part of a small alluvial fan at the mouth of the Rector drainage. Paul Frank's Gemstone Vineyard lies at the southern end of this flat stretch. Frank de-

FIGURE 82. Screaming Eagle vineyard. The wine that comes from this fifty-eight-acre vineyard is made from the best 10 percent of the grapes harvested each year (the rest of the grapes are sold). The rarity and social cachet of this wine brought a price of two hundred fifty dollars a bottle in 2001.

signed the vineyard with the express purpose of growing grapes and making wine that would distinctly reflect the site. He planted Cabernet Sauvignon, Merlot, Cabernet Franc, and Petit Verdot, using types of rootstock and clones that he thought most suitable to the conditions. The wine has been very successful; how well and in what way it reflects the site is more difficult to establish.

As you leave this section of the road, Rector Dam is visible on the right. The next vineyard on the left is Screaming Eagle, source of one of the most expensive and sought-after wines in the valley (Figure 82). Screaming Eagle began as owner Jean Philips's homemade wine; word of mouth and the driving need of many wine aficionados to be in on the most recent discovery quickly transformed it into a phenomenon. The wine is now made by star winemaker Heidi Peterson Barrett from a few select sites that make up perhaps 10 percent of the vineyard.

After Screaming Eagle, the road bends to the right. On that side of the road, Joseph Phelps's Backus Vineyard appears (Figure 83). The lower, older part is terraced, while the newer vines on the steep upper slopes run vertically down the hill. Backus also has an upper section, planted

FIGURE 83. Backus Vineyard seen from the road. Owned by Joseph Phelps, this vineyard was expanded from its original seven acres of terraced vines (on the lower part of the hill) to include the newer vines planted vertically down the slope and another seven acres on the flat above.

FIGURE 84. Backus Vineyard and its upper extension, which it shares with Dalla Valle, Showket, and Vine Cliff. Aerial photography © 2003, AirPhotoUSA, LLC.

on an extensive flat surface, that supports Dalla Valle, Showket, and Vine Cliff (Figure 84). For more than two decades, Backus Cabernet Sauvignon has been one of the most consistently excellent wines in the valley.

Beyond Backus Vineyard, Oakville Crossroad intersects the Silverado Trail on the left. Rudd Estate lies at the corner of this intersection. Geologically, it is related to Backus and the other properties occupying the flat surfaces that cut the slopes of the hills above, all the way up to Stagecoach Vineyards at the top of the Vaca Mountains ridge. The rocks that form the walls that surround Rudd were ripped from the vineyard. Similar, though larger, rocks were ripped from Stagecoach Vineyards, directly above Rudd. Though the two vineyards are separated by some 1,300 vertical feet, geologically they are very similar.

As the road passes Rudd, it descends the northern flank of yet another alluvial fan, which formed at the mouth of a large drainage that cuts into the Vaca ridge a little north of Rector Canyon. Past Oakville Crossroad, the valley opens out to its widest extent. The road runs along the base of the eastern hills, up and down a series of rises and swales that represent older, up-lifted alluvial fans. Looking directly to the left, you can see the short, relatively steep, upper slopes of these fans (Figure 85). Mumm Napa Valley lies near the crest of the largest of these features. Next, a series of small cuts at the side of the road display the mixed character of the alluvial fan sediments—boulders and cobbles lying in a matrix of sand and mud (Figure 86). To the left, you have a fine view of the heavily wooded Mayacamas Mountains across the valley, topped by the triangular peak of Mount St. John (Figure 87).

FIGURE 85. Looking down the slope of a small, uplifted alluvial fan south of Mumm Napa Valley.

FIGURE 86. Alluvial fan sediments on the side of the Silverado Trail, at the bottom of a hill north of Mumm Napa Valley.

FIGURE 87. Mount St. John and the Mayacamas ridge, viewed from the Silverado Trail north of Oakville Crossroad, where the valley widens.

FIGURE 88. Serpentinite mélange on Highway 128 south of Lake Hennessey.

A short side trip east on Route 128 to Lake Hennessey will take you past outcrops of serpentinite mélange, a combination of ocean floor sediment and chunks of ocean crust, described in chapter 1 (Figure 88).

Back on the Silverado Trail, north of the junction with Route 128, a winery with a curved, rock-faced façade is built into a small hill on the left. This is Quintessa, whose vineyards occupy the slopes of a rounded, elongate ridge. Quintessa is one of the few properties in the valley where grapes grow in all exposures—north, east, south, and west (Figure 89). The Quintessa ridge is the northernmost of the hills that formed as toe deposits of the Vaca Mountain displacements.

FIGURE 89. Quintessa vineyards lie slightly north of the intersection of Highway 128 and the Silverado Trail, which runs along the right side of this image. Quintessa has a unique character, a ridge within the valley. Its shape provides diverse microclimates and sun exposure. The Napa River flows west of Quintessa, traveling diagonally through the view from center top to lower left. Aerial photography © 2003, AirPhotoUSA, LLC.

FIGURE 90. Vertical beds of volcanic ash line the road in many places north of Quintessa. This location is north of Deer Park Road.

FIGURE 91. Volcanic ash with layers and pods of obsidian, on the Silverado Trail at Glass Mountain.

FIGURE 92. Black and shiny fragments of volcanic glass in Chabot Vineyard, Glass Mountain.

Once you pass Quintessa, a series of roadcuts reveal some of the volcanic rocks that make up the eastern hills. The road winds past these roadcuts for several miles. They are particularly well exposed at Taplin Road and along a stretch south of Deer Park Road. In many of them, the beds, composed mainly of volcanic ash, are nearly vertical (Figure 90), tilted by the forces that formed the Vaca Mountains. These exposures of volcanic rocks are interrupted only at Deer Park Road, where the rounded pebbles and cobbles of an older, uplifted alluvial fan can be seen in a road bank south of the intersection.

North of Deer Park Road, past Duckhorn Vineyards, you come to a bend in the road, where you can see a massive outcrop of beds of volcanic ash with pods and layers of obsidian (Figure 91). Obsidian, a shiny black, glassy-looking rock that forms when some types of lava cool very quickly, is the material that gave Glass Mountain its name. Collectors of the black volcanic glass have dug holes in this outcrop. Native Americans used obsidian for the heads of spears and arrows. The surface of Chabot Vineyard, owned by Beringer and located up Glass Mountain Road, is awash with glistening fragments of obsidian (Figure 92).

FIGURE 93. In this outcrop opposite the entrance of the Rombauer Vineyards, a zone of what is likely baked soil (orange) is visible below thin beds of tuff and black volcanic glass. The tuff and glass were still extremely hot when they fell to Earth, cooking the rocks or soils on which they landed.

Opposite the entrance to Rombauer Vineyards, one of the most colorful and interesting road-cuts in the valley appears. Here, thin layers of volcanic tuff and obsidian top a bright orange, rubbly rock that probably represents a soil zone baked by the heat of the volcanic ash as it accumulated on the surface (Figure 93).

Up the road and over the hill from this outcrop, the valley opens up again at the mouth of Dutch Henry Canyon. As you pass Larkmead Lane, Three Palms Vineyard, with its three isolated palm trees, is on your left (Figure 94). Here, near the upper reaches of the Napa River, the narrow valley is filled with coarse sediment delivered from the hills that rise steeply on both sides.

The road continues on to Calistoga, winding through the edges of the hills and along a wider flat at the mouths of Simmons Creek and Jericho Canyon. Eisele Vineyard, on Pickett Road, was originally planted by Milton and Barbara Eisele and is now part of Araujo Estate (Figure 95). It

FIGURE 94. Three Palms Vineyard. At the base of the hill behind the center palm tree, an alluvial fan slopes down into the valley at the bottom edge of the Mayacamas ridge.

FIGURE 95. Eisele Vineyard, in Simmons Canyon at the head of Pickett Road. Eisele has been producing critically acclaimed wines for more than thirty years. Aerial photography © 2003, AirPhotoUSA, LLC.

FIGURE 96. Mount St. Helena looms north of Calistoga.

has produced widely acclaimed Cabernet Sauvignon, made by a variety of winemakers, over its history of more than three decades. During the 1970s and 1980s, much of the fruit went to Joseph Phelps Winery for its Eisele Vineyard Cabernet Sauvignon, made by Craig Williams. After Bart and Daphne Araujo bought the vineyard, Tony Soter became the winemaker for some years during the early 1990s. Françoise Peschon now makes the wine, with Michel Rolland as consultant.

The hot springs of Calistoga—remnants of the relatively recent volcanic activity—have attracted visitors since the middle of the nineteenth century. Today, the area of potential volcanic activity centers on the region of Clear Lake, a few miles to the north. As you approach Calistoga, Mount St. Helena rises to the north of the town, providing a suitably majestic backdrop for this narrow northern end of the Napa Valley (Figure 96).

꘎ ꘎ ꘎ *six* ꘎ ꘎ ꘎

THE WINERY

Preserving Character or Shaping Style?

IN MOST OF BORDEAUX, terroir is the focus; the goal in the winery is to capture and preserve the character and quality of the grapes as they arrive from the vineyard, doing only what is necessary to maintain the elements that express the land. The winemaker plays a supporting role, performing a formal dance determined by well-established conventions and long experience, with little room for creativity.

In Napa, the winemaker is more likely to be an active force and to have top billing, with the owner/producer in the supporting role. Just established a new vineyard? If you have enough capital, you can hire consultant winemaker Helen Turley or Heidi Peterson Barrett and guarantee a high price for your wine. Your property must have the requisite potential—these winemakers are choosy and expensive, but their track record of creating sought-after wine is legendary. A few years ago, Randy Dunn, John Kongsgaard, and Tony Soter would also have been on that list, though all are now retired as consultants, working mainly on their own projects. You might have heard of some of the new generation: Mia Klein, Philippe Melka, Ken Bernards, or Karen Culler. It's less likely that you've heard of those who work for a salary—Michael Silacci (Opus One), Joel Aiken (BV), or Ed Sbragia (Beringer), to name only three—but they are in the same league as the high-end consultants. Although each of these winemakers has a distinct personal approach, they possess, together with their counterparts throughout the world, a common set of tools, techniques, and understandings.

The observation that great wine is made in the vineyard has become the cliché of the moment in the Napa wine world. While that notion is surely correct, it's important to recognize as well the power of the winemaker's tools, including the newest additions to the toolbox. This manipulatory power is most often employed to compensate for vagaries of nature or mistakes made in the vineyard, but it can also be used to shape wines that reflect the ambitions of the winemaker as much as or more than the potentials of land and fruit.

The fundamental goal of the winemaker is to preserve the inherent quality and character of the fruit while trying to extract its full potential. Winemakers design every process and experiment to achieve this goal more fully or more efficiently. The intent is to produce a wine of great balance, in which no single element overpowers the others. It's a tricky task, undertaken with what might seem to be crude tools—machines that crush and press, steel and wood vats that hold hundreds of gallons, wood barrels that have changed little over the past century, and hundreds of yards of thick plastic tubing that snake along most winery floors. That the magic in a bottle of fine wine emerges from the aromas and controlled chaos of a winery at harvest may be difficult to imagine, but emerge it does, imprinted with place, vintage, and the human hand. It may even have the exquisite balance that most winemakers seek but few find.

THE PROCESS

At harvest, wineries are aswirl with the sweet, heady aromas of grapes and fermenting wine. Moisture drips and flows everywhere: juice puddles on the floor, water sprays from hoses, the air is heavy with humidity. Cellar rats—the aspiring young winemakers who yearn to be part of the action—slog thick hoses from one vat to another, clean the tanks, and do most of the heavy work. The juice is turning quickly to wine, absorbing color, flavor, and aroma from macerating on the skins before moving to small oak barrels for months of aging. This is the culmination of a season's work in the vineyard, a time of intense activity that caps the year.

The harvest, of course, actually starts even earlier, in the vineyard. Grape pickers squat and stoop at backbreaking angles, slashing bunches from the vines, filling small plastic bins that are emptied into tractor-driven hoppers. As a hopper fills, grapes on the bottom are partially crushed by the weight above, their juice oozing onto the metal floor, exposed to the atmosphere and oxidation.

Maintaining the quality of the fruit begins here, with greater expense ensuring better care. More costly stackable picking boxes deliver fruit intact to the winery. Picking several times instead of once provides more uniform ripeness and maturity. Most important, the process of handpicking allows choice and flexibility. Machines pick ripe and unripe grapes alike and add leaves and shoots for good measure, materials that will bring unwanted characteristics to the wine unless they are eliminated up the line, before crushing. In Napa, where the focus is on quality rather than volume, handpicking is underwritten by the low cost of predominantly Mexican labor and the high price of Napa wine, boosted by the booming 1990s.

This contrast in care—pragmatic reality as opposed to an almost reverent gentility—is carried over into the winery, where some winegrowers go to great lengths to ensure the purity of the fruit and the quality of the juice. But the measures involved, such as sorting by hand and washing the grapes, all add to the cost of production. During the 1990s, with a high-flying economy, many new, small wineries could absorb the expense of these quality-assuring techniques. In a slower economy, with increasing global competition and concern for price, vineyard owners and winemakers will need to find new ways of maintaining quality while reducing expenses.

When the grapes arrive at the winery, a crusher-destemmer breaks the skins and separates fruit from stem. Before crushing, if expense is of little concern, the grapes are sorted by quick hands that pluck out unwanted items, from stems and leaves to the occasional snail. In some wineries, even the jacks—the small three-pronged pieces that attach grape to bunch stem—are removed. And some wash the grapes to remove surface contaminants such as bird droppings, though it's been said—perhaps humorously, perhaps not—that such additions simply provide a bit of complexity and spice.

From the crusher, the must (juice, skins, and other solid material) is pumped to the fermenting tanks. In a technologically ironic twist, a number of new wineries have been built along the lines of their nineteenth-century predecessors, using gravity to move grapes, must, and wine to progressively lower levels and finally to small oak barrels on the ground floor. In earlier years, such a system was based on neccssity; today, it is based in an ideology of gentle treatment.

Grapes come to the winery with natural yeasts, and sometimes other microorganisms, clinging to their skins. In Europe, where terroir rules, wines are commonly fermented on these natural yeasts, on the assumption that they are part of the terroir and thus contribute to its reflection in the wine. In California, winemakers are more likely to add sulfur dioxide to kill these yeasts (and their unwanted friends) and then add cultivated varieties that have specific characteristics and proven track records. Some yeasts are chosen to bring out specific characteristics in the wine, while others work well in the high-alcohol environments that result from ultraripe grapes. Californians argue that most of the natural yeasts come from the winery and have little to do with the terroir of a particular vineyard. Those who favor natural yeasts view the cultivated varieties as a further move toward homogenization of style and character and away from focus on terroir.

FIGURE 97. For many years, Al Brounstein fermented his distinctive Diamond Creek wines in outdoor vats *(top)*. This quaint approach contrasts markedly with the facilities of large-scale producers, such as the Beringer complex shown here *(bottom)*.

During fermentation, the wine resembles a purple stew on slow boil, bubbling vigorously from the release of carbon dioxide as yeast turns grape sugar into alcohol. If you sniff the aroma coming off a vat of bubbling red wine, the assault of CO_2 will snap your head back and sting your nasal passages with a ferocity that brings tears to your eyes and leaves you gasping. Today, however, that's not likely to happen—only the very smallest wineries still ferment in open wood vats, the kind Al Brounstein used outdoors until he built his winery a few years back (Figure 97). Now temperature-controlled stainless steel tanks line the crush pad or fill the winery, giving more the look of an oil refinery rather than the quaint image of the dark and dusty wine cellar.

You actually don't need to crush grapes to make wine—juice will begin fermenting naturally within the berries, reaching up to 2 percent alcohol before the berry dies. As the alcohol increases, skins soften and break, releasing juice that continues to ferment outside the berries. This process is the basis of carbonic maceration, in which whole bunches go through an initial fermentation in the presence of carbon dioxide, which is released from the juice as sugar transforms into alcohol. The weight of the grapes alone crushes the fruit and releases juice, a more delicate process than conventional crushing and pressing. This technique is used mainly in the production of light-bodied, early-drinking wines such as Beaujolais.

Making wine depends mostly on turning grape sugar into alcohol. But great or even good wine comes from extracting color, flavor, and aroma from the grapes. Centuries of winemaking still have not uncovered a single, clearly defined path to this goal. Some winemakers use a cold soak before fermentation, allowing the must to sit at cool temperatures in an environment dominated by water, drawing elements from grape skin and pulp that seem to get lost if extraction occurs only in the alcohol-dominated environment that exists after fermentation begins. Most winemakers prefer to ferment red wine at moderate temperatures, around 85 or 86 degrees Fahrenheit, though some are experimenting with temperatures well into the 90s during certain stages.

Fermentation moves to completion—with all the sugar converted to alcohol—in six to ten days. With high sugar levels from a long hang time, the alcohol level can easily reach 15 percent, a strength that brings some of us dangerously close to making fools of ourselves at the occasional dinner party. High-alcohol wines do have an advantage at professional wine tastings, where the smooth, sweet mouth feel of high alcohol can help to set the wine apart from its competitors.

When the Napa renaissance was young, fermentation tended to be quick and maceration—leaving the skins and other solid components in contact with the wine after fermentation—short. The wines were often hard and sometimes bitter. In part, this came from picking grapes too early, but it also reflected a lack of experience. Many believed that leaving the wine on the skins for too long would bring out harsh tannins and make the wine unpalatable. Now the idea is that extended maceration, often up to forty days, allows short tannin molecules to polymerize (to join together) to form larger ones that provide a smoother character to young wines, making them less biting and astringent.

When fermentation and maceration are complete, the valves of the tanks are opened and the juice drawn off as free-run wine. Skins, seeds, and pulp, saturated with wine, remain in the tank. This material goes to the press, where the remaining liquid is forced out by pressure from steel plates or rubber bladders (the latter is a gentler approach). This so-called press wine is high in tannin and rich with color pigments. Some of it may be blended into the free-run wine to boost color and tannin; otherwise, it is sold as bulk or used for lesser-quality products. The remaining solid matter, the pommace, is returned to the vineyard as a soil enrichment.

All red wines go through a secondary, malolactic fermentation that converts malic acid to lactic acid and carbon dioxide, softening the wine and adding complexity. Malolactic fermentation can occur spontaneously through the intervention of natural bacteria, but more often winemakers encourage it by adding cultivated forms.

After maceration and pressing, the wine is ready for blending—the *assemblage*. Cabernet Sauvignon from lots that have thus far been kept separate is combined with other varieties that provide specific attributes—Merlot for softness; Cabernet Franc for structure, backbone, and flavor; Petit Verdot for color and aroma; maybe even some Malbec—to create the final mix. Over a period of weeks, the winemakers and their assistants will formulate and taste many blends, eliminating some, changing proportions, tasting and retasting, trying to keep it all straight on spreadsheets and in taste memory.

Blending shortly after maceration gives the wine time to "marry in the barrel," to come together with the oak over the months of barrel aging. Many winemakers, however, prefer the greater flexibility of blending after barrel aging, waiting to see what each lot or variety becomes after eighteen or twenty-four months and then blending and allowing the result to marry and mature in the bottle.

If you've ever smelled the pungent, earthy aroma of freshly split oak, you might wonder what it could possibly add to a bottle of wine. But split into staves, dried for a couple of years, crafted into barrels, and toasted with a gentle flame, it adds components that attract money. The buttery taste of Chardonnay, or the hint of vanilla, touch of sweetness, and flavor of wood tannins in Cabernet—all come from aging in oak barrels. Slow movement of oxygen through the joinery of the barrel and through the oak itself softens the wine and adds significantly to its character. The even, cool temperature of caves and their high humidity lead to less evaporative loss, a cost saving that can pay for the cave construction in only a few years. In the cave, alcohol is lost preferentially—a wine that contains 14.5 percent alcohol after fermentation might end up at 13.6 percent, moderating the high alcohol that comes from grapes taken to maturity in the hot Napa sun.

Oak and other woods have been part of winemaking for centuries. In early Napa, winemakers used redwood tanks for aging; a few vintners favored small barrels of American oak. Today, oak *barriques* (small barrels) are used everywhere. Each winery has its favorite type of oak, its own formula for the proportion of new and old barrels, its own preference for degree of toast, its own take on racking and oxygenation. Most Napa winemakers prefer European oak, particularly French, from one or more of five specific forests. Others choose American oak for its more assertive character.

Whatever the source, oak is not a single product—it can vary considerably from barrel to barrel, even if the wood is from the same region, with the same toast, built by the same cooper. Moderate toasting over slow fires is said to draw out the most flavor and aroma components from the oak, while a heavy toast seems to produce more moderate effects. Older barrels are used for lesser wines. Oak is expensive: new French barrels, each holding sixty gallons, cost $650 in 2002.

Once in the barrel, the wine changes slowly and continuously, with solid material—

including the remains of dead yeast—sinking to the bottom. Every few months, the barrels are racked, which involves removing the wine to a clean barrel or vat and sterilizing the dirty one before refilling it. David de Sante likens racking to "opening a drawer, taking out the stuff that's not needed—the old tacks, grocery lists, and other stuff that accumulates—and putting back in just what you want. In the barrel, tannins change, acids fall out, degraded yeast cells settle, the wine starts to come to equilibrium. But it's doing this in a closed container. It can get musty, closed, dark, like an old attic. Racking allows you to open the door, provide a bit of air to open up the wine, fuel the evolution of the tannins, and take the dirty stuff out of the bottom. When you put the wine back in the barrel, the evolution of aging starts in a new and cleaner state." Others, however, consider racking a disturbance, arguing that it risks deterioration rather than improvement.

The decision to filter or fine—the final processes before bottling—is one of the most divisive in winemaking. These processes clarify by removing impurities and help to stabilize the wine; detractors, however, maintain that filtering and fining also damage color, flavor, and aroma. In part, the decision has become a marketing tool, with the label "unfined and unfiltered" indicating to some a higher level of quality and care. Yet many respected Napa winemakers would never release a wine without filtering, believing that a person who buys an expensive bottle should be guaranteed freedom from flaws.

In fining, egg whites or isinglass (very fine mica) slowly sinks through the barrel, gathering any solid and extraneous material that is still suspended in the wine. In filtering, wine is forced through a material—usually diatomaceous earth—that has pore space fine enough to remove small particles. Fining seems to affect flavor and color more than filtration does, softening the wine by removing tannins. When the wine is deemed completely stable and unlikely to exhibit flaws once bottled, it goes to the bottling line for the final step. Some wineries will hold their finest wines for one or two years of bottle aging before distributing them.

NEW TECHNOLOGIES

All along this time-honored path through the winery, decisions that influence the character of the final product bring the winemaker clearly into the realm of terroir. The notion of nonintervention—in which the winemaker's goal is to "stay out of the way"—seems an unattainable ideal. Winemaking is not value-neutral. Every winemaker has a personal and cultural history, a vision, or an intent that is inevitably reflected in the wine. One winemaker might hold that extracting everything possible from the grapes leads to the best expression of terroir, thereby producing a wine of great power and intensity; another might believe that only wines of elegance and restraint allow the nuances of terroir to show through. But all make decisions that shape the character of the product, intruding, however unintentionally, in the process.

While the traditional mix of tools offers considerable opportunity to influence wine character, new techniques based in sophisticated technology are being added at an increasing pace, both in the vineyard and in the winery. We are speaking here not of incremental improvements in existing approaches to grape growing and wine-making, but rather of the incursion of advanced analytical and manipulatory technology into a milieu of long-established tradition. Some of these techniques are being generally applied today; others are creeping into use; and still others are as yet only being considered by winegrowers and winemakers in the Napa Valley. In the use of science and technology, as Napa leads, the rest of California tends to follow, making the valley the cutting edge of "the machine in the garden," as Paul Lukacs has called the application of science and technology to winemaking in America. In the vineyard, the new techniques focus primarily on monitoring; in the winery, they lie more in the realm of manipulation.

The use of monitoring technologies in the vineyards provides winegrowers with scientific verification of what they already know through observation, intuition, and experience. There is a fine line between a vine that is too satisfied with abundant water and one that, in Michael Silacci's terms, experiences urgency short of anxiety. In the vineyard, the feel of a leaf on the skin, the look of a soil, the warmth of the sun, the coolness of the breeze all supply information on vine stress. Now we also have pressure bombs to evaluate the "leaf water potential" by measuring the pressure needed to produce a drop of water from the stem, providing a numeric gauge of water stress. Neutron probe networks monitor soil moisture throughout the season, comparing moisture levels with ideal values. Petiole analysis—measuring chemical uptake by analyzing the leaf stem—indicates which nutrients the plant is actually using and, by implication, which amendments should be added to the soil to provide balanced nutrition.

Remote sensing by airborne instruments that record various wavelengths of the electromagnetic spectrum can provide indirect information about such attributes as vine vigor and the distribution of diseased plants. The Normalized Difference Vegetation Index (NDVI) uses light wavelength data to plot plant vigor. The resulting images (Figure 98) show variation within vineyard blocks, knowledge that can be used in harvesting and remediation work to establish more uniform conditions and crops. Portable Global Positioning Systems (GPS) allow precise "geo-referencing"

FIGURE 98. A map based on the Normalized Difference Vegetation Index (NDVI) reveals variation in plant vigor both within and between vineyards.

of information—that is, with a backpack system, you can locate a position in a vineyard within a few feet. Geographic Information Systems—computer software packages designed to integrate a broad variety of geo-referenced data—provide the ability to manipulate and apply this information. The maps and overlays in this book are the product of geo-referencing and GIS databases; they are powerful tools.

Hemispherical photography, vertical pictures taken up through the plant canopy using a 180-degree lens, offers a precise view of how grape clusters are exposed to the sun. Software that plots the variation of exposure throughout the growing season can aid winegrowers in establishing row direction and choosing canopy management practices to balance fruit exposure and the risk of sunburn, a major problem when fruit is nakedly exposed. Canopy light transmittance measures the amount and character of the light coming through the vine canopy, an indication of shading on leaf and fruit. Excessive shading leads to immature fruit with herbal and vegetal flavors.

Such tools provide an additional measure of confidence in the analytical-intuitive-kinesthetic-emotional mix that is the platform of the winemaker's dance. A few larger operations use them as research and modeling tools in their ongoing attempts to bring greater uniformity to vineyards and greater efficiency to business. The smaller ones either do not need these technologies (because they already take such great care in what they do) or cannot afford them.

The purveyors of technological innovation often present their approach as the new wave, the state of the art, without which you will be left behind in the dust. They tend to consider the pre-technology generations of winemakers old-fashioned and out of date. Data management techniques indeed can integrate an immense amount of diverse input and provide tools for manipulating the information and using it in a variety of forms. In many cases, however, winegrowers and winemakers have limited need for these tools. As winemaker Mia Klein puts it: "Humans integrate so much data—information about soils, sun aspect, heat, what the wine tastes like, what the soil wants to express. If you just measure things and put the data in a machine, all you get is numbers. When I make decisions, they're not based on numbers. They're based on everything I hear, see, taste, feel, *and* the numbers. Otherwise, growing and making wine becomes just a recipe, something you repeat year after year without a real understanding of what is going on around you."

The progress of winery technology over the years has allowed the winemaker, in the words of one winery representative, "to make up for what Mother Nature doesn't give us." Historically, Europeans have employed the practice of chaptalization—adding sugar to the fermenting must—to compensate for lack of sugar in grapes that are not fully mature. Sugar makes alcohol, and alcohol provides body and sweetness to the wine, a mouth feel that otherwise is lacking. Regulation varies with region: sugar can be added in the cooler northern reaches of Europe every year; in more moderate zones, only in poor years; in the warm south, where the climate is much like Napa, not at all. In Europe, it's also legal to add acid when necessary, but only if you don't chaptalize (though French winemakers at best pay lip service to this regulation). In California, it's illegal to add sugar, which is always plentiful in the grapes, but perfectly fine to add acid, which, in Napa's heat, is not. Water, once illegal (though not unused), can now be added to avoid excessive alcohol in years when the grapes are overripe.

Whatever the legalities, modern technology has outstripped them, giving the winemaker tools to achieve goals once blocked by regulation. Alcohol too high? Get rid of it by spinning—using a centrifuge to preferentially separate and eliminate alcohol. Not enough sugar? Concentrate the grape juice by reverse osmosis, a technique that filters out water; or use spinning to reach the same goal, or vacuum distilling. Tannins too tough and green? Soften them through micro-oxygenation, a sophisticated way of adding oxygen to barrels, controlling its delivery through computer technology and thus eliminating the need to rack.

"NATURAL" OR "MANIPULATED"?

Wine professionals and consumers alike sometimes wonder at what level of manipulation, legal or not, the nature of wine moves from the category of "natural" to that of "processed." Perhaps we stepped onto that slippery slope when humans first domesticated the grapevine and began to tend it specifically to make wine. Think of all the "manipulated" elements in winegrowing and winemaking. We begin by ripping vineyards with steel teeth dragged behind a large tractor, disturbing the existing character of soil and commonly mixing it with the sediment or bedrock beneath. Then we plant rootstocks hybridized to bring out certain useful attributes—resistance to phylloxera, drought tolerance, a certain type of root system, an ability to take up potassium or deal with magnesium. We then match variety and clone to the rootstock. The clone has been selected and propagated for its particular character—for the flavor of its grapes, the character of its tannins, or perhaps its yield and productivity.

Soil analysis tells us how much fertilizer the land needs to nurture the vines—nitrogen (from petroleum or urea), phosphorus (from rock phosphate or bird guano), and potassium (mostly from animal bones). We plant the vines and keep the weeds under control with either herbicides or organic methods. We sulfur the plants for powdery mildew and spray for pests, a process that also eliminates natural yeasts.

In the winery, we eliminate bacteria with sulfur dioxide and then add selected strains of yeast to feed the fermentation, choosing the yeast for its ability to live and work in a high-alcohol environment or to draw out certain characteristics of the fruit. We regulate the fermentation temperature in computer-monitored stainless steel tanks to control fermentation, pump over or push down the cap to keep the skins in contact with the juice, macerate for a shorter or longer time to achieve the desired degree of extraction, choose the degree of barrel toast and age in a proportion of new and old oak that will provide the desired flavor profile, let the wine sit for eighteen to twenty-four months, and then bottle the product.

These standard vineyard and winery practices have evolved through the years, a combination of old technology and new, underlying a process that is already a reflection of human intent and intervention. Now, as advanced technology enters the picture at an unprecedented rate, choices become more difficult. If some wineries employ technology to improve on what Mother Nature provides—in difficult years, for example—even those who would like to avoid such manipulation may have to follow suit in order to win a competitive advantage. Yet the differentiation between "natural" and "processed" wines, always indistinct, may already have been irretrievably blurred.

Some consider this of little importance, recognizing the apparently inexorable power of technology. Wine writer Hugh Johnson wrote in 1992, "In a world in which product-liability litigation is a grim reality, in which health concerns grow in direct proportion to our ever-increasing life span, and in which the bureaucratic imposition of unasked-for food standards has become an art form, the romantic ideals [of traditional winemaking] are becoming highly impractical. A high degree of technical knowledge and control is a prerequisite, even it if is directed to a hands-off rather than a hands-on approach to winemaking" (*The Art and Science of Wine,* with James Halliday [London: Mitchell Beazley, 1992], p. 226).

Others such as Paul Draper of Ridge Vineyards and Randall Grahm of Bonny Doon disagree passionately. Wine educator Karen MacNeil, in a *San Francisco Chronicle* article titled "Is Terroir Dead?" (September 18, 2002), quotes Draper (who here uses "hands-off" to mean lack of interference rather than use of technology): "If terroir is going to be expressed, then [the winemaker] has to let the wine more or less make itself. There are very few California winemakers who are truly that hands-off." MacNeil also quotes Grahm: "California wines are generally so tricked-up that if we had terroir, we wouldn't know it. It's almost as if we're the Department of Terroir Prevention."

A key question focuses on the willingness of winemakers to let the public in on what happens in their wineries. If wine labels revealed the use of spinning, reverse osmosis, or other winery manipulation, the public could make its own decisions. That may, of course, be a worry to the winemakers.

In a panel discussion sponsored by the Napa Valley Vintners Association in 2002, Gerald Asher spoke of Jules Chauvet, the revered French winegrower, writer, and teacher, whose core view was that one should not deny oneself the use of technology but should use it only to encourage or perfect the natural process, making it more efficient or precise, for example. Although Asher never knew Chauvet, he believes that the Frenchman would have approved of micro-oxygenation, which allows more precise control than the rougher alternative of racking. The technique was originally introduced in France to deal with the highly tannic wines grown in Tannat and was a successful attempt to reduce the otherwise lengthy barrel aging needed before release. In contrast, Asher believes that Chauvet probably would not have approved of centrifuging to concentrate the juice or reduce alcohol content, seeing this as a rigorous and rough treatment, not part of the natural process.

Whatever the choices made, the winemaker is an integral part of the flow that begins in the contact of vine root with Earth and ends with wine in the bottle. The grape brings with it components of color, flavor, aroma, acid, and tannin; the winemaker seeks to extract these and exhibit them in a wine that has the qualities of balance, harmony, grace, elegance, power, and intensity. With balance, no single component stands out from the others. Harmony implies proportionality, the elements forming a pleasing whole. Grace suggests an experience of beauty and attractiveness. Elegance is defined as restrained opulence or dignified richness. Power is the presence of vigor and strength, while intensity suggests an exceptional or extreme amount, referring most commonly to the hedonistic elements of a wine—its flavor, fruit, or general sensory appeal. Different visions, based on individual experience and outlook, lead one winemaker to try to express terroir through power and intensity, another through elegance and nuance. All perhaps seek balance, harmony, and grace. While the path to the most complete expression of terroir in a wine is still a matter of passionate opinion, power and intensity do tend to overwhelm the nuances and subtle flavors that often distinguish one wine from its neighbor. For each of us, the answers lie in our own experience, in more focused tastings undertaken in the context of better information concerning the elements of terroir.

In Bordeaux and Burgundy, most assume that differences in wine character reflect differences in physical terroir. This may be so, but we wonder whether there has been enough rigorous tasting in the context of detailed information on local terroir to establish that this connection exists for most classified châteaux in Bordeaux or most individual vineyards in Burgundy. We have heard reports that John Wetlaufer in California has led tastings of wines from different Burgundy vineyards made by the same winemaker as well as wines from the same vineyard made by different winemakers. The results suggested that the winemaker had greater impact on the wine than the property did, but the variables were many and the controls few. It is said that adjacent vineyards in Burgundy produce dissimilar wine, usually associated with variations in local terroir, but the interested wine drinker will find little available data concerning substrate and its relation to viticulture and winemaking practices.

In California, the information on physical terroir needed for any attempt to understand these relationships is slowly emerging. In our estimation, at least in North America, we are just beginning to explore the connection of terroir—in all its forms—with wine character. It remains to be seen whether the consumer will be provided enough clear data by winemakers and wine writers to explore these questions freely rather than depending on the opinions, and palates, of the experts.

seven

THE WINEMAKER'S DANCE

ONE DAY AS WE WALKED through Fay and SLV vineyards with Warren Winiarski, he commented on the movement of knee and foot that results in a step. While analyzing our walking patterns, we discussed subjects ranging from the ripeness of grapes, the development of the vines, and hedging techniques to fly-fishing, tendonitis, and whether some wildflowers were Queen Anne's lace or hemlock. (Hemlock is a vector for Pierce's disease, Napa's latest potential scourge, and Winiarski was concerned about this plant appearing anywhere near his SLV vineyard.) It was August, and Winiarski was in the vineyard keeping an eye on the fruit, assessing its development, quality, and uniformity. The sensory, kinesthetic, intuitive, and analytical input he received along the way took his mind down a number of paths, all somehow linked to his concentration on the fruit. It was a living example of the winemaker's dance.

Winiarski thinks poetically and speaks metaphorically. Journalist Rod Smith, in the Fall 2002 issue of *Wine and Spirits* magazine, recounts Winiarski's description of great wine, using the replica of a Greek statue in his office, in symbolic terms, as a model: "The weight is directly under the body, split between two legs, although the forward foot being lifted puts a certain amount of weight forward. Nobody has to explain it—the mind perceives intuitively, at a glance, the balance and the weight slightly forward. A great wine has that kind of balance between the richness and the structure, the soft and the hard. They're so unified that it's like split weight" ("Geology by the Glass," p. 18).

Such also is the balance of the winemaker's dance, one in which apparent opposites—analysis and intuition, fact and hunch, data and the senses, mind and emotion—are woven together in a magical and ineffable way that results in creative response to

PIERCE'S DISEASE AND THE GLASSY-WINGED SHARPSHOOTER

Pierce's disease is the result of a bacterium that reproduces in a plant's xylem—the tissue that carries water—and eventually blocks the flow of water, killing the plant (in the case of grapevines, within one to five years). Pierce's disease has been a problem in California since the 1880s, when it destroyed some forty thousand acres of vines in the Los Angeles basin. Since then, it has been kept under control, but recently it has become more threatening.

Until the late 1980s, the bacterium was spread only by the blue-green sharpshooter, a small insect that lives near watercourses and feeds on vegetation. As it extracts nutrients from a plant through its needlelike feeding mechanism, the sharpshooter injects a substance that can carry the Pierce's disease bacterium, picked up from infected plants. In the late 1980s, a new insect, the glassy-winged sharpshooter, was accidentally introduced to California on nursery stock from the southeastern United States. This variety is larger and more aggressive than the blue-green, flying greater distances and feeding on more plants. It has now spread throughout much of California. As a result, the state's wine grapes are at greater risk.

This problem is being addressed on several fronts, focused both on controlling the glassy-winged sharpshooter and on treating and eliminating Pierce's disease. Some growers have imported stingless, parasitic wasps from Mexico, which lay eggs in sharpshooter eggs, interfering with reproduction. Some local and highly controlled ground spraying has been used in areas of dense infestation. Scientists are investigating other bacteria in hopes of finding one that will kill the Pierce's disease bacterium; they are also mapping the bacterium's genes in search of

(continued)

ongoing events. The dance is not often free of missteps, questions, or confusion—all are part of the winemaker's daily world. We have stood in many vineyards, asked many questions—perhaps about this year's vintage—and heard the answer, "Well, ask me after we've made the wine." There are no guarantees.

The winemaker's dance is perhaps best revealed by statements that reflect the thoughts, decisions, and actions of the dancers themselves as they approach the culmination of the growing season. At that point, the product of the vineyard is in the winemaker's hands. As consulting winemaker Mario Tebbulio puts it bluntly, "I do my best to screw it up as little as possible." And the degree to which it is "not screwed up" is perhaps the degree to which the wine is able to express the terroir, its connection to place and all that has gone into its making.

These days, the goal to which most winemakers seem to aspire is to extract from the grape as clearly as possible this essence of the vineyard, the milieu in which the grape was born and has evolved. In doing so, winemakers also want to create "the best wine possible," a simple phrase that hearkens to a sometimes combative world of passionate opinion. "Yes," says Philippe Melka, "the goal is to make the best wine, but what's best is another story." If the goal is also to express terroir, that's yet another story. Both aims are perhaps revealed not directly but by sidelong glimpses, much as you see, out of the corner of your eye, a small movement in the woods that disappears when you look too closely. So it is with the winemaker's dance—if you look too closely, the whole dissolves into its component parts, which are all you see. The dance is not an object to analyze or even describe; we can only allude to it, most effectively in the words of the winemakers themselves. The diverse approaches to the task of making wine and the vast differences contained in the notion of "what's best" are no better illustrated than by two small wineries, Merus and Dunn.

(continued)

a genetic modification that would kill it off without affecting grapevines. Work to date has already shown that natural zinc, manganese, and copper and iron compounds can inhibit the growth of the disease's bacterium.

MERUS: EXPLORING THE BOUNDARIES

After driving a circuitous route through a well-kept neighborhood in the city of Napa, we pulled up in front of a small, white stucco house, one much like any of its neighbors. We walked up the steps onto a narrow porch littered with wine cartons. The door was open. A large and fierce-looking dog turned out to be friendly, and part wolf, knowledge that ensured our respect. We had arrived at one of Napa's latest boutique wineries, Merus, led there by an article in the *New York Times Magazine* about cult wines (Jim Nelson, "The Cult," December 23, 2001). Our curiosity had been piqued, so we called Merus and arranged a meeting.

Merus is the work, and passion, of Erika Gottl and Mark Herold, a wife and husband who have been making wine for some ten years. Their first commercial vintage, the 1998, was rated highly by Robert Parker, catapulting Gottl, Herold, and Merus into the stratosphere of Napa wine at least briefly; they must still prove their staying power.

Their approach is a curious mixture of low-tech hardware and high-tech concept and approach. Herold, with a Ph.D. in biology, brings analytical intelligence and a deep knowledge of grape physiology and biochemistry. Gottl is perhaps his opposite, a sensitive and intuitive person who speaks of energies in the vineyard and believes that animal and plant life are equal to the lives of humans. "When the fruit comes in, I feel grateful for it, blessed. It's more than grapes just coming in to make wine. The science is always there; the intellectual part needs to be taken care of, separate from feeling. I use my gut to make decisions, but turn to Mark for agreement or disagreement. If we disagree, I reevaluate my decision from a different perspective."

Gottl and Herold do agree that once the fruit comes off the vine, it enters the "zone of depreciation." The goal is to extract as much of the fruit character as they can. Anything less is a flaw. They've already let the fruit hang as long as possible, checking pH and total acidity to get an indication of when the plants begin to say, in effect, "I've done the best I can, given you the best I could—now it's time to take care of myself for next year."

Herold had once intended to be a fish farmer, but he became "obsessed with wine-making." While writing his Ph.D. thesis, he also took courses in enology. After completing his degree, he joined Joseph Phelps winery as a research enologist. There, he introduced the scientific approach to Phelps, conducting experiments with controlled variables, the only way to achieve meaningful results.

Herold ran experiments in cold soaking, for example, the practice of simply letting the crushed fruit sit before inoculating it with yeast. The aim is to gently extract color, flavor, and aroma elements in a water-based environment before pulp fermentation and the harsher extraction by ethanol. He concluded that the process had little effect on extraction, though Phelps is still cold soaking. (When we mentioned this experiment to Winiarski, he expressed interest because it was clear to him, with the certainty of experience, that cold soaking brings out elements that are not touched by the later ethanol extraction during fermentation.)

Eventually, Herold and Gottl decided to establish their own label, a longstanding ambition. And so rose Merus. It's an unconventional operation, this boutique winery in a suburban garage. You walk out the back door onto a concrete crush pad, the driveway. The crusher and fermentation tanks—white plastic containers, large, square, and thick, created originally for some other purpose—sit under a lean-to shed on the side of the garage. The garage itself, now semi-insulated from the heat of summer and the cold of winter, serves as barrel storage.

Despite the rough quarters and low-tech equipment, the couple's winemaking is highly sophisticated, oriented toward perfection. Herold likes "wine on the younger side. I'm a fruit person. Once the fruit's gone, I lose interest. I also like those velvety tannins that come from long hang time and care in crushing."

To make wine of this character, Gottl and Herold work to remove every bit of stem, including the jacks, from the grapes, in order to eliminate the harsh tannins that come from these woody components. Fermentation is whole berry, in which each grape becomes its own fermentation vessel. Aiming for maximum extraction, Herold uses unusually high fermentation temperatures, from 95 to 98 degrees Fahrenheit. He hits the fermentation with a heat spike in the middle, arguing that heat plus water plus ethanol equal high extraction. "If you don't get full extraction, you get more depreciation." And less quality in the wine.

Hot fermentations can sometimes "get stuck," or stop in the middle of the process. Herold avoids this by nurturing the yeast bacteria. One of the problems with fermentation, he says, is that the wild yeasts get a foothold early on but die off when the alcohol rises to about 5 percent. "They sink to the bottom as fat as pigs and sit there hoarding all the available nutrients, so the added yeast can't find sufficient food." To make up for this, Herold feeds the added yeasts a "cocktail" containing niacin, riboflavin, and other vitamins, along with yeast extract. This keeps them happy, healthy, and active, making them strong enough to handle the high alcohols—14, 15, even 16 percent—that come from the high sugar content of fully mature grapes in California.

"You don't need sophisticated equipment to produce high-quality wine," maintains Gottl, backing up the statement with the 93 rating they received from Parker on their first vintage. They are, however, thoughtful and precise in everything they do, attempting to manifest their vision for the wine. They carefully, almost obsessively, sanitize equipment; pick small parcels several times to ensure full ripeness of all the grapes; keep stems out of the fermentation tanks; and use gentle pressing to prevent tannins from being squeezed from seeds. It might all sound a bit precious, but they are not the only ones who are this careful. And you can't argue with success.

DUNN: EXCELLENCE FROM TRADITION

After we left Herold and Gottl, we drove up the valley to Howell Mountain and Dunn Vineyards. Randy Dunn is straightforward, independent, a bit ornery, and an iconoclast. At one point, we were talking about the construction of the Palmaz project, an underground winery with gravity flow buried three levels deep in the Vaca Mountains, where he will be the first winemaker. Dunn told us that Palmaz wanted a sorting table both before and after the crusher to ensure that no stems or jacks enter the fermentation tanks. In his gritty voice, Dunn allowed that you should "sort before the crusher, sure, if you want to. That makes sense if you want to reduce the stems and get the jacks. But after? That's just going to be a mess. Hell, some of the best wines I've ever made, I've thrown the stems back in to ferment."

Dunn's wines have always been known for their extraordinary concentration, intense tannins when young, and the ability to age with elegance. When Dunn began making wine under his own label, in 1984, the wines were so strongly tannic that people wondered whether they would ever come around. But they have aged with surprising grace and beauty, showing the brightness of youth alongside the balance and integration of maturity even after fifteen years.

Dunn is still making wine the same way: "I haven't bought into the early drinking style, haven't changed much how I do things. My new plantings, I've gone vertical—moveable wires, five by nine instead of eight by twelve spacing. I got a new pump, first one ever, two years ago. So things move quicker. It used to take three to four minutes to pump a barrel—now it takes half that. I got a front loader a while back, so we load the fermenting tanks with that now rather than a pitchfork. But, you know, a guy with a [pitchfork] can load a thousand pounds in ten minutes; you can fill a three-ton gondola in an hour and a half. The forklift cost me seventeen thousand dollars, but it's really a waste of money to do anything but [pitchfork] the stuff. I still taste, chew, spit, look at the color. I don't want the grapes to hang forever. I just don't think that more than 14.5 percent alcohol makes a decent table wine, which is what I want to make."

Our conversation about Palmaz reminded us of our meeting with Gottl and Herold and the extreme care and gentleness both seem to associate with making great wine; some others, including Opus One and Harlan, take the same approach. We asked Dunn what he thought about gentle handling.

"I think it's just bullshit. I suppose gravity flow is fine, but I'm sure convinced that it's okay to pump crushed grapes. Wines have been pumped for years. Now people are getting precious about bruising wines from the shear in 'those nasty pumps.' A lot of people pump over gently so they don't bruise the fruit—I use a fire hose. It breaks up the cap and gets the juice moving. I guess gravity flow depends on how much it's worth to you—down at Palmaz, they went that way originally because they thought it was a 'cute marketing gimmick.'" In the winemaker's dance, Randy Dunn is surely the shit-kickin' cowboy whoopin' it up in the local honky-tonk and having the time of his life.

Dunn, on the one hand, and Gottl and Herold, on the other, are highly skilled representatives of two approaches to winemaking in Napa, one deriving from classical roots, the other from the Parker-inspired style of bypassing tradition and exploring, seemingly with greater freedom, the boundaries of winemaking. In a global context, they have been called Old World and New World (or International) styles, a shorthand terminology that too readily separates a continuum of style and character into its two end members. This kind of categorization disregards the gradients that exist and inadvertently encourages wine drinkers to think in simplistic terms rather than focusing on their taste experience. The overlap between these two approaches is generally ignored—and the result is that a palpable tension between them hangs in the atmosphere in Napa, eventually entering most conversations about wine style, wine character, and the association of wine with terroir.

MOUEIX AND BARON: AN INTERPLAY OF AMERICA AND FRANCE

"When I first looked at this soil twenty years ago with my friend Daniel Baron, I thought it was the best soil I had seen in California. I had such a special feeling for the soil and location. It had a sense of history, something very rare in California," recalls Christian Moueix of Napanook, the property originally owned by John Daniel, which has now become Dominus.

Moueix, a major grower and winemaker in Bordeaux, brings the classical French tradition with him to California. "I am not interested here in being a pioneer. In France, perhaps we were the first to thin grapes and drop leaves. . . . But here I like to go back to origins, to understand the best use in a classic way, in spirit, in respect. By classic, I mean slightly rigorous in approach, not exotic. If there had been eucalyptus on the ranch, I would not have been interested. [Eucalyptus is a source of the minty character in some Napa wines, particularly Heitz Martha's Vineyard Cabernet Sauvignon.] We want to produce a wine of world class but one that is clearly Californian, an American wine with a French education, perhaps a bit more sophisticated."

When Moueix was contemplating buying the property, Maynard Amerine, once his professor at Davis, put together a tasting of three pairs, the 1952, 1953, and 1959 Petrus and Inglenook. With four other individuals, they tasted these pairs side by side, blind, ranking the best of each. Inglenook took two out of the three pairings; Moueix says that he could not identify which were French and which were Californian. This experience was key to his decision to buy the property, a transaction in which he originally partnered with John Daniel's two daughters.

"I'm always unsatisfied with the quality. I have in my mind the picture of a perfect wine, and I never seem to reach it. I make a wine for drinking, not for tasting." Moueix maintains that "winemaking is much simpler than anyone thinks, a natural process. You crush the grapes, put it in the vat, and it makes itself. Good grapes make good wine. We do very little in the cellar, just 20 to 25 percent new oak. John Daniel just cared for the vineyard, never acidified, never intervened. Today, there is a cult that has grown around the winemakers. It's a bit embarrassing."

For fourteen years, Daniel Baron made wine at Dominus, arriving after a stay at Petrus, Moueix's premier property in Pomerol. Now at Silver Oak, Baron finds himself making a different style, but he brings to the task the same classical sensibilities that informed his work at Dominus.

Baron describes the connection he and his crew maintain from the vineyard into the winery: "When you work with the same vineyards, the same blocks, you begin to have a dialogue with the vineyard, a conversation. We're out in the vineyards from pruning through harvest, and we develop a picture of what the season has been. When we taste a tank, our experience is infused with a picture of the vineyard at harvest, the leaf color, the character of the stems, the look of the fruit on the vine. If the cellarmaster is not in the vineyard, the tanks are just tanks, just numbers. When it comes to deciding how much time to leave the wine on the skins, his information is limited if he hasn't seen the fruit before it was picked. He and I taste every tank every day. We've both been in the vineyard blocks; we both have a visual feel for the grapes before they were picked. The blocks are all different, we've seen that clone X ripened before clone Y—all of this informs the process.

"Yet, even after years of experience, every vintage feels like childbirth—if we remembered how much it hurt, we might never do it again. And wines are much like our children. Their personality is there from day one, and we can track it through, know its essence even if its behavior at any particular moment seems off. You get a feel from all this of where the fruit has been and where it's going. You have to remember this when you think about judging wines. They're alive and changing moment to moment; they have good days and bad; they show well in a particular glass or with particular food. Judging a wine at any particular moment in its life is like giving a kid a letter grade based on his behavior in the supermarket."

While he was at Dominus, Baron met with Moueix sometimes in France, sometimes in California. He remembers the two of them regularly ordering wine with lunch in France and then a second bottle for the cheese course. A few weeks later, they'd be having lunch in California, noticing that the first glass tasted great but that often the bottle was still half full at the end of the meal. Baron calls the wines that draw you back "come hither" wines, and that's the character he sought to bring out at Dominus—wines that you will reach out for, drawn by the intrigue and interest of an array of flavors and aromas that seem continually new. Danny Schuster says of great wine: "Every one should surprise you. Great wine is haunting—you can't quite put your finger on what it is. It remains a mystery."

How do you achieve these qualities? Dick Grace, who devotes much of his energy to charity events, speaks of the power of intent, a Buddhist notion that the mental picture or background intention you hold in your mind influences the character of what you do. He suggests that if the intent of the winemaker is strictly material—to achieve prestige or to make money, for example—the wine will turn out differently than if the intent has a more social or even spiritual character. By the same token, we might add, if your focus is on classically proportioned and balanced wines rather than on richness and intensity, that will be what you get, because that notion is informing everything you do in the winery.

HOWELL AND MELKA: A FEELING FOR THE LAND

Winemakers who are classically oriented seem to have a distinctive attitude toward the land, something akin to the tradition in Burgundy that holds that if you're making wine in Santenay, for example, your concern is to make the best Santenay you can from the land you farm. You simply don't think of making the best wine in all of Santenay or, as some do in Napa, the greatest wine in the world.

Chris Howell has this view of the land. He arrived at Cain Vineyards in 1990 after earning a degree in viticulture in Bordeaux and working as an intern at several California wineries. He brought with him the key lesson he learned in Europe, that the taste of wine "relies on where it grows." He also brought the very European ethic of working with the land so that its character is clearly expressed in the wines grown on it.

He began at Cain by working to understand the vineyards and trying to gauge their potential. He soon found that they were planted on Franciscan formation mélange, high in magnesium, a composition that creates problems with the vines' uptake of calcium, an element vital to their health. And mélange is highly unstable—saturate it with water, and it slips as quickly as a novice skater on slick ice.

About a year into Howell's tenure, Jim Medlock, the owner of Cain, asked him whether the vineyards could produce the greatest grapes in the Napa Valley. He suggested that if this wasn't possible, perhaps they should go out and find the grapes they needed to produce the greatest wine in Napa. Howell knew that they could contract for grapes from the Rutherford Bench, Stags Leap, or other sources of high-quality fruit, but he told Medlock, "What we need to do is to express the best that this property can produce." And that is what they agreed to do.

Howell added, "Cain is a hillside project, a Cabernet blend, one of the first. It's not about making another great wine. It's about a wine the reflects place. It's been about complexity from the beginning, about taking care of this place and doing it justice, in the barrel, in the bottle, in the glass. And finding people who appreciate it."

The last year their premium wine, Cain 5, was made totally from estate grapes was 1994. Since then, Howell has spent his time replanting the entire property. Not until the 2005 vintage will he once again have enough estate-grown grapes to produce an estate-grown Cain 5. In the meantime, the 1997 Cain 5, made from a mix of estate grapes and grapes from highly selected sources, was named Bordeaux Blend of the Year by *Food and Wine* magazine. The award, barely acknowledged by the self-effacing Howell, helps to expand the notion of "what's best," as Cain 5 is far from the gobs-of-fruit, sock-me-in-the-mouth, knockout wine that seems to be the current favorite of the critics.

In Philippe Melka, the classical approach to the land, which some might see as a reflection of Gallic romanticism, is informed by a deep knowledge of rock, sediment, and soil that comes from his training as a geologist. For Melka, the unique quality of the substrate at each site is the single aspect of terroir that is stable and that also has the potential of imparting individual character to the wine. He even worries that too much irrigation can change the natural quality of the site and what it will provide: "You can't overdo. You need to take care to not hide the natural character of the soil. . . . You just irrigate for the survival of the vine."

Melka has made wine for Quintessa, which is located on an elongate knob in the valley with its own small-scale topography, a series of hills and valleys that corrugate the surface. In that wine, Melka tried "to re-create the atmosphere of the hillside within the valley. The hill in the middle is the core of the wine, with the Merlot from deeper soils to give it some fatness. The Cabernet from the deeper soils on the south is softer, creamy, more civilized; on the hill, it's wild, an explosion of feeling, the backbone of the wine. I want to balance its strength of character with the valley fruit. The vines there are maybe healthier, growing on deeper soil; they bring a creaminess, a silkiness, into the wine. I try to civilize the wine—you know, if the consumer drinks a piece of dirt, it will be tough for him."

Melka approaches Seavey, in Conn Valley, in a different way, though equally focused on balance. Here the soils are poor, gravelly, and sandy, on a steep hillside, exposed and warm. "The Cabernet is exposed to intense heat and shows it, a bit rustic, astringent, concentrated. The owner is a bit the same way—he 'likes wine to kick you a little.' Still, I try to soften it a bit, make it a bit more civilized.

"Diamond Mountain Vineyard is quite different. Lots of natural springs change the profile of the mountain. It has very healthy conditions, almost a valley in the high topography. The wine profile is much the same, very healthy, very pure, beautiful character, very aromatic, perhaps a little more linear.

"Caldwell—it's another story, a piece of rock with barely any soil, needs lots of irrigation and input. But the wines are tremendous. The site is cooler, in the south, on a north-facing slope; and the wine has lots of character. It's irrigated almost like a spring on Diamond Mountain, and the wine shows the same kind of purity and minerality, with lots of intensity, darkness, spiciness."

Melka uses the diverse character of the grapes to build a wine that reflects his mix of scientific and intuitive understanding. To do this, he must sort out and integrate a staggering amount and variety of information. His fellow winemakers all tread the same path, one of opening themselves to the array of available data and allowing the bits and pieces to connect through an almost mystical process that is largely subconscious. Not many have the ability to articulate this understanding, and those who do—people such as Warren Winiarski, Tony Soter, Michael Silacci, Mia Klein, Chris Howell, and Melka himself—often speak poetically and metaphorically, the only forms suitable for describing nonverbal understanding. But all recognize that this subconscious and largely ineffable knowledge informs every decision in the season-long work of making a vintage. The individual's ability to access and use this knowledge is reflected in the wine—whatever the winemaker's vision and intent, the evidence resides in the glass.

Melka alludes to the process of blending, bringing together a variety of elements from a single vineyard to make a wine reflecting the vision that has guided the work of the growing season. Blending is simple to understand but more difficult to accomplish and to appreciate—you mix a measured amount of this Merlot into that Cabernet, add some Petit Verdot and maybe a bit of Malbec, and then taste it and adjust. You work back and forth, creating many blends, recording their composition, tasting each one several times over a period of weeks, before deciding on a final mix. Some choose to blend shortly after maceration; others wait until the components have aged in the barrel for eighteen to twenty-four months.

The intricacy is apparent—blending and tasting specific batches, keeping the blends clear in your taste memory, eliminating them progressively—but the process also depends on an innate feel for how wines of different character work together. This became particularly apparent during a tasting of the 1997 Cain 5 and its components. (For that particular year, the Cain 5 had only four components—the 1997 Merlot did not make the grade.) To make Cain 5, Chris Howell ferments separate lots of each variety, blending them to provide the five elements that make up the wine—Cabernet Sauvignon, Merlot, Cabernet Franc, Petit Verdot, and Malbec. Because he makes the final blend before aging in the barrel, for two or three months following maceration he and his staff put together scores of blends, each tasted several times until they settle on the final mix. Each year, they save a barrel of each one of the elements, to be bottled and stored as an archive.

The tasting was little short of a revelation. None of the four components seemed particularly distinguished. To us, they all seemed a bit dull—Howell termed them "a bit stinky." How could the Bordeaux Blend of the Year come from these unexceptional parts? Yet the blend soared. It was complete, with a welcoming entry, a full middle, and an interesting and extended finish, with marvelous flavor and all the sensory elements you would look for in a fine wine.

Howell says, "We begin with sixty or so different wines. . . . In January or February, we need to begin tasting. Each reaches a certain standard, and as we begin to mix them, the blend begins to become what it can be for that year. Sooner or later, the pieces fit together in a mix that makes sense. We like to blend early and age the blend."

As you contemplate that statement, remember that in blending wine, there is no going back, no unmixing of what has already come together. When you climb a mountain, you can at least retreat if things begin to look bleak. Once you begin mixing wine, you cannot extract even a bit of the Merlot that you have just added to the vat of Cabernet. You're on a mountain, and you can't back down; you can only move forward into something unknown. It must surely be an intimidating moment.

KONGSGAARD AND HARLAN: ON THE EDGE

Randy Dunn, producing wines of unusual power and intensity but with none of the tendency toward soft and supple tannins that is a major focus today, falls somewhere between the classicists and the makers of New World wines. Like the classicists, however, he is not afraid to make wine that needs to sit in the cellar for a few years before you drink it.

Even farther out on the edge, John Kongsgaard is in a group of one. Who else in Napa, especially these days, would declare of his Chardonnay: "My goal is to beat the fruit out of the wine. You only get real expression of the variety when all the fruit is gone, the California melon, the citrus—when it's down to the bare bones of the variety. If I want to taste pineapple, I'll get one at the grocery store." To make sure the site shows through, he leaves the wine in the barrel for two years and comes out with a product that many cannot distinguish from fine white Burgundy.

Kongsgaard's main interest in winemaking is to "find sites that can express themselves through certain varieties. I've never made a living from the Rutherford Bench. I've always looked on the fringe, around the edges, struggling to find places where certain varieties would express the character of the soil. Chardonnay is in ways the most challenging because it's the least challenging. On ordinary ground, you get a normal, generic commodity. But find a site that won't produce five tons an acre, in which you can't always rely on the sun to produce 24 Brix, and you can produce something really distinct. I just think it's more fun to get more bizarre." Kongsgaard's main winemaking guru was Michel Rolland, a Frenchman who has since become one of the world's busiest wine consultants. Early on, Rolland, who is devoted to small yields of mature fruit, told Kongsgaard: "John, in California the sun is the enemy. It makes the grapes ripe too early. If it is too short a time from veraison to harvest, you get poor wines."

The early ripening of fruit in Napa has made this region the center for the ever richer, ever more intense, ever more extracted wines of the New World style. One of the most colorful proponents of this style is Ed Sbragia, winemaster at Beringer. Sbragia likes wine that stands on its own. "You're home on a Saturday afternoon, you're cooking, the family's out. You open a bottle of wine, and then by the time they get home, you suddenly realize the bottle's empty. That's the kind of wine I like."

His preference and winemaking style have evolved over the years. "The more you know the vineyards, the more you know the style of wines that come from them. I've gone more and more to choosing bigger, fatter vineyards to make the kind of wine I've come to like. Yes, I could make the wine more elegant, style it with more nuance by blending in wines from lighter vineyards to balance the richness. But in richness you get flavor, density, mouth feel—the stuff I look for." Sbragia makes Beringer's Reserve wines. It's useful to remember that these wines are blends, mixtures of wine from different locations selected for their contribution to style rather than for relation to place. As good as they may be, if you're interested in terroir, these are not the wines for you.

Bill Harlan set out with a different goal than Sbragia, not to produce a wine that suited his taste (though we presume he did that) but to produce "the best wine from America," an American "first growth" to rival the best of Bordeaux. Harlan wanted a wine of great quality and balance, with consistency, longevity, and a distinctive character that would be true to the place where it was grown. He set out to find property that could produce this kind of wine without requiring him to "fight Mother Nature."

Harlan visited vineyards the world over, trying to extract from his travels a feel for the best land, to look through the "brand" to the soil that underlay its success. What was the most expressive land, and why did it have such character? He decided that the best way to do this in California was "to get history on my side, to find where the best red wine had been produced for a long time." His conclusions were largely topographic, and one of his final arbiters was price—not, by any means, in terms of affordability but as a measure of quality. "Over time, history showed that the best land lay between Yountville and Rutherford, not on the floor of the valley, not in the hills, and not necessarily on the fans, but just up a little way from the bench. Wherever I looked, this seemed to be the most expensive land, so the challenge became to find this setting between Yountville and Rutherford."

It took him ten years to figure it all out. Finally, in 1984, he found the first parcel of land that became Harlan Estate; in 1994, he acquired the last piece. The land lies between 225 feet in elevation and 1,225 feet; the vineyards sit between 325 feet and 525 feet, an area Harlan calls "the Tenderloin," the topographic zone that seemed to attract the highest prices wherever he looked. And to affirm his vision, his wine has also become one of the most expensive, sought after the world over since the first commercial vintage, 1991, hit the market.

Harlan Estate wraps around a ridge that is separated from the Mayacamas Mountains by a narrow, deep valley. The vines face mainly northeast and southwest, but smaller pieces of the vineyard show all ranges of the compass, the variability of perspective requiring considerable sensitivity to sun angles and fruit exposure. The vines yield little fruit, perhaps three tons per acre in a lush year, more often closer to a single ton—and Harlan drops fruit to ensure ripeness and intensity, usually leaving only one cluster per shoot, half the normal vineload. In the winery, they sort before and after the crush, extracting even the smallest hint of stem material. Does this make a difference? Not even the winemakers really know, but everything is done to serve the vision.

The fermentation tanks, French oak, with size and shape designed in a specific ratio of wine volume to tank surface, are of eight sizes, each matched to the yield expected from a specific block. The aging cellars are open to the Earth, with no air movement, the cooling and heating elements in the walls and floors guaranteeing temperature control within one degree throughout the room. Harlan also honors continuity throughout the winemaking process—most of his staff has been with him for more than fifteen years, providing the year-to-year understanding that grows on itself. Harlan has gone a long way to achieve his vision. If demand for his wine is any measure, his success is abundant. The wine is available primarily to a mailing list with a long line of hopefuls, and it costs more than two hundred dollars a bottle retail. At auction, it goes for many hundreds, sometimes thousands, of dollars.

One question lingers, however (which we will address more fully in the next chapter). Although Harlan aims to produce a wine that expresses the land, Harlan Estate is very much a New World wine, bold, with forward fruit, ripe tannins, and incredible intensity—it is surely rich, even opulent. Are such wines able to carry with them the more subtle nuances that come from the land? Or do they reflect mainly the elements that underlie the general style—very mature fruit from long hang time, long maceration giving great extraction, aging mainly in new French oak—any of which might overpower the more delicate flavors and aromas that seem to characterize the land?

BARRETT AND SCHUSTER: A BIT OF CONTEXT

Bo Barrett puts winemaking in a succinct, unvarnished context: "Well, you know, making wine's not rocket science. You take good-tasting grapes, and you can make good wine. If you pick at the right time, press at the right time—do these correctly, and the wine's made, at least if you have a good vineyard. And these days, you can fix just about anything but lack of flavor.

"We dry farm the place, the yields are woeful, about a ton to a ton and a quarter an acre. . . . The Cab starts slow and opens late; it has this steel-titanium core. The Zinfandel is the opposite, opens big, then goes to the back. The Zinfandel is flashier. We crush the Cabernet fruit but try not to break the berries on the Zinfandel . . . it's not good as a seed container, so we try not to knock the seed out of the envelope. We'll drain the juice off to another tank, drain the cap, then put the wine back on top. With the air going in, we get bigger tannins. With our 'A' vineyards, the best ones, we don't have to do much. But in some of the others, where we have some heavy clays, we don't get enough ripe tannins, so we build more forward tannins by putting some air in. It's all art with a cowboy feel—we'll taste it and then say, 'Let's give this one some air.'"

It takes time to know a property. Danny Schuster makes wine in New Zealand and consults for Stag's Leap Wine Cellars in Napa and Antinori in Italy. When he began to work at Stag's Leap, he recalls, "I worked with the people who prune, worked the vineyards, the *assemblage*. I began to ask myself, why does wine from this piece taste like this? I slowly got to know the place, began to feel what's happening in the entire property. I could see how things got created. These consultants that have a hundred clients, they can't do this. They come in, first shock the client, then pull the rabbit out of the hat, show them on the laptop where they're strong and how they're going to help. And then they give the formula: usually, thin the crop, expose the grapes to the sun, be careful how you irrigate. And then they look at their watch and split. You can make lots of money doing this, but I don't think you get to know vineyards very well."

Bo Barrett's comment that "you can fix just about anything but lack of flavor" is similar to Philippe Melka's questioning of "what's best"—both observations contain a world of unspoken meaning. The technological advances that have found their way into the wine industry over the past decade are both powerful and disconcerting. Wine has generally been viewed as a product from the land that comes to the consumer relatively free of anything but the human hand directing natural processes. No longer is this guaranteed. Now technology in the winery allows you to take poor grapes and turn them into decent, even good, wine or take good grapes and turn them into what some might consider great wine. The economics of fine wine requires huge capital investment to establish a winery and maintain a brand. In such conditions, the inclination to manipulate winemaking in lesser years (and yes, California and Napa have lesser years) must be significant. And when the economy is in the tank—its condition as we write these words—the temptation to follow the market rather than your original vision, if these two paths diverge, must be intense. If wine style can indeed overcome the nuances of terroir, then market forces that influence style become an issue in the overall understanding of wine and terroir.

❖❖❖ *eight* ❖❖❖

SOME FINAL, AND FUNDAMENTAL, ISSUES

YOU'VE TRAVELED A LONG PATH with us, from 145 million years ago to the present and from bedrock, sediments, and soils into the winery and beyond. Fundamental to our journey has been the assumption that wines do reflect terroir, in all its natural beauty and complexity. Some dispute this, maintaining that terroir is simply a marketing tool or just plain hogwash. Others wonder whether the technology of winemaking, particularly in California and Australia, hasn't by overuse destroyed any possibility that a wine will reflect terroir rather than the hand of the winemaker. Still others are concerned that extreme styles—in particular, the intense, opulent wines with high alcohol and rich, smooth mouth feel that are so favored today—overshadow any nuance imparted to the wine by place.

We have stated explicitly that wine character and terroir are indeed related, though the relationship between specific aspects of each is still unclear, awaiting more disciplined tasting in the context of the kind of information contained in this book. For us, that's more of a challenge than a problem. When wine producers begin providing clear, useful, and valid information on the terroir in which their wines have been grown, each of us will be able to explore the issue as deeply as we choose. Until then, we must depend on interested and reasonably objective wine writers to dig out the data and share the knowledge with us, or we must dig it out ourselves. For those who are interested, we hope to provide a means of sharing such information at the Web site www.winemakersdance.com.

Exploring the link between terroir and wine, however, primarily involves the senses. In this regard, the many wine lovers whose palates are less sensitive than those of the tasting elite will surely be interested in Diane Ackerman's comments about some human capabilities and limitations. In *A Natural History of the Senses* (New York: Random House, 1990), Ackerman reveals that we can distinguish at least ten thousand odors but have no vocabulary with which to describe them directly: "the physiological links between the smell and language centers are pitifully weak . . . we describe smells in terms of other things" (p. 7). And taste, limited traditionally to four flavors—sweet, sour, bitter, and salty (though we should perhaps mention a fifth, *umami,* which indicates a robust or savory sensation)—follows aroma.

In addition, our sensitivities vary. While there's no denying that some have super-sensitive palates and noses, for most of us the world of taste and aroma is a simpler place, an amalgam of the nuances identified by the great wine tasters of the world. No wonder, then, that many of us have difficulty understanding the writings of those who can distinguish in wine one berry essence (even the subtle blueberry) from another and can identify the aroma and flavor of the nearly odorless and tasteless kiwi.

We can, however, train ourselves to be more sensitive. Ann Noble, for example, retired professor of enology at the University of California at Davis, has trained tasters by placing small amounts of strawberry jam, bell pepper, cassis, or other substances in wine. By smelling and tasting the exaggerated example, one becomes familiar with the aromas and flavors as they occur in unadulterated wine. Although this approach perhaps ties you to the aromas and flavors the experts deem important, it is at least a place to begin.

Nonetheless, the world of terroir and wine, complex as it is, can accommodate all. While it might require an extraordinarily sensitive palate to distinguish the subtle effects of earth, climate, and clone, the rest of us can play the game as well, though under simplified rules.

The view of terroir we present below stems from a comment by Warren Winiarski that emphasizes the fundamental importance of the act of domesticating the wild grapevine. Speaking of the way humans regulate the vine, he observes that "this regulation is perhaps the most encompassing of all the things we do to let the terroir speak." Adapting Winiarski's imagery, we can say that terroir expresses itself through the influences of three major elements and one minor—a chorus of water, of sun, of earth, and of air. (We speak here particularly of the red varieties that are the foundation of Napa's reputation.) If each of these elements of terroir can be heard, the wine may express fully the character of the place in which it grows. If one or more of the elements dominates, the others fade into the background.

The dominance of water produces vigorous plants that develop herbaceous and vegetative notes in their fruit. The dominance of sun leads to overly ripe fruit and the opulent, often exaggerated characters—excessive fruit and high alcohol—that result. The dominance of earth brings the austere, mineral-dominated wines with harsh tannins that reflect less than ideal ripening. Air, in the form of wind and fog, ameliorates, by cooling during summer heat or by warming vines at night; in both cases, air balances sugar and acid levels. Hot winds, however, dehydrate the grapes, leaving sweet juice without the tart balance of acid.

In a system so regulated by the human hand and mind, any notion of "natural balance" strikes us as artificial. But the idea of a balanced wine that reflects each of these elements in proportion holds a truth that can be realized through direct experience. While we have much good and some great wine in the world, truly balanced wines are rare. They stand out in memory as so harmonious that no element of aroma, mouth feel, or flavor intrudes. With such wines, there is no need to emphasize the firm structure, the character of the fruit, the smooth mouth feel, the supple tannins, or the great complexity—the experience is so complete that nothing needs to be said.

These wines usually have some bottle age, and they are more often than not French. The one in our most recent memory was a Bordeaux, not of kingly repute, but a more modest 1988 Château Clerc Milon from Pauillac. By no means an overpowering wine, it nevertheless stopped conversation at the table on the first mouth-filling taste and kept drawing our attention just as vividly throughout a leisurely dinner. Craig Williams, who maintains that the French have used the notion of terroir in part as a marketing tool to sell bad wine from unripe grapes in poor vintages, acknowledges, "The French work hard on proportionality, on balance. They are clearly more experienced at this than we are."

In this context of seeing terroir as a chorus of a few major voices, we can approach the notion of style and fashion from a broader perspective. Instead of arguing whether or not some styles of wine overpower the expression of terroir, we can ask different questions: What balance of the voices of terroir does this wine reflect? Does it favor the sun, with the intense, fruit-forward concentration that such an emphasis produces? Does it favor the earth in which it grew, influenced by mineral elements and strong tannins, with the fruit at least temporarily in the background? Is it dominated by water, with more herbaceous components? Or does it have that rare balance in which no single element holds sway?

Here we recall Dick Grace's notion regarding the power of intent and suggest that the ultimate expression of terroir rests on the intent of the winemaker—the vision of the wine that has been carried throughout the season becomes the guiding rhythm for the chorus and the winemaker's dance. If the winemaker's intent is to "let the terroir speak," then the goal will be to balance the elements. In the vineyard, such winemakers will be careful to give the vines just enough water at just the right times. They will be mindful of the fine line between maturity and excessive ripeness, whose resulting opulence may overpower the voice of earth. They will avoid stressing the vines by withholding water or food to the point that ripening comes into question. In the winery, these winemakers will emphasize good extraction but be aware that too much can overwhelm the nuances. With every decision, their guiding principle is "enough is a feast," based on the understanding that excess of any single element only reduces the expression of terroir. And the winemakers will show care in how they use new technologies, avoiding anything that detracts from that original intent of letting the terroir speak.

Stylistic tendencies and marketplace pressures tend to tip wines away from this balance. In the early days of the Napa renaissance, when the focus was on the winery and grapes were just so much "potter's clay" to be molded into fine wine, water was too often the dominant element, and the resulting wines too vegetal. In the 1980s, the favored style was big, earthy wines—tannic when young, though often with the necessary acid and fruit for an elegant maturity. Today, sun has become dominant, with the focus on fruity, forward wines, with supple tannins. Will sweet youth decline into a vapid old age, or will these wines develop and mature through a long life? Time will tell.

STYLE VERSUS CHARACTER

In the wine world, the slow ascendance of style (a reflection of winemaker choice) over character (what comes from the vineyard) began in 1982, when the young and then little-known Robert Parker so effusively praised the Bordeaux wines of that year, setting off a buying spree at a time of economic affluence and excess. Basing his reviews on the intrinsic nature of a wine rather than reputation or historic trends, Parker turned the world of wine criticism on its head.

Already the archetypes of Cabernet Sauvignon and Pinot Noir—until then based on the style and character of Bordeaux and Burgundy, respectively—had come into question with the astounding results of the Paris wine tasting of 1976. Parker built on this by taking a broader view of varietal character and measures of quality. He proceeded to fulfill the consuming public's need for a guide through the burgeoning forest of wines from regions around the world. Parker's descriptions were strong and clear, and his 100-point rating scale was familiar to Americans, who recognized scores such as 85 and 92 from their grade school days, as opposed to the more narrative descriptive style and 20-point scale of the established British wine critics.

Parker's new view, however, turned out to have its own limitations. He has placed increasing emphasis on power and intensity, personified by big fruit, rich mouth feel, and opulent character—the type of wine he prefers. Distributor, retailer, and consumer alike have come to use Parker less as a guide than as a benevolent dictator, joyfully relinquishing freedom to explore in favor of buying on the basis of Parker's ratings and allowing pleasure in wine to be conditioned by his preference. Winemakers, with an eye on their economic future, can do little other than follow along. Consumers might be better served by a different model, one in which the personal preferences of judges are suppressed in favor of a less subjective view of technical merit and artistic expression. Some wine judging reflects this ethic, but the most influential wine critics apparently continue to reach conclusions based significantly on individual preference.

Colin MacPhail, a Scot who began working in Napa as a tour guide in the mid-1990s and now oversees Leslie Rudd's boutique gin-making venture, says, "Americans have to live up to their newfound confidence in their own sophistication. A lot of people I saw when I was guiding corporate tours were just afraid. They'd come here with an industry group in a competitive environment, and they were terrified of making a mistake, of showing their ignorance. They didn't know anything about wine, so someone at a winery would say, 'Here's our Zin, what do you think?' and they'd be petrified. That fear factor sells wine. A lot of people play on this, implying that if you don't want to appear stupid, you'll buy this bottle for a hundred bucks."

People are similarly afraid of appearing ignorant if they buy a wine with anything lower than a Parker 90, but, as MacPhail emphasizes, "You have to realize that a wine wasn't born with the affliction that it's an 88 or 89 on Parker's scale. People fit wine into fixed strata, but it tends to move around, perhaps from a 92 to an 86, depending on your emotions, the time of day, the kind of food you're eating. All of us pay attention to the numbers, but we really should remember they're only the opinion of one guy."

If they're carefully made, New World or International style wines can exhibit depth and complexity, though lesser versions tend toward a shallow pleasure in which the wine bares all in the shockingly delicious first burst of flavor. Nevertheless, as Parker's influence has grown, wine the world over has swung strongly toward the style he and a few other influential wine critics favor. As a result, many fear that the regional and local character that so often distinguishes wine will be lost. We don't blame Parker for this condition; rather, it more reflects our tendency to distrust ourselves, to depend on the opinions of those whom we consider more informed. And Parker's preferences are not surprising: think of tasting hundreds of wines a day, and imagine what might make an impression on your palate late some afternoon after a week in the tasting trenches. Will it be the subtle wine with nuance and character

A TASTING IN THE MAINE WOODS

It was perhaps less a comparative tasting than an inadvertent coming together of two wines that had no business being next to one another. We had been given a bottle of 1996 Harlan Estate and wanted to get a measure of this wine, which stands out even among that small group of wines whose high quality and small production have made them virtually inaccessible to the vast majority of wine drinkers. We wanted something to taste this against, knowing that comparing the character of wines tends to reveal far more than drinking them alone.

But we were in the Maine woods, with limited resources. The only bottle we could pull out to taste against the Harlan was a 1998 Château Beauregard, a Pomerol made from a different grape, in a different year, in a different style, and of different (quite modest) repute. It was like putting a contender for a regional flyweight wrestling crown in the ring with a world champion sumo wrestler—the Harlan overpowered the Beauregard in a moment, as quickly as the sumo champ would have flung the flyweight from the ring.

This was not a blind tasting, and we laid down no ground rules of remaining mum until everyone had an opportunity to taste and assimilate their experience. Cries of "delicious," "complex," "fabulous" rang out with the first sip of the Harlan, a stunningly rich and powerful wine—"smooth," "bold," "loud," with "no dissonance." "From the first moment, something's happening in my mouth," someone exclaimed, while others commented: "It sparkles"; "It's rich and smooth like good chocolate ice cream"; "It snaps my synapses"; "It has enormous complexity." In comparison, the Beauregard suffered: "hollow," "flat," "empty."

(continued)

that will draw you back again and again over a quiet dinner, or will it be the blockbuster that slaps your mouth to attention?

It may be that the current focus on power and intensity is beginning to fade. In 2001, we visited the California Wine Tasting Championships held at Greenwood Ridge Winery in Mendocino County. The young winegrowers with whom we talked make California but drink French. They are tired of what they consider the overblown nature of California wine, with its lack of subtlety. And some Australian winemakers are moving to cooler parts of that continent to escape the overarching influence of sun and heat.

In the absence of critics' numbers, some consumers will rate wines relative to their own taste, which often differs from that of the experts. In January 2002, we conducted a blind tasting for fifty people, mainly Berkeley professors, their spouses, and friends, presented by the wine club at the University of California. When the tasters were asked which of eight Cabernets they preferred, the votes were spread quite evenly. The wines represented vineyards from one end of the Napa Valley to the other, including such luminaries as Chateau Montelena, Stag's Leap Fay Vineyard, and Dalla Valle Napa, along with lesser-known labels such as Truchard and Caldwell. We expected the more powerful and intense wines to show best here, in the center of New World wine, but instead the personal palate shone through. (We were struck by the diversity of personal experience: one participant found the aroma of one of the wines particularly offensive; whereas another said, of the same wine, "I'd like to have a bowl of that beside my bed, just to smell.") The lesson seems clear—free yourself from the self-imposed tyranny of the experts, experiment, and have fun.

At the 2002 Vintners Association panel discussion mentioned in chapter 6, wine writer Gerald Asher added another dimension to this view, calling on the assembled group of sommeliers, retailers, distributors, and restaurant owners to take back the power they had ceded to the wine critics. "Thirty years ago, a retailer or wholesaler would take up a wine because they believed in it, were willing to invest in it, and make the effort to sell it. . . . You were selling yourself as well as the bottle, hoping the person would benefit from what you said so that you would build your own credibility. . . . Quoting the numbers is a lazy way of selling. You don't have to take any responsibility.

"Today the professionals [such as the group in attendance] listen, taste, try to understand. Often, they are more informed than the wine critics. But by depending on numbers, you have said to the consumer, 'Don't take my word—here's the great poobah's opinion.' Decades ago, things were more leisurely. Now you do things before the wine has had a chance to really show what it will be. But I think the responsibility is on the professionals to stop selling by the numbers and begin once again to guide the consumer."

Asher's view is not free of difficulties—once a wine house has an investment, it must do what it can to sell the product; while the wine critic, presumably independent of financial involvement, can express a genuine opinion—but his point is central. We can depend on one or two people to determine our tastes and to influence the way wine is made,

(continued)

But other interesting comparisons suggested a different kind of experience. "They're like Elizabeth Taylor and Mia Farrow," presumably both beautiful but one more overt than the other. "It's like comparing Peter Paul Rubens with Vermeer," again suggesting shared beauty but distinguishing the obvious from the subtle. One taster who vastly preferred the Harlan noted that it was "much closer to port wine," a view that perhaps mirrored the comments of the group maverick, who detected "burnt" notes in the Harlan fruit and suggested that it might be just too much of a good thing.

We were eating soba (buckwheat pasta) with a sun-dried tomato and cured black olive pesto—no lack of flavor, certainly—but not even this full-flavored food could handle the Harlan. The maverick also suggested that the Beauregard had good balance and integration, deeming the Harlan a bit edgy, a mix of extreme elements that had not yet decided to bond together. To this taster, the Harlan was clearly outdone in the subtle aspects of the grape by the more modest wine.

The bottom line for the maverick was that, although the Harlan outshone the Beauregard in almost every aspect, the latter was certainly the better value, the better wine with food, and in some ways the more intriguing. Having also been the one to provide the wines, he was soundly taken to task for the unfair comparison, just as the promoter who put the flyweight in the ring with the sumo champ would have been castigated in the press. Whether this was just concern for the underdog or recognition of quality overwhelmed by style and intensity we never clearly determined.

❖

or we can become more confident in ourselves and our experience and explore the world of wine with greater flexibility and more pleasure.

The dominance of style over character is a serious and difficult issue. While Parker may not seek the power he wields, he has shown little interest in broadening his perspective, ignoring the potential he has to educate rather than direct. The world of wine retail does not seem inclined to strip shelves of those little cards with the ratings from Parker's *Wine Advocate,* the *Wine Spectator,* the *Wine Enthusiast,* or the other organizations that rank wine.

One of us is fortunate enough to live five miles from a store regularly voted the best wine merchant in the state (Connecticut). It has none of those little cards but does offer dozens of extraordinary bargains from around the world, all tasted and chosen by the proprietors, Bob and Ben Feinn. Until we have more of these dedicated wine merchants and until we as consumers become willing to trust our own taste, Parker and his colleagues will continue to exert undue influence on the way wine is made. Winemakers are a part of the cycle as well, caught in the conflict between dedication to the character of place and vulnerability to the effect of the wine press, the wine critics, and wine auctions. And now technology is entering this arena at an accelerating pace, with unpredictable consequences.

"Americans want to be told what to like. It's part of our national character." Or so says Leo McCloskey, a person who embodies the meeting of technology and wine style. President of Enologix, a consulting firm with clients the world over, he began his technological career conducting wine analyses for Paul Draper of Ridge Vineyards, one of the early converts to the use of wine analysis to help monitor developments in the winery. McCloskey is part wine chemist, part entrepreneur, and part salesman—we spent four hours with him, during which he continually diverted the discussion into ever new and often confusing directions. (Our view of the purpose and direction of Enologix may thus be inaccurate, but it is not from a lack of trying to discern what the company actually does.)

One thing Enologix does exceedingly well is to acquire and manage information. McCloskey oversees a vast storehouse of wine data. He and his colleagues have isolated a number of the phenolic compounds that give wine its color, flavor, and aroma—some fifty-two (half of them fragrances) for whites and thirty-two for reds. The database contains yearly measurements of these compounds for a large number of wines, together with a record of scores from wine critics and retail wine price. McCloskey maintains that quality is defined by the marketplace and can be measured based on wine price, volume sold, and critic ratings. He uses this equation to rate hundreds of wines each year, publishing the results in the magazine *Global Vin-*

tage Quarterly. Enologix also analyzes the relationship between ratings and phenolic profiles, a connection that seems to be at the heart of the business.

All Enologix clients, some sixty at the time we spoke, provide the company with data from all stages in the vineyard and the winery, from bud break to harvest, from fermentation to bottling. Enologix measures phenolic profiles of grapes at various stages of growth and in the winery. By comparing these profiles with those in his database, McCloskey can advise winegrowers and winemakers how closely their profiles match others that have achieved high scores with the critics, or even how well they match specific wines. He can put your wine up against Château Latour, Romanée-Conti, Le Montrachet, La Ladonne, Grange Hermitage, or a host of other wines worldwide. He and his staff also advise their clients on what can be done in vineyard and winery to move the profile into the ranges that attract the highest ratings. McCloskey claims that his clients achieve an average increase of five to six points in ratings within eighteen months of starting his program. He maintains that the ratings he uses come from a broad range of critics.

McCloskey holds things pretty close to the vest. He does not reveal to his clients, who sign nondisclosure agreements, how he reaches his conclusions; nor does he reveal much to visitors, with whom he otherwise chats freely. But the notion that wine quality can be measured by sales volume, price, and critical ratings neglects the obvious connection between the first two items and the third. If a wine gets a high rating from Parker or the *Wine Spectator,* it flies off the shelf, thus justifying higher prices and ensuring large sales volume. McCloskey's quality metric, then, appears to reflect to some unknown degree the judgment and opinion of the *Wine Advocate* and the *Wine Spectator,* both of which project a preference for New World wines.

In providing winemakers with a route to higher ratings and better sales, McCloskey is also promoting, however inadvertently, a particular style. If Enologix's client base grows significantly, this influence could well become an issue in analyzing the forces that determine prevailing wine styles. For any wine that purports to reflect the terroir of its origin, however, the dominance of style over character—the influence of the winemaker overshadowing what comes from the vineyard—fundamentally negates any such claim.

The current generation of winemakers—Tony Soter, Mia Klein, Philippe Melka, Rosemary Cakebread, Chris Howell, Michael Silacci, Bo Barrett, Heidi Peterson Barrett, Joel Aiken, Daniel Baron, Karen Culler, Ken Bernards, Cathy Corison, Steve Rogstad, Sarah Gott, Ed Sbragia, and their many compatriots—trained and learned in an environment that was relatively free of technology, in a tradition that has come to emphasize close connection to the vineyard. They have the ability and confidence to approach winegrowing with the intuitive tools developed from observation and experience and to combine this approach with new technologies as they arise.

The next generation and the next after that will grow and learn in a milieu progressively permeated by sophisticated technology. Will they be able to maintain the intuitive approach that has so clearly been successful in producing a broad variety of distinctive wines? Or will they become dependent on, and a reflection of, technological advance? And how will this affect the character of the wine that their minds and hands produce?

MOVING TOWARD SUSTAINABILITY

A force that might be an effective balance to the advance of technology is now inching its way into the nooks and crannies of vineyard and winery. Some winegrowers are becoming convinced that modern, chemically based agriculture ultimately destroys the productive potential of vineyard substrate, the most vital and valuable component of terroir, the one that many believe plays a decisive role in wine character. In response to these concerns about long-term agricultural and environmental sustainability, some winegrowers are moving toward more traditional approaches to the land—from the simple act of reducing the use of pesticides and herbicides to the more complex methodology of biodynamics.

"From the beginning, we have considered ourselves stewards of an extraordinary property, approaching everything we've done with the intent of honoring the past— the fruit and the wines that have come from this land," says Bart Araujo. Bart and his wife, Daphne, bought the Eisele vineyard in 1989, knowing that this land had produced exceptional wine since its first planting in 1971.

"We wanted to see if we could improve on what had been done before, with the idea of creating a legacy that might even be better. For the first five years, our idea was to farm sustainably, to follow organic farming practices but to retain the right to use chemicals as a last resort. In the mid-nineties, we decided that was a cop-out, and we went fully organic in '98. Then, in 2000, we decided on practicing biodynamic agriculture."

Daphne Araujo adds, "We didn't like the foliar sprays we were applying in the middle of the summer. We seemed always to overdose on something. We would deal with one symptom, and then a different one would arise. We decided there was a better way to farm, based in the soil." She predicts that "the whole valley ultimately will go sustainable—not if, but when."

Based on the works of philosopher/mystic Rudolph Steiner, biodynamics is a complex blend of science and mysticism grounded in the peasant farming practices of nineteenth-century eastern Europe. Biodynamic practices tend toward the esoteric, timing the acts of planting, cultivation, and other processes to phases of the moon and utilizing various concoctions that "energize" compost. But don't let this out-on-the-edge side of the approach close your mind—some aspects of biodynamics might well lead to the reinforcement of terroir, by making its practitioners pay attention to the land in all its aspects and in all seasons, bringing an enriched awareness to the work of farming.

Biodynamics stresses that any piece of land should be autonomous, depending on itself rather than outside sources for soil amendments. This is certainly an interesting notion in the context of terroir—the more the land is free of material added from the outside, the more likely are the grapes grown on it to reflect local character. Philippe Pessereau, who is experimenting with biodynamics at Joseph Phelps, emphasizes that biodynamics "restores the links with other plants and microorganisms, reenlivens the soils, making them healthy. The plants become healthier, each is unique in common with the site, and the typicity will be more pronounced, more reflective of location."

John Williams farms organically and flirts with biodynamics. When he bought the land that now surrounds Frog's Leap Winery, "it was a toxic waste dump, only two trees left and all the vines suffering from phylloxera. It had been irrigated and fertilized heavily based on the view that the root systems needed more stuff. But that was wrong—it was like feeding them Coke and candy bars. . . . I set about replanting a couple of acres at a time, working with the rest of the property to restore the soils, to build soil structure. You can see these plants look pretty healthy, but they were about dead when I started." The vines did, indeed, look pretty healthy, though they were still infected with phylloxera and slated to be replaced soon. Williams and others who have taken up organic and biodynamic practices maintain that healthy vines come from healthy substrate and that healthy substrate comes from working with the most natural, nonchemical approaches, which will sustain the land for generations to come.

Sustainability of land use and the environmental effects of vineyard development are central and contentious issues in the ongoing history of the Napa Valley. In a peculiar way, Napa provides a microcosm of a world situation. As populations expand, the value we place on land continues to rise, and a variety of viewpoints compete for attention—environmental sustainability, economic viability, aesthetic values, among others. This is the context in which the terroir of Napa vineyards exists, and the way these issues play out will affect the future of winemaking in the valley. The

Napa Valley is a rare place, one of the few areas producing wine of a quality that attracts the attention, interest, and cash of the entire wine world. It is perhaps unique among such areas in its diversity of microenvironments and in the potential diversity of wine character, an attribute that is vulnerable to today's trends.

In earlier decades, much of Napa's potential was swallowed up in the volume of blended wine that was produced, to the detriment of the individual, site-specific wines that could be made from the best components—think of a painting in uniform brown (the result of mixing all the colors on a palette), as opposed to one filled with distinct and vibrant colors. But diversity is of interest only if wine character takes precedence over style. Vineyard-designated wines have little point, and less justification for added cost, if they all seek to please the palates of a small number of critics and their devoted public, using recipes designed to create phenolic profiles that bring high ratings or mimic famous wines. Imitating one another will destroy distinctive character in wines and lead to regional mediocrity, an egregious misuse of the bounties of Napa.

The strength of a few individuals—Al Brounstein, Tom Burgess, Mike Grgich, Joseph Heitz, Robert Mondavi, Joseph Phelps, John Shafer, Warren Winiarski, and a few others—laid the foundation for the Napa renaissance and the explorations that continue today. Now it may be time for the Napa community to reevaluate its purpose and direction, to reset itself on a course of leadership rather than trudging farther down the road of reaction to fad and fashion, a sure path to a lesser position in the wine world than the one to which it aspires.

In the 1730s, during what Chris Howell describes as "a furor of planting in Bordeaux," the king of France issued a decree forbidding further vineyard development. It had little long-term effect: today Bordeaux, with six times the area of Napa, stands as the world symbol of great wine. Now a similar move is on to limit the development of new vineyards in Napa, driven by a variety of concerns that include problems arising from dependence on a single crop; environmental decline caused by erosion in the hills and siltation of the Napa River; "visual pollution" created by vineyards in the hills; the transformation of a quiet rural paradise into a bustling center of world tourism; and the simplistic notion that Napa already has too much land devoted to vineyards. At a time when Napa is entering the same rarefied level enjoyed by Bordeaux, however, limiting vineyard development by overly restrictive regulation might turn out to be a short-sighted path. Wine may not be an ideal rallying point around which to build community, but it is the heart and soul of the Napa Valley—without it, the region would be either a sleepy farm community raising prunes and pears or a once-beautiful place developed with housing, shopping centers, and parking lots.

A productive path might be for all parties to accept the Napa Valley for what it is—one of the world's great and unique wine-growing regions—and work together to create a model of agricultural, environmental, and aesthetic sustainability that would honor the legacy of the past and provide an outstanding example of cooperation and clarity. And while they are doing so, we can only hope that the winemakers of Napa will continue to please our palates with wines of similar character—truly great wines of balance and integrity from land farmed with concern for future generations.

BIBLIOGRAPHY

Ackerman, Diane. *A Natural History of the Senses*. New York: Random House, 1990.

Bakker, Elna S. *An Island Called California: An Ecological Introduction to Its Natural Communities*. Second edition, revised and expanded. Berkeley: University of California Press, 1984.

Brook, Stephen. *The Wines of California*. London: Faber and Faber, 1999.

Carpenter, E. J., and Stanley W. Cosby. *Soil Survey of the Napa Area, California*. Series 1933, no. 13. Washington, D.C.: U.S. Department of Agriculture, Bureau of Chemistry and Soils, January 1938.

Clarke, Oz. *Oz Clarke's Wine Atlas*. Boston: Little, Brown, 1995.

Coates, Clive. *An Encyclopedia of the Wines and Domaines of France*. Berkeley: University of California Press, 2000.

Gladstones, John. *Viticulture and Environment*. Adelaide: WineTitles, 1992.

Graymer, R. W., D. L. Jones, and E. E. Brabb. *Geologic Map and Map Database of Northeastern San Francisco Bay Region, California*. Miscellaneous Field Studies Map. 26 pp. Scale 1:100,000. U.S. Geological Survey, in preparation.

Graymer, R. W., D. L. Jones, E. E. Brabb, Jason Barnes, R. S. Nicholson, and R. E. Stamski. *Geologic Map and Map Database of Eastern Sonoma and Western Napa Counties, California*. U.S. Geological Survey, in preparation.

Halliday, James, and Hugh Johnson. *The Art and Science of Wine*. London: Mitchell Beazley, 1992.

Howell, D. G., and J. P. Swinchatt. "A Discussion of Geology, Soils, Wines, and the History of the Napa Valley Region." *California Geology* 53, no. 3 (2000): 4–12.

Johnson, Hugh, and Jancis Robinson. *The World Atlas of Wine*. Fifth edition. London: Mitchell Beazley, 2001.

Kramer, Matt. *Making Sense of California Wine*. New York: Willliam Morrow, 1992.

Lambert, G., and J. Kashiwaga. *Soil Survey of Napa County, California*. Washington, D.C.: U.S. Department of Agriculture, Soil Conservation Service, 1978. (An updated 1999 version of the soils map, digitized and revised, is available at www.ftw.nrcs.usda.gov/ssur_data.html.)

Laube, James. *California Wine.* New York: Wine Spectator Press, 1999.

Lukacs, Paul. *American Vintage: The Rise of American Wine.* Boston: Houghton Mifflin, 2000.

Pomerol, Charles, ed. *The Wines and Winelands of France: Geological Journeys.* Orléans: Editions du BRGM, 1989.

Robinson, Jancis. *Vines, Grapes, and Wines.* New York: Knopf, 1986.

Smart, Richard, and Mike Robinson. *Sunlight into Wine.* Adelaide: WineTitles, 1991.

Smith, Rod. "Geology by the Glass." *Wine and Spirits,* Fall 2002.

Stevenson, Robert Louis. *The Silverado Squatters.* San Francisco: Mercury House, 1996. (Originally published in 1883.)

Sullivan, Charles. *Napa Wine: A History from Mission Days to the Present.* San Francisco: Wine Appreciation Guild, 1994.

Swinchatt, Jonathan. *The Foundations of Wine in the Napa Valley: Geology, Landscape, and Climate.* Cheshire, Conn.: EarthVision, Inc., 2002.

Swinchatt, Jonathan, and D. G. Howell. *EarthNectar—The Wines of Napa Valley and the Earth from Which They Arise.* 50-minute video. Cheshire, Conn.: EarthVision, Inc., 1990.

Wilson, James E. *Terroir: The Role of Geology, Climate, and Culture in the Making of French Wines.* Berkeley: University of California Press, 1999.

Winchester, Simon. *The Map That Changed the World: William Smith and the Birth of Modern Geology.* New York: HarperCollins, 2001.

Winkler, A. J. *General Viticulture.* Berkeley: University of California Press, 1962 (2nd rev. ed., 1974).

INDEX

Page numbers in *italics* indicate figures, tables, and maps. Page numbers annotated with *s* indicate sidebar material (e.g., 7–9s).

Concord grapes, 141
Conn Creek area, 100, 192
Constant (wine), 99
consumers: dependence on wine critics, 203,
    205–206, 207; guidance, need for, 202, 205,
    206; informed on technology use, 180;
    informed on terroir, 76–77, 181–182, 199.
    See also personal taste
Cooks Illustrated, 77–78s
Coombsville, 59–60, *59,* 113
cordon pruning, 142, *143*
core stones, 80–81, *81–82*
Corison, Cathy, 73, 99, 102
cost: of oak barrels, 174; of planting acre of
    vines, 130; of shared wine tasting, 104s.
    See also market forces; prices
cover crops, 42
critics. *See* wine critics
crop estimation, 147
crop load, 147
crop thinning, 146–147, 189; as described by
    Columella, 147
crop yields: balanced vines as quality indicator,
    147–149; Bo Barrett on, 197; growing
    conditions and, 141–142; as prescribed
    by critics, 148; spacing of vines and, 142;
    thinning to lower, 146–147, 189; under-
    balancing, 147
crushing and destemming, 171, 172, 186, 187,
    196
crust (Earth), 13, *13. See also* oceanic crust
crustal bulges, 15, *19,* 21
crystalline basement, *19, 23*
Culinary Institute of America (CIA), 68–69
Culler, Karen, 169
cult around winemakers, 189
cult wines: names of, 73, 185–187, 196; prices
    of, 73; small-label growth issues and, 154
culture and history of place, 6, 105

Dalla Valle Vineyards: cult wine of, 73; displace-
    ment surfaces and, *57;* as landmark, 50, *51;*
    location of, *161;* vine balance and, 141–142
Daniel, John, Jr., 40, 65, 189
data management techniques, 178
Davis clones, 74, 153
DAYMET, 110–111, 113, 117
De re rustica (Columella), crop thinning described
    in, 147
Deer Park Road, 165
DEM (digital elevation model), 30–31, *31*
deposition. *See* erosion/deposition process

deserts, rain shadows and, 11, 12
Diamond Creek Vineyards: early recognition
    of terroir and, 4; microenvironments of,
    48–49s, 112–113s; residual EPUs and, 99;
    vineyards of, 48, *48*
Diamond Mountain AVA, 120, 121; map
    showing, 7
Diamond Mountain Road, 70
Diamond Mountain Vineyard, 192
digital elevation model (DEM), 30–31, *31*
digital orthoquad photo (DOQ), 31–32, *31*
diseases: phylloxera, 125, 130–132, 209; Pierce's,
    183, 184–185s
Disney family. *See* Silverado Vineyards
displacement surfaces, 53–60, *53–59,* 155–156,
    156; flat surfaces and, 57–60, *57–59;* knobs
    and hills as toe deposits of, *52,* 53–54, *54–
    55, 159;* tours viewing, 155–156, *156,
    159, 159*
Dominus Estate: alluvial EPUs and, 99; crop
    yields and quality of, 147–148; founding
    of, 150; Great Valley sequence rock and,
    40; location of, *64, 65*
DOQ (digital orthoquad photo), 31–32, *31*
drainage: erosion control and, 42; soil texture
    and, 92; vigor dependent on, 99, 129
Draper, Paul, 4, 180
drip irrigation, 116, 146
dropping clusters. *See* crop thinning
Dry Creek, 45, 63
dry farming, 146, 197
Duckhorn Vineyards, 165
Dunn, Randy, 137, 169, 187–188, 194
Dunn Howell Mountain (wine): and Caldwell
    vineyard, 137; early recognition of terroir
    and, 4; residual EPUs and, 99
Dunn Vineyards, 187
Dutch Henry Canyon, 69, *70,* 110, 111, 166
Dutch Henry Creek, 50

early-drinking wines, 172. *See also* accessibility
earth: as element of balance in terroir, 200–202.
    See also bedrock; geologic history; soil;
    substrate
earthquakes: asymmetry of Napa Valley demon-
    strated by, 89; San Andreas fault system,
    21–25, 36–37, *37, 40*
earthworms, 90
economic considerations. *See* market forces
ecosystem compared to terroir, 6
egg whites, in fining, 175
Eisele, Milton and Barbara, 166, 168

geologic history (continued)
of, 25–26, 26, 36–38, 37; nature of
our knowledge of, 14s; San Andreas
fault system, formation of, 21–25, 36–
37, 37; Sierra Nevada, formation of,
12–15, 13; Vaca Mountains, formation
of, 25–26, 26, 36–38, 37. See also geologic mapping
geologic mapping, 33–36, 34–37, 35–36s; complexity of rock geometry and, 25–26; story
of soil and, 79
geologic structure. See rock architecture
geologists vs. soil scientists, 78–79
geology. See geologic history; plate tectonics;
rock architecture; volcanics
Girard, Steve, 133
GIS (Geographic Information Systems), 114–
115, 177
Gladstones, John, 95–96, 122
Glass Mountain, 164, 165, 165
glassy-winged sharpshooter, 184s
Glen Ellen formation, 25, 62
Global Vintage Quarterly, 207
Gods of Wine, 75, 148. See also wine critics
Gottl, Erika, 185–188
GPS (Global Positioning System), 114–115,
176–177
grace, as wine quality, 181
Grace, Dick, 138, 190, 201
Grace Family clone, 137–138
Grace Family Vineyards, 69, 137–138; cult wine
of, 73
grafting, 138–139
Grahm, Randall, 180
granite, 17, 79–81
grape growers. See winegrowers
grape pickers, 139s, 170–171. See also workers
and working conditions
grapes. See fruit; phenolic profiles; ripening;
vines
Gravelly Meadow (vineyard), 48–49s, 48
gravity flow, 65, 171, 187, 188
Great Basin, 11
Great Britain: critics in, rating scale of, 202;
"grip" as term in, 116s
Great Valley sequence: formation of, 16–19,
19, 21; geologic maps showing, 34, 103;
mineral character of, 17; Napa terroir and,
24, 38–41, 40, 102, 158–159, 158; and
Napa volcanics, 22–23, 23, 24, 26; San
Andreas fault and movement of, 37, 40
Greystone Cellars, 1, 68

Grgich, Mike, 2, 71, 210
growing degree day, 112–115, 114–115
Gulf Stream, 105

handpicking, 140s, 170–171
hang time, defined, 146
hardpan, 92
Harlan, Bill, 195–196
Harlan Estate: cult wine of, 73, 204–205s; land
of, 195–196; location of, 65, 65; residual
EPUs and, 99
harmony, as wine quality, 181
Hartwell Vineyards, 157
harvest, 140s, 170–171
Haynes, Arthur, 131–132
Haystack Mountain, 50, 51
hedging, 67, 183
Heitz, Joe, 2, 4, 210
hemispherical photography, 177
hemlock, 183
Hennessey drainage, 45, 87, 89, 100, 111
Herold, Mark, 185–188
The Hess Collection (winery), 40
Highway 29, 23, 50, 83, 108; tour along, 62–71
hills and knobs, 50–54, 52, 55, 159
history. See culture and history of place;
geologic history
Howell, Chris: blending and, 193–194; Franciscan formation and, 19–20, 191; on French
attempts to limit vineyard development,
210; land as focus of, 191–192; on rootstock
choice, 135
Howell Mountain AVA, 32, 121; map showing, 7
Hudson, Lee, 89, 92, 134
Hudson River, 108
"hungry" water, 42, 43

ice sheets, as glaciers, 51
identity, geographic: market forces and, 154
Inglenook Vineyards, 1, 39. See also Niebaum-
Coppola Estate Winery
integrated pest management (IPM), 91, 184–
185s
intention of winemaker, 190–191, 201–202
International style. See New World style; style
in wines
intuition. See winemaker's dance
irrigation: drip, 116, 146; dry farming vs., 146;
by hand, 116, 146; natural balance of vines
and, 142; substrate protection and, 192.
See also water

precipitation. *See* rainfall

press wine, 173

pressure bombs, 176

prices: crop yields and, 147, 148; of cult wines, 73; for grapes, niche creation and, 153; for land, 76, 195–196. *See also* cost; market forces

Pride Mountain Vineyards, 151

Prohibition, 1–2

provenance analogy, 10

pruning, 139–146, *143, 144*

pyroclastic flows, 16, 24

Quintessa (vineyard; winery), 100, 163, *163,* 192

racking, 175, 181

rainfall: as attribute of terroir, 2; drip irrigation and, 116; at harvest, 116–117; kinetic energy and, 42; in Napa, city of, 117; regional patterns of, 117, *117–120. See also* irrigation; water

Ramey, David, 116*s*, 147–148

Rattlesnake Ridge, *107*

Rector Canyon: alluvial fan of, 87, 89, 161; formation of, 45, *46;* soils and, 80; temperature maximums and, 111

Rector Creek, 45

Rector Dam, 50, *51,* 153, 160

Rector Reservoir, 153, 159

Red Rock Terrace (vineyard), 48–49*s, 48*

redwood tanks, 174

regulations governing wine making, 178–179, 180

residual materials (EPUs), 80–81, 87, *88, 91,* 98–99, 149

reverse osmosis, 179

Rhone region, 130

Richard Perry Vineyards, 59, 60

Ridge Vineyards, 4

ripening: physiological maturity as concern in, 150–152, 154; regulation of vine and, 129–130; sugar content and, 150, 151–152, 154; taste and, 151; temperature equitability and quality of grape, 122; too early, 194–195; veraison as signal for, 133; vintage of 1974 and, 150; water withholding and, 146. *See also* phenolic profiles; sugar; vines

rivers. *See* watercourses; *specific rivers*

Robert Mondavi Winery: association of terroir to wine character and, 99, 102; district designations and, 73; growing degree designations and, 113, *115;* location of, *66, 67, 157;* rainfall measurements by, 117, *117;* ripeness and, 151; spacing and hedging of vines for, 67. *See also* To Kalon Vineyard

rock, weathering of, 79–81, *81–82*

rock architecture: cross-section mapping of, 35–38, *35–37;* defined, 33, 34; folded, 15, *16, 36–38, 36;* tilted on edge, 15; volcanic action and, 15

Rocky Mountains, 11, 21

Rogstad, Steve, 73

Rolland, Michel, 168, 194–195

Rombauer Vineyards, 166, *166*

roots: clay in soils and, 92–93; penetration of, 85, 92, 146, 149

rootstock: California-specific, development of, 132; drip irrigation and, 146; dry farming and, 146; grafting clones onto, 138–139; hybridization of, 179; location, matching to, 135; phylloxera-resistant, 131–132

Route 128, 70, 163

Rubicon (wine), 67

Rudd, Leslie, 133

Rudd Vineyards & Winery, 86, 100, 133, 161

Rutherford AVA: Franciscan formation and, 38; map showing, *7;* soil types in, *94*

Rutherford Bench. *See* Rutherford fan

Rutherford fan: architecture of, *85;* association of terroir to wine character and, 99, 115; bedrock feeding, 100, 102, *103;* Franciscan formation and, 39, 102; growing degree days and, 115; Oakville considered distinct from, 102; watershed feeding, 100, *101*

Sacramento River, 43, 45

Sage Creek, 45

San Andreas fault system, 21–25, *26,* 36–37, *37,* 40

San Francisco Bay, 12, 25, 43, *44,* 51

San Francisco Chronicle, 180

San Pablo Bay, 43–45, 86

sandstone, 17

Sante, David de, *143,* 146, 150, 175

Sauvignon Blanc: and growing degree days, 115; rainfall at harvest and, 117; of Spottswoode, 68

Sawyer (cult wine), 73

Sbragia, Ed, 96, 169, 195

Schuster, Danny, 127–128, 190, 197

science and terroir, 95–98. *See also* technology

Screaming Eagle (vineyard), 100, 160, *160;* cult wine of, 73 sea level changes, erosion/deposition and, 43–45, *44, 50*–52

Seavey (wine), 192

sediments. *See* EPUs; soil; substrate

senses. *See* personal taste; wine tasting

serpentinites, 20, 41, 95, 163, *163*

Shafer, John, 100, 210

Shafer Hillside Select (cult wine), 73, 159

Shafer Vineyards, 100, 159

Shaulis, Nelson, 140–141

Showket Vineyards, *57, 161, 161;* cult wine of, 73

Sierra Nevada, 11, 12–15, *13*

Silacci, Michael, 146, 151, 169, 176, 193

Silver Oak Cellars (winery), 189–190

Silverado Trail, 15, 23, 41, 50, 86, 108, 153; tour along, 155–168

Silverado Vineyards, 41, 52, 158–159, *158*

Simmons Canyon, 121, *167*

Simmons Creek, 166

slope aspect, diversity of, 108, *109*

SLV (Stag's Leap Vineyard), 100, 126, *157*

Smart, Richard, *112s,* 140–141, 148–149

smell, sense of, 199–200

Smith, Rod, 183

Smith, William, 35–36s

Soda Canyon Road, 155

Sogg, Daniel, 127

soil, 73–104; as attribute of terroir, 2; Chardonnay as tool for extracting flavor from, 4; color of, microenvironments and, 49, *49;* consumer knowledge of, 76–77; correlations of wine character and, 95–96; as element of balance in terroir, 200–202; fertilizer needs and, 179; geologists vs. soil scientists and, 78–79; geology as primary influence on, 29, 79; ideal, 92–93, 134; layers of, 90–92, *91,* 93; mature, 79, 91–92; natural balance in, 90–91, 208–209; new focus on, 32, 73–74; profiles of, 90–93, *91;* studies, large-area, 93–95, *93–94;* study pits, 84, 89–90, 92, 134–135; tilth, 90; youthful, of Napa Valley AVA, 45, 79, 91, 102, 104. *See also* bedrock; EPUs; substrate

soil profiles, 90–93, *91*

soil study pits, 84, 89–90, 92, 134–135

soil surveys, large area, 79, 93–95, *93–94*

Sonoma Volcanics, 22. *See also* Napa volcanics

Soter, Tony: as consultant, 169; Eisele Vineyard wine and, 168; and ineffability of knowl-

edge, 193; ripeness and, 150; soil preferred by, 73

spinning, 179, 181

Spottswoode Estate (vineyard; winery), 68, *69,* 99, 151

Spring Mountain AVA, 121; map showing, 7

springs, 99, 168, 192

Spurrier, Steven, 8

St. George rootstock, 132, 146

St. Helena, 50, *68–69*

St. Helena AVA: association of terroir to wine character and, 99; growing degree days of, 112, 113; map showing, 7

St. Helena fan: acid values distinguishing, 192; bedrock feeding, 100, 102, *103;* watershed feeding, 100, *101*

staff. *See* workers and working conditions

Stagecoach Vineyards: bedrock and, 32; choice of location for, 133; displacement surfaces and, *56–57;* geological relations of, 161; as landmark, 50, *51;* microenvironments and, 49–50; soil depth, 80–81. *See also* Krupp, Jan

Staglin Family Vineyard, 99

Stags Leap AVA: association of terroir to wine character and, 100, 115; Cabernet and, 126–127; Great Valley sequence and, 41; map showing, 7; palisades above, *33;* tour of, 155–159, *155–159;* wind patterns in, 121, *122*

Stag's Leap Wine Cellars: association of terroir to wine character and, 100; caves of, 158; and displacement surfaces, 59, 60; early recognition of terroir and, 4; location of, *157;* and Napa volcanics, 41; and Paris wine tasting of 1976, 8; Danny Schuster and, 197. *See also* Winiarski, Warren

Steiner, Rudolph, 208–209

Sterling Vineyards, winery of, 70, *70,* 110

Stewart, Lee, 2

Strasser, Rudy von, 99

streams. *See* watercourses; *specific creeks*

style in wines: ascendance of, 202; categorization of, as limiting, 188; changes over time in, 74, 75, 202; vs. character, 74–75, 202–208, 210; defined, 202; market forces and, 75, 198, 202, 203, 205–207; technology promoting, 207; terroir overshadowed by, 75, 181, 195, 196–197, 199, 203, 207. *See also* character of wine; New World style

subappellations: boundaries of, 8–9s; diversity of terroir within, 77; map showing, 7. *See also specific subappellations* subduction, 13–22, *13*

substrate: as attribute of terroir, 2, 208; erosion/deposition process and, 81, 83–84, *84–85;* Glen Ellen formation, 25, 62; granite weathering, 79–81; human influence on, 102, 104, 179; irrigation and protection of, 192; as parent material, 78–79; particle size in, 80; residual materials, 80–81, 87, *88, 91,* 98–99, 149; root growth-patterns and, 85; as stable aspect of terroir, 192; sustainability and, 208–209; of vigorous sites, 144, 145; vineyard design and changes in, 128; vineyard illustration comparing, 149; youthful soils and importance of, 79. *See also* alluvial fans; bedrock; EPUs; soil

sugar: addition of, 152, 178; air as balancing, 201; alcohol content related to, 173, 187; clone influence and, 136; excessive, 152, 154, 194; fermentation of, 172, 173; focus on, 150–152; France and, 150, 152, 178; historical lower levels of, 140, 150, 152; physiological maturity compared to level of, 150–152; shading of vines and reduction of, 141, 149; technologies to concentrate, 179, 181; veraison and redirection of, 133–134. *See also* alcohol content; fermentation; ripening

Sulfur Creek, 68

sulfur dioxide, 171, 179

sun: as attribute of terroir, 2; as current stylistic focus, 202; as element of terroir balance, 200, 201–202. *See also* temperature

Sunlight into Wine (Smart and Robinson), 112

sustainability, 90–91, 208–211

Syrah, 96–98, 126

Tannat region, 181

tannins: airing and building of, 197; crop yields and balance of, 147–148; destemming and, 186, 187; fining and, 175; food accompaniment and, 116–117*s;* maceration times and, 173; mature vs. youthful, 116–117*s;* micro-oxygenation to soften, 179, 181; physiological maturity and, 150, 151, 152; stress on vine and, 146; temperature and development of, 100, 115; water withholding and, 146

taste: ripening based on, 151; sense of, 200. *See also* personal taste

Taylor, Charles, 134

Tebbulio, Mario, 184

technology: balance for terroir and, 202; character of wines lost through, 74–75, 180, 198, 199, 206–208; consumer awareness and, 180; dependence on, and loss of intuitive approach, 207–208; Enologix, 206–207; Merus and concept approach, 185–187; "natural" vs. "processed" wine and, 179–181, 198; necessity of, debate on, 178, 180–181; regulations outstripped by, 179; soil and climate analysis using, 114–115; vineyard design accommodating, 128; winemaking process using, 176–179

tectonics. *See* plate tectonics

temperance movement, 1

temperature, 109–112; Cabernet vineyards and, 110, 126; correlations/associations of site to wine character and, 97, 115; equitability of, and quality of grape, 122–123; of fermentation, 173, 186; of France compared to Napa, 109–110; north-south gradient not supported by data, 110–111, *111;* and tannin development, 100, 115; topography linked to variation in, 111–112

terroir: biodynamics reinforcing, 208–209; blending as overshadowing, 195, 210; as concept, 2, 3–6, 8; culture and history of place and, 6, 105; disputed as relevant, 199, 201; as earth, vines, and people, 6, 10; EPU map as tool in understanding, 89; great wine produced by wide range of, 104, 105; information sharing on, 199; intention of winemaker and, 190–191, 201–202; natural elements of, 200–202; physical, defined, 3; regional excellence and, 2; style overshadowing, 75, 181, 195, 196–197, 199, 203, 207; technology as homogenizing, 74–75, 180, 198, 199, 206–208; Wilson's inconsistent use of term, 3–4. *See also* character of wine; EPUs; geologic history; microenvironments; rainfall; soil; substrate; sun; temperature; terroir influence, associations and correlations; topography; vines; winemaker's dance

Terroir: The Role of Geology, Climate, and Culture in the Making of French Wines (Wilson), 3–4

terroir influence, associations and correlations: experimentation to explore, 96–98, 149; microenvironment diversity and, 48–49*s,* 49–50; personal experience and, 48–49*s,*

volcanics: crustal bulges and, 15; erosion of, 16–17; eruptions, 14, 24; lateral tectonic plate movement and, 22–24; mudflows (lahars), 16, 24; pyroclastic flows, 16, 24; rock architecture and, 15, *16;* shapes formed by, 15; subduction of tectonic plates and, 12–14. *See also* Napa volcanics

washing grapes, 171
water: acidic, erosion by, 32–33, 80, *81;* adding to fruit, 152, 178–179; as element of balance in terroir, 200–202; excessive growth of vines and, 99, 129; "hungry," erosion and, 42, 43; springs, 99, 192; urgency of vines and, 146; withholding, 146, 202. *See also* drainage; irrigation; rainfall; watercourses
watercourses: bank erosion of, 86–87; erosion/deposition process of, 42–45, *43–44,* 81, 82–84, *84–85;* flood plains, 86–87; profile of, 42–43, *43;* watersheds, 89, 100, *101, 103. See also specific rivers and creeks*
watersheds, 89, 100, *101, 103*
Web sites: for climate data, 110–111; for downloadable tours, 62; for growing degree days information, 113; for questions to authors, 62; for terroir information sharing, 199
Weber, Ed, 147
Wetlaufer, John, 181
Whitford Cellars, 59
Wild Horse Valley AVA, 62; map showing, 7
wildlife, 51
Williams, Craig, 168, 201
Williams, John, 86–87, 144, 146, 209
Wilson, James E., 3–4
Winchester, Simon, 36s
wind patterns, 121–122, *122,* 200–201
Wine Advocate, 206, 207
Wine and Spirits, 77s, 183
wine critics: British, 202; Brix-degree standards and, 152; consumers dependent on, 203, 205–206, 207; crop yields standardized by, 148; diversity lost due to preferences of, 75, 202–206, 207; Enologix and improving ratings from, 207; merchants and, 205–206; power and intensity preferred by, 75, 202–204, 207; winemakers dependent on, 203, 206
Wine Enthusiast, 206
wine making process, 170–175; balance for terroir in, 202; barrel aging, 174–175, 179–180, 181, 193, 196, 197; blending, 173–174; bottling and bottle aging, 175;

cold soaking, 173, 186; crushing and destemming, 171, 172, 186, 187, 196; filtering and fining, 175; harvest, 140s, 170–171; maceration, 172–173, 179, 186; "natural" vs. "processed," 179–181; regulations governing, 178–179, 180; technological developments in, 175–179; washing, 171. *See also* blending; fermentation
wine merchants, personal taste vs. that of critics and, 77, 205–206
Wine Spectator, 75, 126–127, 206, 207
wine tasting: alluvial fan comparison, suggested, 102; balance and, 181; of Cain 5 and its elements, 193–194; changeability of wines and, 190; by critics, and preference for blockbusters, 203–204; diversity of individual experience in, 77–78s, 204–205, 204–205s; for French terroir, 181–182; of Harlan Estate and Beauregard, 204–205s; high-alcohol content and, 173; natural elements of terroir and, 200–201; of Petrus and Inglenook, 189; structured, suggestions for organizing, 104, 104s; super-sensitive palates and, 9–10, 199–200; training for, 200; by University of California, Berkeley, wine club, 204–205; wind-effects comparison, suggested, 121. *See also* character of wine; Paris wine tasting of 1976; personal taste; style in wines
Wine Tasting Championships, California, 204
wine writing: terroir descriptions in, 77–78s; terroir information sharing and, 199; variation in palate sensitivity and, 200
winegrowers: as attribute of terroir, 6, 8; Nathan Fay as, 126–127; vision of, 133. *See also* vines; vineyards; *specific growers*
winemakers: as attribute of terroir, 6, 8; balance sought by, 170, 181, 183–184, 201–202; confidence gained by, 125; consultants, 169, 197; fading focus on power and intensity by, 204; goal of, fundamental, 170, 184–185; intention of, 190–191, 201–202; manipulative power of, 169–170; nonintervention ideal and, 175–176, 189; qualities sought by, 181; vision of, 6, 8, 175–176, 181. *See also* balance; market forces; technology; wine critics; winemaker's dance; wine making process; *specific makers*
winemaker's dance: as attribute of terroir, 38–39; balance of, 183–184; defined, 3; diversity of, 184–185, 188; at Dominus, 189–190; at Merus, 185–187; microclimate

distinctions and, 112–113s; technology adding confidence to, 178

winery design, gravity flow, 65, 171, 187, 188

Winiarski, Warren: and Cabernet geography of the valley, 126–127; on cold soaking, 186; on Nathan Fay, 127; and fruit improvement, 125–126, 127–130; and old vine syndrome, 125–126, 127, 129; and Paris wine tasting of 1976, 8, 125; as pioneer, 2, 210; on regulation of the vine, 200; and Danny Schuster, 127–128; "3 Gs" concept of, 6; on wind patterns, 121. *See also* Stag's Leap Wine Cellars

Winkler, A. J., 112–113, 132

workers and working conditions: continuity of, 196; vineyard, 138–139, 139–140s, 170–171; winery, 170, 171

yeasts, 171, 179, 186–187

young soils, 105, 108

young topography, 105

Yount, George, 1

Yountville AVA, map showing, 7

Yountville Hills, 54, 56, 159, 159

Zinfandel: and growing degree days, 115; handling of, 197; as heavy bearing, 126

Zinfandel Lane, 41

DESIGNER	Victoria Kuskowski
COMPOSITOR	Integrated Composition Systems
INDEXER	Victoria Baker
TEXT	11/15.75 Bembo
DISPLAY	Myriad
PRINTER AND BINDER	Friesens Corporation